International Perspectives on Child Abuse and Children's Testimony

International Perspectives on Child Abuse and Children's Testimony

Psychological Research and Law

Bette L. Bottoms
Gail S. Goodman
editors

SAGE Publications
International Educational and Professional Publisher
Thousand Oaks London New Delhi

For information address:

SAGE Publications, Inc.
2455 Teller Road
Thousand Oaks, California 91320
E-mail: order@sagepub.com

SAGE Publications Ltd.
6 Bonhill Street
London EC2A 4PU
United Kingdom

SAGE Publications India Pvt. Ltd.
M-32 Market
Greater Kailash I
New Delhi 110 048 India

Printed in the United States of America

Library of Congress Cataloging-in-Publication Data

Main entry under title:

International perspectives on child abuse and children's testimony :
    psychological research and law / editors, Bette L. Bottoms, Gail S.
    Goodman.
        p. cm.
    Includes bibliographical references and index.
    ISBN 0-8039-5627-4 (cloth : acid-free paper). — ISBN
    0-8039-5628-2 (pbk. : acid-free paper)
        1. Child abuse—Law and legislation. 2. Child witnesses.
    3. Psychology, Forensic. I. Bottoms, Bette L. II. Goodman, Gail S.
    K5189.I58 1996
    347'.066'083—dc20
    [342.766083]   96-9953

This book is printed on acid-free paper.

96 97 98 99 10 9 8 7 6 5 4 3 2 1

Production Editor: Michèle Lingre
Typesetter/Designer: Christina Hill
Cover Designer: Lesa Valdez

For Gary and Phil

Contents

1

International Perspectives on Child Witnesses

An Introduction to the Issues

BETTE L. BOTTOMS
GAIL S. GOODMAN

Professionals worldwide face many common problems in their attempts to combat child abuse. These problems include the need to deal judiciously with abuse allegations, especially claims of sexual violations against children. Shared problems raise shared questions: Can professionals validly assess children's credibility? How should children be interviewed? What are the best ways to present children's evidence in court? How can society safeguard defendants' rights while ensuring adequate child protection? These problems are difficult, at best. Their solutions are important, however, because they are fundamental to assuring justice for both victimized children and innocent defendants.

Although numerous problems are shared across societies, the legal traditions for approaching these problems vary considerably from one country to another. Differences in legal systems constrain solutions to

1

societal problems, such as child abuse, in important ways. For instance, in the United States, defendants' Sixth Amendment rights to confrontation require cross-examination of witnesses. The Sixth Amendment also assures that trials are open to the public, which results in children often testifying about personally traumatic events before an audience of strangers. In countries that do not honor such rights, greater freedom to attempt procedural alternatives and to experiment with different approaches is possible.

Cross-cultural differences also exist in the relative emphasis societies place on the problem of child abuse. In India, children are considered lucky to have a roof over their heads and any caretaker at all, regardless of whether the caretaker is less than kind. In contrast, spanking a child is illegal in Sweden. In America, society is currently focused on the issue of false reports, with occasional startling realizations of the destructiveness of actual abuse. It is dogma in the United States that it is better for 100 guilty people to go free than for one innocent person to be falsely incarcerated. Consistent with this view, the American legal system is geared to protect innocent defendants through, for example, the presumption of innocence. Other countries differ, emphasizing more the common good and society's interests rather than personal freedom. It is important to understand how these differences are manifested in legal approaches, legal reforms, and scientific research.

Legal Trends

Many of the cultures represented in this book were highly influenced by the British legal system and, in fact, were English territories at one time (e.g., Australia, Canada, Hong Kong, India, Israel, United States). Nevertheless, each society has added its own local twists in attempts to protect children from abuse and from possible stress during legal proceedings. For example, some countries have established mandatory reporting laws to ensure societal intervention in child abuse cases. Such countries have seen dramatic increases in the reporting of child abuse, which has fueled interest in child witnesses. Some of these same countries have dropped laws requiring corroboration of child sexual abuse as a prerequisite for prosecution and have relaxed child competence laws. Innovations to ease children's provision of testimony also have been implemented. Of considerable interest, use of closed-circuit television (CCTV) for child witness testimony is being employed in a number of countries and was ruled constitutional under certain conditions in United States criminal courts (*Maryland v. Craig,* 1990). CCTV permits children to testify from a room adjacent to the courtroom and spares the child face-to-face confrontation with the accused, although still permitting direct and cross-examination of the child witness. Although CCTV is rarely employed in the United States, it is becoming commonplace in other countries, such as England. Thus, some countries have attempted substantial innovations over the past few years. Professionals worldwide have much to learn from the results.

In contrast to attempts to protect child abuse victims, skepticism toward child witnesses has increased recently in the United States, resulting in laws to protect innocent defendants from false accusations and nonabused children from a false belief that they were abused. Such skepticism is based largely on concerns about children's susceptibility to suggestion and parental coaching. For example, one state (New Jersey) has instituted taint hearings in which attorneys can challenge the way in which children were interviewed (*State of New Jersey v. Michaels,* 1994). If a judge determines that an interview was so leading that a child's memory is likely contaminated, then the child will not be permitted to testify, and the case may well be dropped. In the future, we can learn about the consequences of such hearings on child abuse prosecutions: Such legal trends may help guard against the consequences of overzealous interviewing, but the results may not all be positive. Will new legal trends, such as the implementation of taint hearings, aid justice or thwart societal efforts to stop child abuse? Although the legal pendulum swings back and forth in any one country, efforts in other countries can contribute to a balanced perspective.

Social Science Research

Psychological research on child witnesses and child abuse also reflects the issues raised and the values represented in each country. In the United States, children's suggestibility has been the primary focus of research, in part reflecting important links to theoretical issues within academic psychology, but also reflecting U.S. society's concerns with false reports and individual freedom. However, U.S. researchers also have examined jurors' reactions to child witnesses and how those reactions are affected by legal reforms and expert testimony. Concerns in other countries have differed. For example, research in New Zealand has focused more on techniques that can help children provide accurate testimony, such as use of props and drawings in interviews. In England, considerable research has concentrated on field studies to evaluate the effect of reforms implemented to protect children who testify in court.

There is often an interplay between researchers' interests (e.g., children's suggestibility, procedural reforms to protect children in court) and a country's policies concerning child witnesses. For instance, researchers who view their countries' child protection policies as having contributed to false reports of abuse are likely to study children's suggestibility and the dangers of leading interviews. Laws in such lands are then influenced by the research findings. New laws may then create new problems (e.g., children who do not receive societal protection because they are not believed), which then again stimulate relevant research endeavors. Because each country has unique laws and policies toward child protection, this interplay can lead to different research foci internationally.

Former International Efforts

We are not the first to express an interest in international perspectives on child witnesses. In 1989, Spencer, Nicholson, Flin, and Bull (1990) held a conference at Cambridge University, England, which included speakers from such diverse countries as Israel, Scotland, England, Germany, Norway, France, and the United States. In the early 1990s, a NATO-sponsored conference was held in Italy, involving many countries and lively discussion. The International Society for Prevention of Child Abuse and Neglect holds regular conferences in which speakers from all over the world present papers on child abuse treatment, prevention, social policy, and research. The society's journal, *Child Abuse & Neglect,* frequently includes articles by authors from around the world. These are valuable resources and information outlets for readers interested in international issues relevant to child abuse and child witnesses. We have attempted to add to these existing sources by creating this edited volume.

The Present Book

The theme around which we have organized this book is one that we believe is both timely and important. Specifically, we have collected international submissions detailing (a) the status of child witness research internationally, (b) legal innovations currently used to accommodate child witnesses in courtrooms, and (c) research investigating the effectiveness and implications of such innovations. Thus, we have brought together knowledge from around the world to build an important and useful information base for the education of scholars and legal professionals in all countries.

Represented in this volume are the works of an impressive array of authors writing about child witness research and legal systems affecting children in many societies. The authors have addressed a wide range of issues: Historically, what role have children played in their legal systems? What special laws have been instituted to ensure the rights of parties involved in child witness cases? What special techniques have been, or could be, introduced in their countries to accommodate child witnesses (e.g., to aid children's recall of past events of legal relevance, to prepare children psychologically for the experience of testifying, or to make their involvement in the legal system less stressful)? What has been the effectiveness of such techniques? What information has been gained regarding discrepancies between needs of child witnesses and needs of courts? What is the status of child witness research in various countries?

We are proud to say that all of the contributions to this book are grounded in innovative scientific work of high quality. To ensure interdisciplinary communication, the chapters have been written for a wide audience, with clinical and forensic implications drawn. For most of the chapters, social scientists and legal scholars collaborated to produce works that are both legally and empirically sound.

We invited the present authors to contribute to this book out of respect for their research and writings. Although we do not necessarily agree with everything presented in this book, we believed that it was important to permit authors to take their own perspectives and develop them as they saw fit. We preferred to have all the authors represent their and their countries' approaches to child witness and child abuse research rather than to take a strong editorial hand in molding the contents of the book. We believe that this approach worked well to create an exciting set of chapters that truly represents the diversity of approaches taken in dealing with children in legal systems worldwide. As a result, this book should be of interest to a wide international readership, from practitioners, researchers, and students to mental health, social service, medical, and legal professionals concerned with child abuse or children's testimony.

Many chapters have a two-part format: (a) a comprehensive, historical overview of the development of a nation's recognition of and legal response to child abuse and (b) a description of research related to key issues in the country's struggle to accommodate children's testimony. The chapters move conceptually from those addressing the accuracy and suggestibility of children's testimony, with emphasis on pretrial investigative interviewing, to ones detailing a variety of techniques developed to accommodate child witnesses in the courtroom.

Our book opens with Warren and McGough's review of the latest research findings relevant to obtaining accurate information from children during a forensic investigation. Their comprehensive review of the child witness literature is organized in a practical and accessible way. Although contemporary literature on children's testimony sometimes focuses exclusively on highlighting children's weaknesses, the authors have taken a step toward underscoring the implications of research for improving children's eyewitness testimony. Children, like adults, have limitations, but they also have wide-ranging competencies that can be maximized with informed interview techniques. From this review, it is clear that future researchers face the challenge of identifying more of those competencies and developing interviewing techniques that will capitalize on children's abilities. Researchers interested in meeting this challenge are given numerous ideas about where to start. Readers from legal and social service disciplines are provided with a sophisticated understanding of current research that should be useful in their efforts to implement the best possible interviews.

Lamers-Winkelman and Buffing introduce readers to the Dutch response to child abuse, which historically has been to treat abuse as a family, not societal or legal, problem. Child abuse cases that do enter a Dutch courtroom virtually never include the testimony of child witnesses. Thus, the Dutch focus of concern and of research is on precourt interviewing of child witnesses and the credibility of their statements. The authors detail the results of Lamers-Winkelman's investigations of the effectiveness of statement validity analysis, a controversial but increasingly studied technique for determining the credibility of a witness's statements through content analysis.

As in the Netherlands, children rarely testify in countries such as Israel or Germany. Instead, specially trained experts interview child witnesses,

then testify themselves regarding children's statements. Although a justification for this approach is to shield children from the trauma of testifying, Sternberg, Lamb, and Hershkowitz reveal the disadvantages of this
system for the successful prosecution of child abuse in Israel. Even so, the
Israeli legal system provided the authors with a unique research opportunity: documented records of actual child victim statements that could be
compared to objective indications of credibility such as perpetrator confessions. The authors present an overview of their investigations into
statement validity analysis and the effect of interview style on the accuracy
and completeness of actual child victims' statements.

The next group of chapters are from countries with more liberal policies
toward the admission of children's courtroom testimony. With these policies has come the necessity to accommodate children's special needs in
the courtroom. Our contributors describe the ways in which research in
their countries has kept step with legislative changes designed to make
children's court experiences less stressful and more productive. Innovations from Canada, Great Britain, Scotland, Australia, New Zealand, South
Africa, Hong Kong, and the United States are reviewed, including precourt
preparation programs, CCTV or "live link" testimony, and expert testimony on child abuse. Sas, Wolfe, and Gowdey lead off this section with
Chapter 5, detailing Canadian reform efforts. In particular, the authors
describe their work in developing and implementing an extensive child
witness preparation program. They report how their model program for
courtroom preparation successfully achieves its objectives through child
witness education and stress reduction.

Few countries have legal systems so receptive to and informed by social
science findings as Great Britain and Scotland. In Chapter 6, Bull and
Davies write about the English and Welsh experience with child abuse and
children's testimony. After detailing government directives regarding the
videotaping of children's interviews, the authors report findings from their
research aimed at improving forensic interviews, for example, their investigations of the effectiveness of the cognitive interview, a technique
developed by American researchers R. Edward Geiselman and Ronald
Fisher (see, e.g., Geiselman, Saywitz, & Bornstein, 1993). Bull and Davies
also discuss their research concerning the use of CCTV testimony, point-
ing out the importance of examining the effects of CCTV not only on
children's emotional demeanor and accuracy but also on jurors' perceptions of the testimony.

In Chapter 7, Flin, Kearney, and Murray detail their "generally fruitful, if at times challenging, working relationship" with the legal system of Scotland. Their research program has been fruitful indeed: In their chapter, the reader learns about the findings of Flin and Murray's broad research programs addressing children's perceptions of court involvement, children's legal knowledge, the effects of delay on children's memory, and the effect of instituting live-link testimony on the perceptions and reactions of those involved in child abuse cases. Their energetic efforts have had a remarkable effect on the Scottish approach to child witnesses.

Next, Shrimpton, Oates, and Hayes describe legal reforms recently instituted in Australia, as well as the research that informed those changes. For example, findings from Oates and Shrimpton's research on the effects of delay on children's memory led to recommendations that adjudication of child witness cases be expedited. Other Australian research has led to an appreciation of problems presented by legal language and the intimidating atmosphere of the courtroom. Among the resulting innovations have been court preparation programs, CCTV, and a unique program of pretrial diversion that "sentences" some offenders to treatment rather than criminal prosecution.

In New Zealand, radical reform in laws regarding children's evidence recently inundated the courts with a wide variety of courtroom innovations. Pipe and Henaghan describe the nature of these innovations and the results of their survey research that documented New Zealand's reactions to the changes. Their findings can inform professionals in other countries who are seeking to understand how similar innovations might be received in their own jurisdiction. The authors show that although legal and social service professionals in New Zealand identify both strengths and weaknesses in the new legislation, they generally embrace innovative techniques for child witnesses and perceive such techniques to be successful in reducing the trauma of children's courtroom testimony.

Against a backdrop of internal political and societal turmoil, countries such as South Africa have only recently been the setting for child witness research and reform. Much like American law, South African law is adversarial in nature and, as such, has been slow in obliging the needs of children. Louw and Olivier describe the only child witness studies conducted in South Africa to date and the notable influence of that research on legislation. They end with directives for future work that might ensure continued reform in their country.

Ho profiles children's experiences in the legal system of Hong Kong, a country currently "failing children who are victims of abuse." Although Hong Kong has experienced rapid growth in child abuse awareness over a relatively short time, its legal and social service systems still present great obstacles to reporting and prosecuting child abuse. Although children are infrequent participants in Hong Kong courtrooms, Ho documents legal cases illustrating the country's struggle with issues of competency, corroboration requirements, admissibility of expert testimony, and so forth. Thus far, Hong Kong's reception of innovation has been cautious, at best. Even so, Ho provides reason for optimism: As in South Africa, a special commission has recently made recommendations for reform in the Hong Kong legal system. These suggestions, such as minimizing the delay between disclosure and trial and the use of CCTV, may positively affect the country's future legal approach to children.

In the wake of its Supreme Court decisions such as *Coy v. Iowa* (1988) and *Maryland v. Craig* (1990), the United States has actively pursued changes that might positively affect children's participation in the legal system. Psychological and legal perspectives on these changes are the substance of the next two chapters. Kovera and Borgida's extensive review of American research allows the reader to understand jurors' perceptions of children's testimony from a social psychological perspective. The authors also overview findings from their own experimental research program examining how witness preparation, expert testimony, and CCTV presentation of testimony influence jurors' reactions to testimony. The reader will be left with an appreciation of the psychological processes behind jurors' reactions to children's evidence.

Completing our group of chapters on special techniques for children in the courtroom is a broad-reaching contribution by Myers, a leading U.S. legal authority on child abuse and children's testimony. Myers brings together previous chapters by providing a historical overview of the distinctions between common law and civil law systems, and how the underlying assumptions of these systems have determined the course of legal reform pertaining to children's testimony internationally. He proceeds with an in-depth review of virtually all reforms that have been considered worldwide, providing a particular emphasis on reforms relevant to the U.S. legal system. Finally, Myers unveils a unique contribution to the field: a proposed legal code that could be used to guide courts in assuring that children receive all possible support in the courtroom environment. The adoption of this code would be a substantial advance for the cause of child witnesses.

In the book's closing chapter, Segal reminds us of an important yet easily over looked perspective: In Third World countries, profound difficulties in providing even basic life necessities to children largely override concerns about child abuse. Segal details the very beginnings of a country's social and legal recognition of children's human rights and their need for legally mandated protection. In considering Segal's depiction of children's plight in modern-day India, readers in developed countries can, on the one hand, feel fortunate with their own country's strides toward children's justice. But on the other, readers can soberly recognize how much more work is needed on behalf of children worldwide, especially in underdeveloped countries. Segal's chapter also reminds us of the importance of international dissemination of knowledge gained from societal struggles to understand child abuse, to maximize children's capabilities as witnesses, and to give them a voice in a legal system designed for adults.

With these remarks, we invite you to this book's forum for information exchange among an international group of researchers and practitioners. It is our hope that you, and eventually children within legal systems worldwide, will find it of benefit.

Acknowledgments

We wish to thank the many people who made this book possible. First, the authors of each chapter worked diligently to help us produce this high-quality collection. C. Terry Hendrix and Dale Grenfell of Sage Publications were a delight to work with. Chapters 2, 3, 4, 5, 7, 9, and 13 also appear in a special issue of the journal *Criminal Justice and Behavior* (Vol. 23, No. 2, June 1996). We thank the journal's editor, David Glenwick, for inviting us to create that special issue, which has grown into the present book. We also thank a number of academic reviewers who gave their time to provide feedback that made the contributions substantially stronger. Finally, conversations with our colleagues and students have also helped shape the volume.

References

Coy v. Iowa, 487 U.S. 1012 (1988).

Geiselman, R. E., Saywitz, K. J., & Bornstein, G. K. (1993). Effects of cognitive questioning techniques on children's recall performance. In G. S. Goodman & B. L. Bottoms (Eds.), *Child victims, child witnesses: Understanding and improving testimony* (pp. 71-94). New York: Guilford.

Maryland v. Craig, 110 S.Ct. 3157 (1990).

Spencer, J. R., Nicholson, G., Flin, R., & Bull, R. (1990). *Children's evidence in legal proceedings: An international perspective.* Cambridge, England: J. R. Spencer.

State of New Jersey v. Michaels, 642 A.2d 1372 (1994).

2

Research on Children's Suggestibility
Implications for the Investigative Interview

AMYE R. WARREN
LUCY S. McGOUGH

In 1984, Loftus and Davies argued that the relevant question was not simply, "Are children suggestible?" but "Are children more suggestible than adults?" Their question serves to remind us that suggestibility and other forms of distortion are inherent to all human remembering. Many American empiricists responded to their challenge by conducting research on children's comparative capabilities as witnesses. Indeed, by 1993, Ceci and Bruck observed, "In the past 10 years, more research has been conducted on the suggestibility of child witnesses than in all of the prior decades combined" (p. 403). Furthermore, American social scientists accurately perceived an opportunity to influence courts' assessment of

AUTHOR'S NOTE: Portions of the research reported in this chapter were funded by a University of Chattanooga Foundation Faculty Research Grant to the first author.

This chapter is reprinted from *Criminal Justice and Behavior,* Vol. 23 No. 2, June 1996 269-303.

children's credibility as trial witnesses and, consequently, explicitly sought to design "ecologically valid" research with clear applicability to the American trial process (e.g., see Goodman, Rudy, Bottoms, & Aman, 1990). This social science research, reported either through expert testimony at trial or through amicus briefs for appellate courts, has influenced judges and legislators to a degree never before achieved in three centuries of American law development.

Public and professional interest in reforming American trial processes affecting child witnesses was sparked by a series of failed child sexual abuse prosecutions in the 1980s, beginning with the notorious McMartin Pre-School case in California (*People v. Buckey,* 1984; for a review of those developments, see McGough, 1994; Myers, 1994). Initially, the goal was to reform trial procedure by providing additional insulation from face-to-face confrontation with the accused perpetrator for children who were sexual abuse victims. In a pair of decisions, the U.S. Supreme Court subsequently approved the use of novel devices, including closed-circuit television, to shield traumatized child witnesses from the defendant during their trial testimony (*Coy v. Iowa,* 1988; *Maryland v. Craig,* 1990).

Gradually over the past decade, however, the reform emphasis shifted from trial procedure to the earlier pretrial interviewing process. In another case, the Supreme Court reviewed the reliability of a critical interview conducted by a pediatrician asked to evaluate whether a $2\frac{1}{2}$-year-old had been sexually abused. At trial, the young child did not testify. Instead, the trial jury heard only the doctor's report of the child's "hearsay" statements accusing her stepfather. (The doctor admitted that although he had dictated notes to summarize his conversation with the child, they were not detailed and did not record any changes in the child's affect or attitude.) A defense expert witness had countered that the reported interview was replete with suggestive questions that could have contaminated or even produced the child's accusation. The Supreme Court was persuaded to reverse the conviction, finding that the doctor's account of the child's accusation was unreliable and inadmissible as evidence (*Idaho v. Wright,* 1990).

Most recently, a conviction in a New Jersey prosecution of a day care teacher for child molestation was reversed because the appellate court accepted as its central inquiry whether

interview techniques used by the State in this case were so coercive or suggestive that they had a capacity to distort substantially the children's recollections of actual events and thus compromise the reliability of the children's statements and testimony based on their recollections. (*State v. Michaels* N.J. 1994 at 1377)

Throughout its opinion, the New Jersey Supreme Court relied heavily on an amicus brief that had been submitted by 45 American researchers. That brief not only presented a theoretical review of research but also specifically analyzed audiotapes of many interviewing sessions with the alleged child victims in the *Michaels* case and strongly criticized the interviewing techniques used. There can be little doubt that empirical data demonstrating the causative link between the use of improper, highly suggestive interviewing techniques with children and their skewed memories influenced the Court to vacate the conviction.

When a conviction is reversed, the possibility exists that the accused can be retried. In the *Michaels* case, the New Jersey Supreme Court held that on retrial, the children could testify only if the prosecutor could prove that they still retained their fresh, "untainted" memory of their experiences. The prosecutor announced a decision not to retry Michaels, presumably because that hurdle seemed insurmountable and, as is typical, there was little evidence aside from the children's allegations (Whitcomb, 1992). The extant empirical research seems to support the prosecutor's decision: Once children have been exposed to and have incorporated misleading information or interpretations from interviewers into their memories, the implanted false portions may be extremely difficult to uproot. As Fehrer (1988) has hypothesized,

> The repeated reinforcement of [altered perceptions] creates in the child a "subjective reality" that an event did happen even if it never did. This enables the child to relate such experiences on the witness stand without "lying." She actually believes the event happened, and no conventional trial tactics should be able to show that she is "lying," because she is not. (p. 233)

Building on the source confusion studies of Foley and Johnson (1985), Ceci, Huffman, Smith, and Loftus (1994) have demonstrated that some very young children are resistant to efforts aimed at removing implanted inaccurate events, even when later told by experimenters and parents that the implanted events did not occur. However, Poole and Lindsay (1995) reported that preschoolers in their study demonstrated more knowledge about the difference between actual and implanted events during a debriefing than they had indicated in their performance on a traditional source-monitoring task. Certainly, more research is needed on this vital issue facing the American legal system.

In summary, reflecting the growing body of suggestibility research, the focus of reform of American legal procedures affecting child witnesses has dramatically shifted from the courtroom to the investigatory interviewing process. The quality of the interviews will affect whether the child or interviewer can give reliable trial testimony. It is likely that researchers will appear with increasing frequency at trials as expert witnesses on the reliability risks inherent in interviewing children.

Before attempting to summarize the research on suggestibility, we must note four caveats. First, we acknowledge that those who interview child witnesses have an extremely demanding and difficult job and that often they must conduct interviews under less than ideal conditions. In the real world, the lines between encouraging candid disclosure and suggesting a response, between fact-finding and assumption, and between investigation and therapy are not clearly marked and require split-second judgment calls. Second, we recognize that the reliability of any memory is a complex equation composed of cognitive, social, emotional, and moral elements in a delicate, constantly interactive balance. In a chapter of the present length, there is the danger of oversimplification. Other, more expansive, reviews exist, to which the reader is referred (e.g., Ceci & Bruck, 1993). Third, we must acknowledge that the research base on which we rely is limited in its ecological validity and applicability to children who are victim/witnesses of sexual abuse. Sexual abuse is certainly unlike most staged laboratory events. It is more salient and more stressful, occurs in a context of secrecy and threat, is often a repeated event, and has long-term ramifications for children and their families (see Goodman et al., 1990, for a discussion). However, it also should be kept in mind that many of the studies we report were, in fact, designed to apply to nonabused children, who under certain conditions may report information that leads us to believe they have been abused. Finally, we have chosen to feature research on suggestibility as an unconscious tendency of children. Thus, we have concentrated on the research involving child respondents who, although exposed to interviewer influence, are yet conscientiously attempting to provide accurate accounts of events. This is the most common forensic application of suggestibility research. However, given their dependence and greater vulnerability, children also may be more susceptible to coaching to deceive than are adults (e.g., Tate, Warren, & Hess, 1992). We acknowledge the existence of a growing body of research on children's capability and practice of conscious deception, but those studies are beyond the scope of the present chapter (see Ceci, Leichtman, & Putnick, 1992, for a review).

Mindful of those limitations, we target the investigative interview and offer a summary of relevant research. What are the optimal conditions for securing an account of a child's remembered experience that will be as reliable or more reliable than that of an adult? How, when, where, and by whom should a child witness be interviewed to diminish potential distortions and enhance the trustworthiness of the child's remembered account? Our intent is to encourage researchers to assume a more socially proactive role by discovering and recommending interviewing protocols that will minimize opportunities for the contamination of children's accounts. The purpose of this chapter is to begin laying that foundation.

The Role of the Interviewer: The "Who" of the Interview

In Wells's (1989) memorable aphorism, focusing exclusively on the abstract cognitive capabilities of a child and thereby failing to consider the child's interactive process with the interviewer is like studying the sound of one hand clapping. Every child who is a potential trial witness will be interviewed before trial by at least one and typically several adults. For example, in a criminal prosecution, interviewers include the investigating police officer, the prosecutor's staff, the prosecutor, the defense investigator, and the defense counsel. Indeed, service providers testified before the Attorney General's Task Force on Family Violence (1984) that child victims of intrafamily violence are subjected to at least a dozen investigative interviews before all interrelated legal proceedings are resolved (Whitcomb, 1992). The same phenomenon occurs in civil cases as the child is variously interviewed by counsel for both parties, as well as by insurance adjustors or psychologists or physicians, depending on the nature of the dispute and the importance of the child's testimony.

In a legal system based on adversariness, interviewer partisanship is a considerable problem, perhaps even an explicit role expectation. Although the ethical obligations of all lawyers and experts are clear—to serve justice and to avoid misleading the court—the limits of zealous advocacy are less well lighted. Two studies document the power of interviewers who purposely attempt to extract a skewed report from a child through the use of biasing statements. A confederate "baby-sitter" played a game with 4-year-olds in Tobey and Goodman's (1992) study. Eleven days later, the children returned to the laboratory for an interview and were divided into two groups. The first group was interviewed by an actor costumed as a police officer, who introduced the session by saying, "I am very concerned that something bad might have happened the last time that you were here when you played with the baby-sitter. We need your help. My partner is going to come in now and ask you some questions about what happened." Thereafter, another actor-police officer questioned each child. The second group never met with a police officer but, instead, were simply questioned by a "neutral" interviewer. The children cautioned and interviewed by the police gave fewer accurate statements and more inaccurate statements about their experience than those who were interviewed by the neutral interviewer. As Goodman (1993) subsequently summarized the findings, "One should be concerned not only with the actual questions but also with the context of the interview. An accusatory or intimidating context leads to increased errors in children's reports" (p. 15).

The earlier work of Clarke-Stewart, Thompson, and Lepore (1989) had reached similar results, although through the use of more aggressively manipulative questioners. They sought to determine whether 5- and 6-year-old children could be swayed by an authoritative adult to alter their impressions and interpretations of a staged live event involving an actor who played the role of "Chester the Janitor." The interviewers were fully informed confederates, who purposefully assumed either an accusatory, exculpatory, or neutral interpretation of Chester's activities when probing children's memory of their actual personal observations. When questioned by a neutral interviewer or one whose interpretation of Chester's activities was consistent with what the children had seen, the children's accounts were accurate. In contrast, when the interviewer contradicted what a child had seen, the child's version quickly conformed to the suggestions or interpretative biases of the interviewer. Even when questioned by their parents, the children's answers remained consistent with the interviewers' biases.

The bias of the interviewer need not be explicit, nor must the interviewer intentionally pursue that bias to affect the accuracy of a child's remembered account. In the investigation of reported crime or evaluation of a civil dispute, the substance, chronology, and details of events are un-known, and the interviewer must extract an accurate account in the dark. In contrast to laboratory experiments, as Davies and Flin (1988) have explained, "[Real life] events can be much more ambiguous and question-ing takes the form of hypothesis testing as the interviewer builds up a comprehensive picture of what transpired as information is slowly elic-ited" (p. 25). Even experienced interviewers such as teachers or police officers can unwittingly induce inaccurate accounts through their inter-viewing techniques:

> The most consistent counterproductive strategy [used by experienced interview-ers] involved reaching a premature conclusion regarding the shape of events or appearance of the actors and then appealing to the child, through a series of suggestions or leading questions, to confirm their beliefs. Such strategies on occasion led to serious misunderstandings and consequent false reports. (Dent, 1978, quoted in Davies & Flin, 1988, p. 25)

Professional role biases and preconceived hopes about a witness's account can influence the interviewer's mode and tone of inquiry and, in turn, shape the respondent's responses. Even experienced professionals may lack the skills and sensitivity essential to the production of an unbiased, accurate account (Warren, 1992).

Two recent experiments documented this more subtle danger. Pettit, Fegan, and Howie (1990) staged a presentation to preschool children, during which an apparently unrelated event occurred as one of the actors "accidentally" knocked a cake from the table to the floor. The "accident" abruptly ended the presentation. Two weeks later, the children were questioned about the episode by interviewers, who had been primed with varying preinterview information. The interviewers were divided into three groups: The first group received an accurate report of the child's experience, the second an inaccurate report, and the third no information at all. Each interviewer was instructed to question the child until the interviewer found out what actually had happened. Despite the caution to avoid leading questions, 30% of all interviewers' questions were leading, and half of these were misleading, that is, based on false assumptions about what actually had transpired. The interviewers primed with inaccurate information asked four to five times as many misleading questions as did the other interviewers. More important, the children interviewed by the inaccurately biased interviewer gave the most inaccurate information, agreeing with 41% of the embedded inaccurate information contained in their questions.

In another experiment involving preschoolers (Ceci, Leichtman, & White, 1995), children participated in a game ("Simon Says") that involved some touching. The children were interviewed 1 month later. Each interviewer was supplied with a one-page summary of what might have occurred; some of the information was accurate, and some was inaccurate. The interviewer was instructed to examine the children to determine how much of the information they could still recall and to begin by asking the child for free recall. However, thereafter, the interviewer was instructed to use "whatever props she felt necessary to elicit the most factually accurate recall from the child" (p. 16). When the interviewer's questions were based on accurate information about the child's experience, she extracted most of the details of the experienced event with no false reports. In contrast, when the interviewer was misinformed, 34% of the 3- and 4-year-olds and 18% of the 5- and 6-year-olds corroborated one or more false events that the interviewer believed had occurred.

Avoiding Biasing Responses

Skillful interviewing technique requires an appreciation of the distinction between the adoption of a generalized, supportive attitude that encourages recall of the child's actual memories and the use of techniques that bias the child toward certain selected responses. Goodman, Bottoms, Schwartz-Kenney, and Rudy (1991) reported positive effects of "reinforcement"—giving cookies and juice at the beginning of the interview, followed by a warm, friendly interviewer attitude coupled with frequent and random praise, such as "You're doing a great job" or "You've got a great memory," regardless of the accuracy of the child's statements (p. 78). In their study, 3- to 4-year-olds and 5- to 7-year-olds who had received inoculations at a medical clinic were interviewed about the event 2 or 4 weeks later or both times. Half of the children received such reinforcement during the interviews, and the other half did not. Goodman et al. (1991) found that reinforcement did not increase inaccuracies. In fact, reinforcement eliminated age differences in commission errors to misleading questions suggestive of abuse, whereas younger children in the nonreinforced group made more commission errors than their older counterparts.

In contrast to the benign comfort of a snack at the beginning of an interview is the offering of bribes to obtain a particular admission, such as "You told us everything once before. Do you want to undress my dolly? Let's get done with this real quick so we could go to Kings to get popsicles [*sic*]" (*State v. Michaels*, 1993). Or as one commentator observed about the McMartin pretrial process:

> The interviews would prove to be the undoing of the prosecutor's case. . . . [The interviewer's] technique seemed Pavlovian: emotional rewards to the child who accused the teachers, rebuffs to those who did not. "What good are you? You must be dumb," she said to one child who knew nothing about the game Naked Movie Star. (Carlson, 1990, p. 26)

On a more subtle level, a clinician has claimed that an interviewer can perhaps unwittingly shape a response by his or her body language, for example, by giving intense attentiveness to some responses or details while appearing distracted or ignoring other responses (*State v. Giles,* 1989). There is a thin line between being warm and supportive of a child, particularly one who allegedly has been traumatized, and actively encouraging or discouraging only particular types of responses by word or gesture.

In contrast to randomly sprinkled praise and support of a child is the induction of negative stereotypes by the interviewer. In Lepore and Sesco's (1994) study, children ranging in age from 4 to 6 years of age played some games with a confederate adult. Half of the subsequent interviews of the children were conducted in a neutral mode, and the other half were conducted in an "incriminating" mode. In the incriminating mode, for example, the interviewer reinterpreted a child's descriptions of the adult's actions by stating, "He wasn't supposed to do [or say] that. That was bad. What else did he do?" At the conclusion of these incriminating procedures, the children heard three misleading questions about things that in fact had not occurred: "Didn't he take off some of your clothes, too?" "Other kids have told me that he kissed them, didn't he do that to you, too?" "He touched you and he wasn't supposed to do that, was he?" The children in both conditions then were asked a series of direct yes/no questions about what each actually had experienced. Children who had been interviewed in an incriminating manner not only were more inaccurate than those who had been neutrally interviewed, but also one third of them embellished their answers with details that conformed to the interviewer's incriminating suggestions. The accuracy of a child's account clearly depends on the interviewer's skill and sensitivity to children's special vulnerabilities to questioning and to inadvertent suggestion as well as purposeful manipulation. All direct questioning inherently involves a demand characteristic (Dent & Stephenson, 1979). Some types of exchange, such as cross-examination or police interrogation, are explicitly authoritarian forms of discourse. In other types of questioning, the demand is softened or may be inferred by children. As King and Yuille (1987) observed, an adult asking a child whether a person had blond, brown, or black hair indirectly suggests that hair color is important and is information the child should be able to provide. "An adult may resist this implicit demand; a younger child may misinterpret the interviewer's intentions and end up providing what he or she feels is an appropriate answer" (King & Yuille, 1987, p. 27).

Interviewers should take greater care to establish the ground rules of the interview to counter the child's predictable assumptions. As Brennan and Brennan (1988) noted, quizzing by a schoolteacher may be the child's only past experience with forced interactions conducted by a nonfamily member. Thus, a child may well assume that there is a "right" or "wrong" answer. Recent research (Toglia, Ross, Ceci, & Hembrooke, 1992) has demonstrated that when children are presented with misleading information by someone who appears to be knowledgeable about the event, they are more likely to succumb to the suggestions. In contrast, when the person attempting to mislead the child either states in advance that he or she has no knowledge of the event, or appears to be less knowledgeable (e.g., a 7-year-old child), children are less likely to be misled (Ceci, Ross, & Toglia, 1987a, 1987b; Toglia et al., 1992). The interviewer should explain the range of permissible responses, expressly informing the child that "I don't remember," "I don't know," and most important, "I don't understand the question" are perfectly acceptable (Geiselman & Padilla, 1988). Studies by Warren, Hulse-Trotter, and Tubbs (1991) and Saywitz, Moan, and Lamphear (1991; cited in Saywitz, 1995) have demonstrated that advance warnings that questions might be "difficult" or "tricky" and that one should answer only with what is truly remembered can reduce suggestibility in adults and children alike. When such warnings are combined with instructions to answer "I don't know" rather than guessing, suggestibility may be further decreased (e.g., Buhrman & Warren, 1994) Unfortunately, such instructions are not a panacea (Moston, 1987). Children may not realize that questions are "difficult" or "tricky" (Perry et al., 1993), or they may become overly cautious after such instructions, thereby increasing their errors of omission (Saywitz et al., 1991).

Children may change their answers to repeated questions because they feel that the repetition implies an unacceptable first answer, or because a slightly rephrased second question is interpreted as a different question requiring a different type of response (e.g., Warren et al., 1991). Poole and White (1991, 1993) asked 4- and 8-year-old children and adults a series of seven questions three times each during a single interview session, and then reinterviewed the subjects again after 1 week and after 2 years. Young children more frequently changed their answers to the closed-ended (yes/no) questions, and all respondents seemed to become more certain of their answers with question repetition. In a study by Warren et al. (1991), after children and adults heard a story, they were asked a set of questions, some of which were misleading. They were then told that their answers were not all correct, and asked the same questions again. Children were much more likely to change their answers, even to the nonmisleading questions, than were adults. These studies suggest that an interviewer should attempt to keep track of questions that have been asked previously (Walker & Warren, 1995) and avoid repetition. If repetition is necessary, the child should be reassured by comments indicating that the interviewer is attempting to clarify understanding of an earlier answer rather than seeking a different one.

Perhaps more effective than any didactic explanation of the child's role as an interviewee is modeling of those expectations in role-play, what Geiselman, Saywitz, and Bornstein (1993) have called a "practice interview." As a part of their cognitive interview, they have role-played the interviewing process by asking children first to describe some sort of neutrally experienced event like brushing their teeth that morning or what they did while waiting to be interviewed. Any misconception the child predictably may have about what is expected and about the task of remembering, such as guessing or making up a detail, can be flushed out and corrected in discussion before the important memory retrieval process begins.

In view of the risks of partisanship, some commentators have urged the appointment of nonpartisan, independent professionals who would conduct the critical early interview of any child witness (Libai, 1969;

McGough, 1994; Parker, 1982). This reform would mirror similar appointments made in other legal systems, such as those of Israel, Norway, France, and Germany (see Sternberg, Lamb, & Hershkowitz, 1996 [this volume]). Admittedly, such a reform is still considered revolutionary in the American legal system (Montoya, 1993), even though England now has moved away from a purely adversarial system when the witness is a child.

Short of such a major systemic reform, certainly more can be done to provide better training for those professionals who regularly interact with child witnesses: prosecutors, mental health practitioners, protective services workers, police investigators, and juvenile court personnel. There is a need for standard interviewing protocols, such as those developed by professional groups and by the government in England (Home Office, 1992).

Timing and Frequency: The "When" of the Interview

Early Interviewing

Delays between an experience and a trial can be considerable in the American legal system. For example, in the failed McMartin preschool prosecution in California, 7 years passed before the alleged abuse victims gave their testimony at trial (Carlson, 1990). In less sensational child abuse cases, Goodman et al. (1992) found that the average time from initial complaint to trial was $10\frac{1}{2}$ months, even though such cases ordinarily receive docket priority. In noncriminal or civil cases, trial testimony can be postponed even longer. As but one example, the parents of a 6-year-old boy sued a manufacturer for selling them a bicycle with defective brakes that they gave their son at Christmas. Nineteen months after a serious bike-riding accident, the child's deposition was taken. Six months after that the parents sued. The trial began almost 9 years after the accident (*Walden v. Sears, Roebuck, & Co.*, 1981).

In an attempt to contain the risk of memory-fade, the American pretrial process provides several mechanisms for preserving a witness's memory when it is more fresh, for example, by taking a statement informally or formally by a sworn and cross-examined deposition or by affidavit (i.e., answers to interrogatories). Even so, the triggering event for these earlier recordings of the witness's account is the report of his or her involvement in some event such as a crime or civil dispute. When the victim of a crime is a child, the child may delay reporting the event. This is especially true when the crime involves a secret sexual assault of the child (*State v. Michaels,* 1994; Summit, 1983). Even when the child is a bystander witness, an investigation may be stalled for a considerable time before the existence or identity of a particular child witness becomes known. Nonetheless, even when everyone knows that a child has relevant evidence, the plaintiff in a civil lawsuit may not secure the services of an attorney who could schedule the child's interview until long after, for example, the accident occurred or the divorce and contest over the child's custody becomes inescapable. Thus, the real-world obstacles to securing an "early" interview are formidable.

Delayed interviews may pose a comparatively greater burden for children than adults. Children appear to forget all types of information (relevant, irrelevant, central, and peripheral details) at faster rates than do adults (Brainerd, Reyna, Howe, & Kingma, 1990; Poole & White, 1993; Warren, Hagood, & Jackson, 1993), and the younger the child, the faster the forgetting rate may be (e.g., Baker-Ward, Gordon, Ornstein, Larus, & Clubb, 1993). Thus, children's recall errors may increase over time even when they are not exposed to misleading questions or other possible contaminants. For example, Poole and White (1991, 1993) found that in an immediate interview children and adults did not differ in the proportion of inaccurate information reported, but after a 2-year delay, the children averaged 20% inaccurate information, compared to 7% for the adults. Flin, Boon, Knox, and Bull (1992) found that the amount of accurate information reported by 6- and 9-year-old children decreased significantly over a 5-month delay, whereas adults' accurate recall levels were stable over the same period. Furthermore, errors increased significantly over the delay, especially for the 9-year-olds.

Quicker and greater forgetting may also put children at greater risk of susceptibility to misleading information presented after a delay. The greatest levels of children's (and adults') suggestibility, and specifically, memory-impairment-related suggestibility, typically have been found in studies that delay the presentation of misinformation (e.g., Ceci et al., 1987a, 1987b; Poole & Lindsay, 1995; Warren & Lane, 1995). Weak memory traces, whether weakened by time or by insufficient original encoding, may be more vulnerable to integration with or overwriting by nonevent information (e.g., Brainerd et al., 1990; Myles-Worsley, Cromer, & Dodd, 1986; Warren et al., 1991).

An early interview not only captures memories when they are fresh, it may reduce further forgetting later, a phenomenon known as "inoculation against forgetting" (Brainerd et al., 1990). Warren and Lane (1995) and many other researchers (e.g., Goodman et al., 1991; Tucker, Mertin, & Luszcz, 1990) have reported that early questioning results in more complete and accurate accounts later. However, early questioning does not always prove beneficial (Baker-Ward et al., 1993) and may not provide any practically significant advantages after a lengthy interval of months or years (e.g., Flin et al., 1992; Poole & White, 1993).

If early interviews can inoculate against forgetting, then it is possible that early interviews can also inoculate against suggestibility. Tucker et al. (1990) showed that children interviewed with both neutral and misleading questions shortly after witnessing a videotaped event were more resistant to later misleading questioning than children who were questioned only after a delay. Furthermore, Warren and colleagues (Warren & Hulse, 1994; Warren & Lane, 1995) demonstrated that an early, entirely neutral interview significantly reduced children's later suggestibility.

Repeated Interviewing

In some studies, a single early interview is insufficient for reducing forgetting and later suggestibility. Neutral "booster" interviews spread out over the retention interval may help in maintaining the completeness and accuracy of an account over a long period (Brainerd & Ornstein, 1991). There is strong evidence from the laboratory that multiple recall attempts produce more accurate information than single recall attempts, and that more information is reported on later recall trials than initial recall trials (Brainerd et al., 1990; Howe, 1991). Furthermore, within a single interview, children may disclose very little information, and what they do report may not be repeated in a later interview. For example, Fivush, Hamond, Harsch, Singer, and Wolf (1991) found that 2-year-olds interviewed twice, with a 6-week interval between interviews, were very accurate in what they recalled during a single interview, but very inconsistent across interviews, recalling less than 20% of the same information on both occasions. Thus, repeated interviewing may be necessary to obtain complete pictures of events from young witnesses.

Unfortunately, repeated questioning, even when it is entirely neutral, may ultimately do more harm than good (Warren & Lane, 1995). In studies with both adults and children, intrusion errors have increased over trials, not just over time (Eugenio, Buckhout, Kostes, & Ellison, 1982; Fivush & Hamond, 1989). Memory reports become more complete and elaborate with repeated questioning, but both accuracies and inaccuracies increase.

Exposure to repeated misleading interviews may exacerbate the problem. Ceci et al. (1995) repeatedly questioned preschoolers over a period of several weeks regarding an event that had occurred in their nursery school. Over time, these children made many false allegations and fabricated details about the event that were consistent with misleading suggestions of the interviewers. In another study by Ceci and his colleagues (Ceci, Loftus, Leichtman, & Bruck, 1994), children were repeatedly asked to think about and visualize both events that actually had happened in their lives and events that they never had experienced. After weekly interviews over 12 consecutive weeks, many children (43% compared to 29% initially) reported the nonevents as actual experiences, and some provided elaborate narrative accounts of the nonevents.

On the other hand, Goodman et al. (1991) found that children interviewed twice with suggestive and neutral questions were actually less suggestible the second time, but no different in overall suggestibility from the once-interviewed children. Tucker et al. (1990) observed that twice-interviewed children were superior to singly (delayed) interviewed children in answering misleading questions accurately, but their performance did not change from the first to the second interview. Last, Warren and Lane (1995) and Warren and Hulse (1994) found that children suggestively interviewed twice were no more suggestible (when asked direct questions) than those suggestively interviewed only once after a delay, and they concluded that the timing of the initial interview is more important than the number of interviews.

Even if the empirical evidence regarding the effects of repeated interviews on suggestibility, accuracy, and completeness is inconsistent, it is common sense that interview repetition provides greater opportunity for contamination of children's reports. Additionally, Flin (1991) cautioned that repeated questioning can reduce witness cooperation and motivation and can diminish witness credibility if it appears that the witness has been overrehearsed. Most important, when the interview concerns child sexual abuse or other assaults, repeated interviewing can be stressful and may impair performance (Flin, 1991).

Minimizing the number of pretrial interviews requires coordination and consolidation of responsibility between investigative agencies. Some communities have assigned a single professional who assumes all responsibility for a case and controls all official interactions with the child from initial assignment through final disposition of all proceedings (Whitcomb, 1992).

Furthermore, we believe that whenever a child is interviewed by a professional, that interview should be preserved on videotape. Like other countries, notably England, Scotland, and Canada (see Flin, Kearney, & Murray, 1996, and Sas, Wolfe, & Gowdey, 1996 [both in this volume]; Spencer & Flin, 1990), American jurisdictions should mandate that all investigative interviews be videotaped. Although some mental health professionals have expressed concern about such a procedure (MacFarlane, 1985), the dividends of accurate fact-finding and potential reduction of stress for the child (due to reducing the need for repeated interviews) far outweigh the often-cited deficits of exposing the expert interviewer to unwarranted criticism or of breaching the child's privacy (Flin, 1991; McGough, 1995; Spencer & Flin, 1990). The Child Victim Witness Investigative Pilot Project (CVWIPP; California Attorney General's Office, 1994) found that participating professionals, including prosecutors, defense counsel, police, and social service providers, enthusiastically endorsed videotaping as a component of a comprehensive program aimed at providing enhanced protection of child abuse victims through improved interviewer training and interagency cooperation.

A videorecorded interview also can serve to refresh a child's memory of what she or he had earlier remembered. Preliminary findings of Yuille, Porter, and Tollestrup (1993) indicate that second and third graders' recall of action-oriented details was enhanced when they were reinterviewed after seeing their earlier videotaped accounts of a staged experience. In addition to refreshing memory, the CVWIPP suggested six other advantages of videorecording: It can reduce the number of interviews (and interviewers); it provides an incentive for interviewers to use proper techniques; it preserves the child's exact statements, emotions, and demeanor at the moment of disclosure; it encourages capitulation of the accused, either through a confession or guilty plea; it is useful in assessing the strength of the key witness for the prosecution and thus facilitates decisions about whether to pursue a prosecution; and it aids in preparing the child for testimony at trial.

Finally, and perhaps more important for the ideal of justice, a videore-corded interview serves as a benchmark of the child's earliest report against which the reliability of later versions can be weighed. If details are omitted or added, a more informed judgment can be made about whether the changes result from reminiscence (the accurate later recall of information not recalled earlier; e.g., Tucker et al., 1990) or flashbacks (Loftus & Kaufman, 1992) or, instead, from memory-fade or improper suggestion.

The Interviewing Process:
The "How" of the Interview

The skillful interviewing of children is a very complex task, and the myriad issues embedded in interviewing have been reviewed in depth elsewhere (e.g., Garbarino & Stott, 1989; Jones & McQuiston, 1988). Thus, we will narrow our focus in this chapter to a few critical points about which current empirical research suggests problems and solutions.

Encouraging a Spontaneous, Free-Recall Report

It is well documented that children's spontaneous, free-recall reports are more accurate, although less complete, than those elicited by specific questioning (e.g., Dent, 1991). Therefore, almost all interview guidelines contain recommendations about establishing rapport and "warming up," which may increase the amount of information that children provide spontaneously (e.g., American Professional Society on the Abuse of Children, 1990). However, anxious interviewers may be tempted to skip free-recall or general, open-ended questioning altogether and jump directly to specific questioning regarding the alleged abuse. In one recent examination of 23 child sexual abuse interviews conducted by child protective services personnel, Elliott (1995) found that only 10 had any rapport-building period, and only 1 began with free-recall or general questioning prior to specific questioning about the abuse.

Steller and Boychuk (1992) suggested starting an interview with narrative prompts such as "I understand something may have happened to you. Tell me as best you can about that so I understand" (p. 50). They also recommend the use of "cue questions," which may trigger the child's memory of an event, and following up such cue questions with open-ended questions relevant to the answers. For example, if a child replied, "In the bedroom," when asked, "Where did something happen?" the interviewer should follow up with another general question, such as "Tell me as much as you can remember about what happened in the bedroom" (Steller & Boychuk, 1992, p. 50).

A similar approach known as the stepwise interview is advocated by Yuille, Hunter, Joffe, and Zaparniuk (1993). The stepwise interview begins with rapport building, then moves to a request for recall of two specific (but neutral and unrelated to the alleged abuse or crime) events. A free-narrative session regarding the "target event" (suspected abuse) follows, during which the child is asked to describe the event "without leaving out any details" (p. 107). According to Yuille, Hunter, Joffe, and Zaparniuk (1993), during this phase, the interviewer acts as a facilitator, not an interrogator, and refrains from interrupting, correcting, or challenging the child's statements. The free narrative is then followed by general questions, which should be based on information the child has already provided. Finally, specific questions and interview aids are introduced if necessary. Preliminary results of a study designed to evaluate the effectiveness of the stepwise interview are promising, in that use of this format appears less likely to result in interviews that yield "scant or contaminated information" (Yuille, Hunter, Joffe, & Zaparniuk, 1993, p. 111).

As Yuille, Hunter, Joffe, and Zaparniuk (1993) acknowledged, although the ideal situation is for children to provide all known, relevant information in response to free-recall prompts or general questions, in actuality most children's spontaneous recollections are woefully incomplete. However, rather than resorting to specific questioning to draw out additional information, some researchers are attempting to develop new techniques to boost the completeness of children's free recall without compromising their accuracy. For example, the cognitive interview (Geiselman & Fisher, 1992), first developed for use with adult witnesses, is now the topic of extensive research with children. The cognitive interview includes several mnemonic devices shown to be effective in boosting free recall in laboratory memory research, such as asking respondents to recall events in forward and backward order, asking them to take another person's perspective when attempting to recall the event, attempting to reconstruct the original circumstances surrounding the event, and emphasizing the importance of recalling all information, whether or not it is considered important. In addition to proposing the cognitive interview's specific mnemonic techniques, Geiselman and Fisher (1992) suggested that interviewers should allow witnesses to fully divulge their knowledge by allowing them sufficient time to answer questions and by avoiding interruptions.

In a study of the cognitive interview's effectiveness with third-grade and sixth-grade children, Geiselman et al. (1993) found that the cognitive interview was markedly superior to a standard interview in eliciting accurate information. McCauley and Fisher (1992) found similar results, using a revised version of the cognitive interview with 7-year-olds. In another recent study (Milne, Bull, Köhnken, & Memon, 1994), 8- and 9-year-old children interviewed with the cognitive interview recalled significantly more accurate details than children interviewed by standard procedures. More important, the cognitive interview did not appear to increase reporting of inaccurate information, and when administered prior to a set of misleading questions, it also improved the children's resistance to suggestibility.

Unfortunately, the cognitive interview may be inappropriate for younger and less verbal children, who may not possess the skills necessary to use the alternative perspective component or to reorder the sequence of events. Moreover, a recent meta-analysis of studies has shown that the cognitive interview significantly increases the amount of inaccurate, as well as accurate, information reported (Köhnken, Milne, Memon, & Bull, 1994). Although the cognitive interview is not likely to be a cure-all, its overarching goal of boosting witnesses' free recall rather than prying out information with direct questions is compatible with all known empirical data.

Avoiding Specific and Leading Questions

The major issue confronted by interviewers is likely to be the paradox that young children need help recalling experiences, but that direct, specific questions and other recall prompts may produce distortions and suggestibility. Research consistently has demonstrated that younger children provide much less information than older children or adults in free-recall accounts of events or in response to general questions (e.g., Dent, 1991; for a review, see Goodman et al., 1991). To obtain complete event reports from young children, then, it may be necessary to ask more specific questions and provide more retrieval support and prompting. Unfortunately, when specific questions are asked, although younger children's reports do become more complete, their accuracy often decreases (Dent, 1991).

Recent studies have found that investigators rely on specific questions almost exclusively when interviewing children. Warren (1992) and her colleagues (Boyd, 1993; Hulse, 1994; Warren, Boyd, & Walker, 1992) have analyzed the child sexual abuse investigative interviews conducted by child protective services professionals in one state. Approximately 90% of all questions were specific questions; in fact, the majority (64%) called only for a yes or no response, and this held true across the wide age range of the children interviewed (2 to 13 years). Children rarely were asked questions to which they could respond with multiword or narrative answers, but when such questions were asked, the children responded accordingly. Consistent results have been seen in a recent analysis of interviews conducted by specially trained Israeli "youth investigators" (Lamb et al., in press; Sternberg et al., 1996). Only 2.2% of the interviewers' utterances were "invitational," defined as those encouraging an open-ended, narrative response from children. When invitational utterances were used, however, they did evoke longer and more detailed responses from the children.

Interviewers' apparent overuse of specific questions may be due to the sensitivity involved in child sexual abuse interviews. For example, in a study that required children to give information about a genital exam, even older children required specific questioning to disclose information (Saywitz, Goodman, Nicholas, & Moan, 1991). Ironically, however, these findings also may suggest that interviewers were limiting the information that children could provide by asking for very specific details and allowing only one-word replies. In the aforementioned interview studies by Warren and her colleagues, 64% of the interviewers' questions were yes/no questions, and accordingly, approximately 64% of the children's utterances during the interviews were only one word long. The interviewers also took longer "turns" when speaking than did the children. They averaged four utterances in one turn (before the child responded or was allowed to respond), whereas the children averaged only a little over one utterance per turn. Overall, the interviewers spoke approximately 15 words to every 4 spoken by the children.

The finding that interviewers appear to assume control of the interview process by using a primarily direct question-answer format and asking several questions without waiting for responses has several troubling implications with respect to child witnesses. Specific questions are more likely to be leading questions, and young children (particularly pre-schoolers) may be more likely to go along with these leads than are adults (e.g., Cassel, 1991; Ceci & Bruck, 1993; Goodman & Reed, 1986). Children are not necessarily more suggestible than adults, but certain social and cognitive factors, including, as previously discussed, the social context of the interview and the delay since the to-be-remembered event, can create conditions that increase children's relative suggestibility (Ceci et al., 1987a; Goodman & Reed, 1986). Additional influences on susceptibility to misleading questioning include the linguistic form of, and the types of information addressed by, the questions. For example, Goodman and Reed reported that children were more resistant to misleading questions involving central-event details or actions as opposed to peripheral details. Similarly, King and Yuille (1987) suggested that children are more resistant to questions involving event details they find salient, but that details that are interesting or salient for children may not be those found salient by adults. Regarding the effects of question form, Dale, Loftus, and Rathbun (1978) found that when objects had not been presented in a film, preschoolers were more accurate in responding to questions using an indefinite article ("Did you see *a* stop sign?") rather than a definite article ("Did you see *the* stop sign?"). Cassel (1991) reported that children were more influenced than adults by tag questions, which take the form of a statement followed by a question, such as "The man had brown hair, didn't he?"

Another concern surrounding the use of specific, direct questions is that children attempt to provide responses to almost any adult question, even if they do not clearly understand their meanings (Moston, 1990; Warren & McCloskey, 1993). In fact, children and, to a lesser extent, adults even will respond to meaningless or bizarre questions such as "Is red heavier than yellow?" if they are asked by an authoritative experimenter (Hughes & Grieve, 1980; Pratt, 1990). Further exacerbating the problem, children rarely ask for clarification when they do not understand what is being asked of them (see Warren & McCloskey, 1993) and often fail to realize that they do not comprehend the questions (Perry et al., 1993). Thus, asking children a series of direct questions is likely to result in a series of responses, but the validity of these responses may be questionable.

Using Anatomically Detailed Dolls
and Other Nonverbal Recall Aids

The tradeoff between completeness (when using specific questions) and accuracy (when using general and free-recall questions) has led to the development of nonverbal means of eliciting information. Most of the attention, empirical and otherwise, has been focused on the use of ana-tomically detailed dolls. Use of these dolls in child abuse interviews is widespread (Boat & Everson, 1993), but there is equally widespread concern about their potential suggestiveness (Wolfner, Faust, & Dawes, 1993), which has led to a ban on their use in some jurisdictions (Bruck, Ceci, Francoeur, & Renick, 1995). Although anatomical dolls may be used simply to assess children's anatomical and sexual knowledge or their terminology for body parts (Boat & Everson, 1993), most research efforts have been aimed at assessing the dolls' potential to facilitate or distort children's recall.

In one of the earliest of these studies, Goodman and Aman (1990), using anatomically detailed dolls, questioned 3- and 5-year-old children and found that the dolls neither enhanced nor decreased accuracy. Saywitz, Goodman, et al. (1991) questioned 5- and 7-year-olds about previous medical examinations, which, for half the children, had included genital exams. When asked to reenact the exam with props (scale-model medical instruments) and anatomically detailed dolls, the children doubled the amount of information they had reported in free recall. However, errors also significantly increased. In an exclusively verbal interview session, more than three fourths of the children who had received the genital exam failed to disclose genital touching. That rate was not improved when dolls were provided. Only when the interviewer pointed to the doll's genitalia and directly asked "Did the doctor touch you here?" did a majority of children report the genital contact. Conversely, those children who had not received a genital exam did not falsely report genital touching in either their verbal recall or doll-aided free-recall reports, but a very small percentage did falsely report genital touching when the interviewer pointed to the doll's genitalia and asked a direct question.

More recently, Bruck et al. (1995) conducted two studies that expanded upon the Saywitz, Goodman, et al. (1991) research. In their first study, 3-year-old children were given medical exams (half of them received genital exams) and then were immediately directly questioned using anatomically detailed dolls and medical (e.g., a stethoscope) and other (e.g., a spoon) props. In the second study, an additional 20 children received genital exams and then were questioned using the anatomically detailed dolls. In both studies, children were equally accurate when using their own bodies or the dolls to recall the exam. Furthermore, children's reports of genital touching were often inaccurate, both with and without the dolls. Not only did children fail to report genital touching when it had occurred, but they were equally likely to falsely report genital touching when it had not occurred.

Given the controversy over anatomically detailed dolls, some advocate the use of more "neutral" props, including nonanatomically detailed dolls, puppets, drawings, and toys. Gordon et al. (1993) asked 3- and 5-year-olds to describe a recent doctor's visit using nonanatomical dolls. The 5-year-olds were aided by the use of the dolls, recalling more accurate details, but their accounts were no more elaborate overall than those elicited without dolls. Pipe and her colleagues (Gee & Pipe, 1995; Pipe, Gee, & Wilson, 1993; Salmon, Bidrose, & Pipe, 1995) studied the effectiveness of various types of props with three groups of children (ages 3, 5-6, and 9-10). Under certain conditions, props enhanced accurate recall for all age groups, but the use of toy props rather than real props, and the use of irrelevant or distracter props also increased errors, especially after a delay. Because an interviewer may not know which props might be relevant and irrelevant in actual child witness cases, the advisability of using any props becomes dubious.

Suggestibility issues aside, research on the benefits of dolls and props for the younger, less verbal children for whom they were devised is inconclusive. Gordon et al. (1993) found that dolls enhance recall for 5-year-olds but not for 3-year-olds. Similarly, Salmon et al. (1995) found that props do not enhance 3-year-olds' verbal recall of events. In fact, recent studies (e.g., DeLoache, 1995) suggest that children who are 3 years old and younger may be unable to use the dolls to represent themselves or scale models and props to represent real-world objects. If so, then young children's behaviors with dolls and props may be random, play actions rather than accurate demonstrations of earlier actual events.

Using Age-Appropriate Language

Until the effectiveness and potential suggestibility of nonverbal interview aids is better documented, interviewers may be forced to rely on purely verbal means of eliciting information. The developmental appropriateness of the interviewer's language then becomes of paramount concern. Several researchers have documented the use of complex and confusing language by attorneys questioning children during trials (e.g., Brennan & Brennan, 1988; Kranat & Westcott, 1994; Walker, 1993). Perry et al. (1993) demonstrated that such complex questions have deleterious effects on children's and adults' answers. In their study, kindergartners, fourth graders, ninth graders, and college students were asked about a videotaped incident with questions phrased either in "lawyerese" (including negatives, double negatives, multifaceted constructions, specific or difficult vocabulary, and complex embedding of propositions) or in matched, simplified versions. Across age groups, twice as many simply phrased questions were answered correctly as were lawyerese forms of the questions. Also, respondents of all ages accurately judged how well they understood and could answer the lawyerese questions only 55% of the time, whereas they accurately judged their ability to answer the simplified questions 90% of the time.

The questions asked of a child earlier in the legal process may be even more important than those asked in the courtroom, as they can determine whether the case will be pursued, whether a child will be protected from further abuse, and whether an innocent person is falsely accused. As mentioned previously, Warren and her colleagues have analyzed child protective services professionals' investigative interviews of allegedly sexually abused children between the ages of 2 and 13 (Boyd, 1993; Hulse, 1994; Warren, 1992; Warren et al., 1992). They found that question complexity did not appear to differ depending on the age of the child being interviewed. They also found many examples of complex syntax and age-inappropriate vocabulary, and questions concerning abstract and complex topics that the children being interviewed would be unlikely to understand. For example, one child was asked if she knew "what those warts were transmitted by?"

Walker (1994) provided several concrete recommendations, well grounded in empirical research as well as common sense, for achieving the goal of age-appropriate questioning. For example, she recommended that interviewers avoid complex question forms, including those containing multiple propositions, negatives, passives, and embeddings. Interviewers always should be alert to any signals of comprehension difficulty, for example, inappropriate responses, ambiguous responses, lack of response, and "I don't know" answers (Walker, 1994; Walker & Warren, 1995). Interviewers should avoid "big words" in general and legal jargon in particular. Many studies (e.g., Saywitz, Jaenicke, & Comparo, 1990; Warren-Leubecker, Tate, Hinton, & Ozbek, 1989) have shown that children have difficulty with terms such as *court* and *jury,* confusing them with "a place to play basketball" and "something you wear around your neck," respectively. These confusions are not limited to legal terms, however, because children may use words in quite limited and literal ways. For example, a child may say that she was not wearing any "clothes" when she was wearing a bathing suit (Hulse, 1994).

In summary, interviewers wishing to elicit accurate reports, especially from young children, should encourage children to spontaneously and freely report information by establishing rapport, allowing sufficient time for responses, and refraining from interruptions or premature use of specific questions. Although nonverbal means of eliciting information may be appealing, especially with younger children given the typical paucity of their verbal reports, the use of dolls, props, and, in particular, anatomically detailed dolls should be thought of as a last resort and approached with extreme caution. Finally, in all interviews, whether strictly verbal or a combination of verbal and nonverbal techniques, the language used throughout the interview should be developmentally sensitive.

The Interview Context:
The "Where" of the Interview

There is a long-standing assumption among clinicians that the environment in which an interview takes place is an important factor facilitating both a child's willingness to interact and his or her ability to relate reliable information. Many clinicians take great pains to make their interviewing rooms inviting and reassuring, often creating a facility that is indistinguishable from a playroom at any nursery school (Hall, 1989). Goodman and Helgeson (1985) similarly suggested that a comfortable interviewing environment contributes to more accurate recall: "Because stress interferes with the retrieval process, and because retrieval failures predict heightened suggestibility, it is possible that . . . the adversary process may not be the best means of obtaining the truth from children" (pp. 203-204). As part of the recent reforms of the pretrial processing of child sexual abuse cases, many communities have created special interviewing spaces for child victims. For example, in Huntsville, Alabama, the Children's Advocacy Center is located in a house rather than an office building because "it symbolized a non-institutional approach" to the handling of such cases (Cramer, 1985, p. 213). This concept has been replicated nationwide (Whitcomb, 1992).

In truth, there is scant research exploring the linkage between the physical interviewing environment and the accuracy of the child's account. Most studies conflate the place of questioning with the mode or tone of interviewing. In a study by Hill and Hill (1987), older children (ages 7-9) were shown a videotape of an encounter and then divided into two groups and asked identical questions about what they had seen. The critical difference between the two groups was the setting and manner in which the children's statements were extracted. Members of the "interview group" were questioned and tape-recorded by a single interviewer in a private room fitted with one-way mirrors and a microphone; members of the "courtroom group" were questioned on direct examination by a law student and cross-examined by another law student in a courtroom setting presided over by a "judge" and in the presence of other individuals, including the actor "defendant." Children in the interview group tended to relate more central items in free recall, answer specific questions correctly more often, and respond with "I don't know" or give no answer when asked specific questions significantly less often than did members of the courtroom group.

Saywitz and Nathanson (1993) examined the association between 8- to 10-year-old children's perceived stress of the interview/testimonial environment and their ability to testify accurately. Two weeks after participating in a physiology lesson/activity, children were questioned either in a room at their own school or in a courtroom. Children questioned in the courtroom performed worse on free recall and on misleading questions than their agemates questioned at school, and they rated the courtroom as more stressful. In addition, perceptions of the stressfulness of the environment were negatively correlated with correct free recall. Although more research isolating the effect of the place variable is needed before any definitive conclusions can be drawn about the importance or influence of the interviewing environment, preliminary data suggest that a comfortable setting may contribute to children's recall performance.

Conclusion

American researchers have now moved beyond the challenge posed by Loftus and Davies (1984). We believe that the research question for the next decade is: How can children be empowered to resist suggestiveness and to recall their experiences more accurately and completely? Many states have formed special, professional task forces to develop child witness interviewing strategies and protocols. Among others, in California the CVWIPP (California Attorney General's Office, 1994) has found that when child interviewing specialists are trained in child development and forensic issues, such training results in improved fact-finding, reduced system-induced trauma to children, and also ensures that children in need of services are identified and referred appropriately. Empirical research can contribute not only to the redress of unjust accusations but also, and perhaps more important, to the prevention of injustice and the enhancement of children's credibility.

References

American Professional Society on the Abuse of Children. (1990). *Guidelines for psychosocial evaluation of suspected sexual abuse in young children.* Chicago: Author.

Attorney General's Task Force on Family Violence. (1984). *Final report.* Washington, DC: U.S. Department of Justice.

Baker-Ward, L., Gordon, B. N., Ornstein, P. A., Larus, D. M., & Clubb, P. A. (1993). Young children's long-term retention of a pediatric examination. *Child Development, 64,* 1519-1533.

Boat, B. W., & Everson, M. D. (1993). The use of anatomical dolls in sexual abuse evaluations: Current research and practice. In G. S. Goodman & B. L. Bottoms (Eds.), *Child victims, child witnesses: Understanding and improving testimony* (pp. 47-69). New York: Guilford.

Boyd, C. J. (1993). *The investigatory child sexual abuse interview: Questioning techniques of child protective service workers.* Unpublished master's thesis, University of Tennessee at Chattanooga.

Brainerd, C. J., & Ornstein, P. A. (1991). Children's memory for witnessed events: The developmental backdrop. In J. Doris (Ed.), *The suggestibility of children's recollections* (pp. 10-20). Washington, DC: American Psychological Association.

Brainerd, C. J., Reyna, V. F., Howe, M. L., & Kingma, J. (1990). The development of forgetting and reminiscence. *Monographs of the Society for Research in Child Development, 55* (3-4, Serial No. 222).

Brennan, M., & Brennan, R. (1988). *Strange language: Child victims under cross examination.* Wagga Wagga, Australia: Charles Sturt University-Riverina.

Bruck, M., Ceci, S. J., Francoeur, E., & Renick, A. (1995). Anatomically detailed dolls do not facilitate preschoolers' reports of a pediatric examination involving genital touching. *Journal of Experimental Psychology: Applied, 1*(2), 95-109.

Buhrman, A. K., & Warren, A. R. (1994, August). *Reducing suggestibility in normal and learning disabled child witnesses.* Paper presented at the Third International Conference on Practical Aspects of Memory, College Park, MD.

California Attorney General's Office. (1994). *Child Victim Witness Investigative Pilot Project: Research and evaluation final report.* Sacramento: Author.

Carlson, M. (1990, January 29). Six years of trial by torture. *Time, 140,* 26-27.

Cassel, W. S. (1991). *Child eyewitness testimony: The search for truth and justice in the American way.* Unpublished master's thesis, Florida Atlantic University, Boca Raton, Florida.

Ceci, S. J., & Bruck, M. (1993). The suggestibility of the child witness: A historical review and synthesis. *Psychological Bulletin, 113,* 403-439.

Ceci, S. J., Huffman, M. L., Smith, E., & Loftus, E. F. (1994). Repeatedly thinking about a non-event: Source misattributions among preschoolers. *Consciousness and Cognition, 3,* 388-407.

Ceci, S. J., Leichtman, M., & Putnick, M. (Eds.). (1992). *Cognitive and social factors in early deception.* Hillsdale, NJ: Lawrence Erlbaum.

Ceci, S. J., Leichtman, M. D., & White, T. (1995). *Interviewing preschoolers: Remembrance of things planted.* Unpublished manuscript.

Ceci, S. J., Loftus, E. F., Leichtman, M. D., & Bruck, M. (1994). The possible role of source misattributions in the creation of false beliefs among preschoolers. *International Journal of Clinical and Experimental Hypnosis, 62,* 304-320.

Ceci, S. J., Ross, D. F., & Toglia, M. P. (1987a). Age differences in suggestibility: Narrowing the uncertainties. In S. J. Ceci, M. P. Toglia, & D. F. Ross (Eds.), *Children's eyewitness memory* (pp. 79-91). New York: Springer-Verlag.

Ceci, S. J., Ross, D. F., & Toglia, M. P. (1987b). Suggestibility of children's memory: Psycholegal implications. *Journal of Experimental Psychology: General, 116,* 38-49.

Clarke-Stewart, A., Thompson, W., & Lepore, S. (1989, May). *Manipulating children's interpretations through interrogation.* Paper presented at the biennial meeting of the Society for Research on Child Development, Kansas City, MO.

Cramer, R. E., Jr. (1985). The district attorney as a mobilizer in a community approach to child sexual abuse. *University of Miami Law Review, 40,* 209-216.

Coy v. Iowa, 487 U.S. 1012 (1988).

Dale, P. S., Loftus, E. F., & Rathbun, L. (1978). The influence of the form of the question on the eyewitness testimony of preschool children. *Journal of Psycholinguistic Research, 7,* 269-277.

Davies, G., & Flin, R. (1988). The accuracy and suggestibility of child witnesses. In F. G. Davies & J. Drinkwater (Eds.), *The child witness: Do the courts abuse children?* (pp. 21-34). Leicester, England: British Psychological Society.

DeLoache, J. S. (1995). The use of dolls in interviewing young children. In M. S. Zaragoza, J. R. Graham, G. C. N. Hall, R. Hirschman, & Y. S. Ben-Porath (Eds.), *Memory and testimony in the child witness* (pp. 160-178). Thousand Oaks, CA: Sage.

Dent, H. R. (1978). Interviewing child witnesses. In M. Gruneberg, P. Morris, & R. Sykes (Eds.), *Practical aspects of memory* (pp. 236-243). London: Academic Press.

Dent, H. (1991). Experimental studies of interviewing child witnesses. In J. Doris (Ed.), *The suggestibility of children's recollections: Implications for eyewitness testimony* (pp. 138-146). New York: Springer-Verlag.

Dent, H. R., & Stephenson, G. M. (1979). An experimental study of the effectiveness of different techniques of questioning child witnesses. *British Journal of Social and Clinical Psychology, 18,* 41-51.

Elliott, K. C. (1995). *An evaluation of interview guidelines and child sexual abuse interviews.* Unpublished master's thesis, University of Tennessee at Chattanooga.

Eugenio, P., Buckhout, R., Kostes, S., & Ellison, K. (1982). Hypermnesia in the eyewitness to a crime. *Bulletin of the Psychonomic Society, 19,* 83-86.

Fehrer, T. L. (1988). The alleged molestation victim, the rules of evidence, and the Constitution: Should children really be seen and not heard? *American Journal of Criminal Law, 14,* 227-255.

Fivush, R., & Hamond, N. R. (1989). Time and again: Effects of repetition and retention interval on 2-year-olds' event recall. *Journal of Experimental Child Psychology, 47,* 259-273.

Fivush, R., Hamond, N. R., Harsch, N., Singer, N., & Wolf, A. (1991). Content and consistency in early autobiographical recall. *Discourse Processes, 14,* 373-388.

Flin, R. (1991). Commentary: A grand memory for forgetting. In J. Doris (Ed.), *The suggestibility of children's recollections* (pp. 21-23). Washington, DC: American Psychological Association.

Flin, R., Boon, J., Knox, A., & Bull, R. (1992). The effect of a five-month delay on children's and adults' eyewitness memory. *British Journal of Psychology, 83,* 323-336.

Flin, R., Kearney, B., & Murray, K. (1996). Children's evidence: Scottish research and law. In B. L. Bottoms & G. S. Goodman (Eds.), *International Perspectives on Child Abuse and Children's Testimony: Psychological Research and Law* (pp. 358-376). Thousand Oaks, CA: Sage.

Foley, M. A., & Johnson, M. K. (1985). Confusions between memories for performed and imagined actions: A developmental comparison. *Child Development, 56,* 1145-1155.

Garbarino, J., & Stott, F. M. (1989). *What children can tell us.* San Francisco: Jossey-Bass.

Gee, S., & Pipe, M.-E. (1995). Helping children to remember: The influence of object cues on children's accounts of a real event. *Developmental Psychology, 31,* 746-758.

Geiselman, R. E., & Fisher, R. P. (1992). *Memory-enhancing techniques for investigative interviewing: The cognitive interview.* Springfield, IL: Charles C Thomas.

Geiselman, R. E., & Padilla, J. (1988). Cognitive interviewing with child witnesses. *Journal of Police Science and Administration, 16,* 236-242.

Geiselman, R. E., Saywitz, K. J., & Bornstein, G. K. (1993). Effects of cognitive questioning techniques on children's recall performance. In G. S. Goodman & B. L. Bottoms (Eds.), *Child victims, child witnesses: Understanding and improving testimony* (pp. 71-94). New York: Guilford.

Goodman, G. S. (1993). Understanding and improving children's testimony. *Children Today, 22,* 13-15.

Goodman, G. S., & Aman, C. (1990). Children's use of anatomically detailed dolls to recount an event. *Child Development, 61,* 1859-1871.

Goodman, G. S., Bottoms, B. L., Schwartz-Kenney, B. M., & Rudy, L. (1991). Children's testimony about a stressful event: Improving children's reports. *Journal of Narrative and Life History, 1,* 69-99.

Goodman, G. S., & Helgeson, V. S. (1985). Child sexual assault: Children's memory and the law. *University of Miami Law Review, 40,* 181-208.

Goodman, G. S., & Reed, R. S. (1986). Age differences in eyewitness testimony. *Law and Human Behavior, 10,* 317-332.

Goodman, G. S., Rudy, L., Bottoms, B. L., & Aman, C. (1990). Children's concerns and memory: Ecological issues in the study of children's eyewitness memory. In R. Fivush & J. Hudson (Eds.), *Knowing and remembering in young children* (pp. 249-284). New York: Cambridge University Press.

Goodman, G. S., Taub, E. P., Jones, D. P. H., England, P., Port, L. K., Rudy, L., & Prado, L. (1992). Testifying in criminal court. *Monographs of the Society for Research in Child Development, 57* (5, Serial No. 229).

Gordon, B. N., Ornstein, P. A., Nida, R. E., Follmer, A., Crenshaw, M. C., & Albert, G. (1993). Does the use of dolls facilitate children's memory of visits to the doctor? *Applied Cognitive Psychology, 7,* 459-474.

Hall, M. D. (1989). The role of psychologists as experts in cases involving allegations of child sexual abuse. *Family Law Quarterly, 23,* 451-464.

Hill, P. E., & Hill, S. M. (1987). Videotaping children's testimony: An empirical view. *Michigan Law Review, 85,* 809-833.

Home Office. (1992). *Memorandum of good practice on video recorded interviews with child witnesses for criminal proceedings.* London: Home Office with Department of Health.

Howe, M. L. (1991). Misleading children's story recall: Forgetting and reminiscence of the facts. *Developmental Psychology, 27,* 746-762.

Hughes, M., & Grieve, R. (1980). On asking children bizarre questions. *First Language, 1,* 149-160.

Hulse, D. A. (1994). *Linguistic complexity in child abuse interviews.* Unpublished master's thesis, University of Tennessee at Chattanooga.

Idaho v. Wright. 775 P.2d 1224 (Id. 1979), affirmed, 497 U.S. 805 (1990).

Jones, D. P. H., & McQuiston, M. G. (1988). *Interviewing the sexually abused child.* London: Gaskell.

King, M. A., & Yuille, J. C. (1987). Suggestibility and the child witness. In S. J. Ceci, M. P. Toglia, & D. F. Ross (Eds.), *Children's eyewitness memory* (pp. 24-35). New York: Springer-Verlag.

Köhnken, G., Milne, R., Memon, A., & Bull, R. (1994, March). *Recall in cognitive interviews and standard interviews: A meta-analysis.* Paper presented at the biennial meeting of the American Psychology-Law Society, Santa Fe, NM.

Kranat, V. K., & Westcott, H. L. (1994). Under fire: Lawyers questioning children in criminal courts. *Expert Evidence, 3,* 16-24.

Lamb, M. E., Hershkowitz, I., Sternberg, K. J., Esplin, P. W., Hovav, M., Manor, T., & Yudilevitch, L. (in press). Effects of investigative utterance types on Israeli children's responses. *International Journal of Behavioral Development.*

Lepore, S., & Sesco, B. (1994). Distorting children's reports and interpretations of events through suggestion. *Journal of Applied Psychology, 79,* 108-120.

Libai, D. (1969). The protection of the child victim of a sexual offense in the criminal justice system. *Wayne State Law Review, 15,* 977-1032.

Loftus, E. F., & Davies, G. M. (1984). Distortions in the memory of children. *Journal of Social Issues, 40,* 51-67.

Loftus, E. F., & Kaufman, L. (1992). Why do traumatic experiences sometimes produce good memory (flashbulbs) and sometimes no memory (repression)? In E. Winograd & U. Neisser (Eds.), *Affect and accuracy in recall: Studies of "flashbulb" memories* (pp. 212-223). New York: Cambridge University Press.

MacFarlane, K. (1985). Diagnostic evaluations and the use of videotapes in child sexual abuse cases. *University of Miami Law Review, 40,* 135-165.

Maryland v. Craig, 497 U.S. 836 (1990).

McCauley, M., & Fisher, R. (1992, March). *Improving children's recall of actions with the cognitive interview.* Paper presented at the biennial meeting of the American Psychology-Law Society, San Diego, CA.

McGough, L. S. (1994). *Child witnesses: Fragile voices in the American legal system.* New Haven, CT: Yale University Press.

McGough, L. S. (1995). For the record: Videotaping investigative interviews. *Psychology, Public Policy, and Law, 1,* 1-17.

Milne, R., Bull, R., Köhnken, G., & Memon, A. (1994, September). *Child witness suggestibility and cognitive interviewing.* Paper presented at the annual meeting of the British Psychological Society, Developmental Psychology Section, Portsmouth, England.

Montoya, J. (1993). Something not so funny happened on the way to conviction: The pretrial interrogation of child witnesses. *Arizona Law Review, 35,* 927-987.

Moston, S. (1987). The suggestibility of children in interview studies. *First Language, 7,* 67-78.

Moston, S. (1990). How children interpret and respond to questions: Situational sources of suggestibility in eyewitness interviews. *Social Behavior, 5,* 155-167.

Myers, J. E. B. (1994). Taint hearings for child witnesses? A step in the wrong direction. *Baylor Law Review, 46,* 873-946.

Myles-Worsley, M., Cromer, C. C., & Dodd, D. H. (1986). Children's preschool script reconstruction: Reliance on general knowledge as memory fades. *Developmental Psychology, 22,* 22-30.

Parker, J. Y. (1982). The rights of child witnesses: Is the court a protector or perpetrator? *New England Law Review, 17,* 643-717.

People v. Buckey, No. A-750900 (Cal. Crim. Dist. Ct. 1984).

Perry, N. W., Claycomb, L., Tam, P., McAuliff, B., Dostal, C., & Flanagan, C. (1993, March). *When lawyers question children: Is justice served?* Paper presented at the biennial meeting of the Society for Research in Child Development, New Orleans, LA.

Pettit, F., Fegan, M., & Howie, P. (1990, September). *Interviewer effects on children's testimony.* Paper presented at the International Congress on Child Abuse and Neglect, Hamburg, Germany.

Pipe, M.-E., Gee, S., & Wilson, C. (1993). Cues, props, and context: Do they facilitate children's event reports? In G. S. Goodman & B. L. Bottoms (Eds.), *Child victims, child witnesses: Understanding and improving testimony* (pp. 25-45). New York: Guilford.

Poole, D. A., & Lindsay, D. S. (1995). Interviewing preschoolers: Effects of nonsuggestive techniques, parental coaching, and leading questions on reports of nonexperienced events. *Journal of Experimental Child Psychology, 60,* 129-154.

Poole, D. A., & White, L. T. (1991). Effects of question repetition on the eyewitness testimony of children and adults. *Developmental Psychology, 27,* 975-986.

Poole, D. A., & White, L. T. (1993). Effects of question repetition and retention interval on the eyewitness testimony of children and adults. *Developmental Psychology, 29,* 844-853.

Pratt, C. (1990). On asking adults and children bizarre questions. *First Language, 10,* 167-175.

Salmon, K., Bidrose, S., & Pipe, M.-E. (1995). Providing props to facilitate children's event reports: A comparison of toys and real items. *Journal of Experimental Child Psychology, 60,* 174-194.

Sas, L. D., Wolfe, D. A., & Gowdey, K. (1996). Children and the courts in Canada. In B. L. Bottoms & G. S. Goodman (Eds.), *International Perspectives on Child Abuse and Children's Testimony: Psychological Research and Law* (pp. 358-357. Thousand Oaks, CA: Sage.

Saywitz, K. J. (1995). Improving children's testimony: The question, the answer, and the environment. In M. S. Zaragoza, J. R. Graham, G. C. N. Hall, R. Hirschman, & Y. S. Ben-Porath (Eds.), *Memory and testimony in the child witness* (pp. 113-140). Thousand Oaks, CA: Sage.

Saywitz, K. J., Goodman, G. S., Nicholas, E., & Moan, S. (1991). Children's memories of physical examinations that involve genital touch: Implications for reports of sexual abuse. *Journal of Consulting and Clinical Psychology, 59,* 682-691.

Saywitz, K., Jaenicke, C., & Comparo, L. (1990). Children's knowledge of legal terminology. *Law and Human Behavior, 14,* 523-535.

Saywitz, K. J., Moan, S., & Lamphear, V. (1991, August). *The effect of preparation on children's resistance to misleading questions.* Paper presented at the annual meeting of the American Psychological Association, San Francisco.

Saywitz, K. J., & Nathanson, R. (1993). Children's testimony and their perceptions of stress in and out of the courtroom. *Child Abuse & Neglect, 17,* 613-622.

Spencer, J. R., & Flin, R. (1990). *The evidence of children: The law and the psychology.* London: Blackstone.

State v. Giles, 772 P.2d 191 (Idaho 1989).

State v. Michaels, 625 A.2d 489 (N.J. App. 1993), *aff'd,* 1994 WL 278424 (N.J. Sup. 1994).

Steller, M., & Boychuk, T. (1992). Children as witnesses in sexual abuse cases: Investigative interview and assessment techniques. In H. Dent & R. Flin (Eds.), *Children as witnesses* (pp. 47-71). Chichester, England: Wiley.

Sternberg, K. J., Lamb, M. E., & Hershkowitz, I. (1996). Child sexual abuse investigations in Israel: Evaluating innovation. In B. L. Bottoms & G. S. Goodman (Eds.), *International Perspectives on Child Abuse and Children's Testimony: Psychological Research and Law* (pp. 322-337). Thousand Oaks, CA: Sage.

Summit, R. (1983). The child sex abuse accommodation syndrome. *Child Abuse & Neglect, 7,* 177-192.

Tate, C. S. , Warren, A. R., & Hess, T. (1992). Adults' liability for children's "lie-ability": Can adults coach children to lie successfully? In S. J. Ceci, M. Leichtman, & M. Putnick (Eds.), *Cognitive and social factors in early deception* (pp. 69-87). Hillsdale, NJ: Lawrence Erlbaum.

Tobey, A., & Goodman, G. S. (1992). Children's eyewitness memory: Effects of participation and forensic context. *Child Abuse & Neglect, 16,* 779-796.

Toglia, M. P., Ross, D. F., Ceci, S. J., & Hembrooke, H. (1992). The suggestibility of children's memory: A social-psychological and cognitive interpretation. In M. L. Howe, C. J. Brainerd, & V. F. Reyna (Eds.), *Development of long-term retention* (pp. 217-241). New York: Springer-Verlag.

Tucker, A., Mertin, P., & Luszcz, (1990). The effect of a repeated interview on young children's eyewitness memory. *Australian & New Zealand Journal of Criminology, 23,* 117-124.

Walden v. Sears, Roebuck & Co. (5th Cir. 1981).

Walker, A. G. (1993). Questioning young children in court: A linguistic case study. *Law and Human Behavior, 17,* 59-81.

Walker, A. G. (1994). *Handbook on questioning children: The linguistic perspective.* Washington, DC: American Bar Association.

Walker, A. G., & Warren, A. R. (1995). The language of the child abuse interview: Asking the questions, understanding the answers. In T. Ney (Ed.), *True and false allegations of child sexual abuse: Assessment and case management* (pp. 153-162). New York: Brunner/Mazel.

Warren, A. R. (1992, May) *Interviewing child witnesses: Some linguistic considerations.* Paper presented at the NATO Advanced Studies Institute on the Child Witness in Context: Social, Cognitive, and Legal Perspectives, Il Ciocco, Italy.

Warren, A. R., Boyd, C., & Walker, A. G. (1992, March). *Interviewing child witnesses: Beyond leading questions.* Paper presented at the biennial meeting of the American Psychology-Law Society, San Diego, CA.

Warren, A. R., Hagood, P. L., & Jackson, J. (1993, March). *Forgetting relevant and irrelevant details: Age and repeated testing effects.* Paper presented at the biennial meeting of the Society for Research in Child Development, New Orleans, LA.

Warren, A. R., & Hulse, D. A. (1994, September). The effects of initial questioning on later susceptibility to suggestion. In A. Memon (Chair), *Can the child witness be easily misled?* Symposium presented at the annual meeting of the British Psychological Society, Developmental Section, Portsmouth, England.

Warren, A. R., Hulse-Trotter, K., & Tubbs, E. (1991). Inducing resistance to suggestibility in children. *Law and Human Behavior, 15,* 273-285.

Warren, A. R., & Lane, P. (1995). Effects of timing and type of questioning on eyewitness accuracy and suggestibility. In M. S. Zaragoza, J. R. Graham, G. C. N. Hall, R. Hirschman, & Y. S. Ben-Porath (Eds.), *Memory and testimony in the child witness* (pp. 44-60). Thousand Oaks, CA: Sage.

Warren, A. R., & McCloskey, L. A. (1993). Pragmatics: Language in social contexts. In J. B. Gleason (Ed.), *The development of language* (3rd ed., pp. 195-237). New York: Macmillan.

Warren-Leubecker, A., Tate, C. S., Hinton, I., & Ozbek, I. N. (1989). What do children know about the legal system and when do they know it? First steps down a less traveled path in child witness research. In S. J. Ceci, D. F. Ross, & M. P. Toglia (Eds.), *Perspectives on children's testimony* (pp. 158-183). New York: Springer-Verlag.

Wells, G. S. (1989, June). [Commentary on the state of research on children's suggestibility]. Paper presented at the Cornell Conference on the Suggestibility of Children's Recollections, Ithaca, NY.

Whitcomb, D. (1992). *When the victim is a child* (2nd ed.). Washington, DC: National Institute of Justice.

Wolfner, G., Faust, D., & Dawes, R. (1993). The use of anatomical dolls in sexual abuse evaluations: The state of the science. *Applied and Preventative Psychology, 2,* 1-11.

Yuille, J. C., Hunter, R., Joffe, R., & Zaparniuk, J. (1993). Interviewing children in sexual abuse cases. In G. S. Goodman & B. L. Bottoms (Eds.), *Child victims, child witnesses: Understanding and improving testimony* (pp. 95-115). New York: Guilford.

Yuille, J. C., Porter, S., & Tollestrup, P. (1993). *The effects of children reviewing their initial videotaped interviews on subsequent recall for an interactive event.* Unpublished manuscript, University of British Columbia, Vancouver, Canada.

3

Children's Testimony in the Netherlands
A Study of Statement Validity Analysis

FRANCIEN LAMERS-WINKELMAN
FRANK BUFFING

In the Netherlands, many agencies are supposed to deal with child sexual abuse. Whether they actually do so is another question. Agency policies, therapeutic philosophy, and a strong belief in the "family" are responsible for the primary approach to child abuse as a family problem rather than a criminal act. Mandatory reporting has not been established, and everyone can decide individually how to respond to a suspicion. Nevertheless, child sexual abuse can be, and is, reported to the police, and sexual abuse victims are interviewed both by the police and by court-appointed experts. Victims of physical abuse are hardly ever interviewed about the alleged events and, therefore, are rarely witnesses. Consequently, the debate regarding children as witnesses in the Netherlands is restricted to sexual abuse victims.

This chapter is reprinted with permission from *Criminal Justice and Behavior,* Vol. 23 No. 2, June 1996 304-321. © 1996 American Association for Correctional Psychology.

In this chapter, we first discuss the various Dutch agencies that deal with child abuse and neglect and child sexual abuse. In the second section, we report statistics on child abuse and neglect and child sexual abuse in the Netherlands. The third section deals with the assessment of children's allegations of sexual abuse. We review studies on statement validity analysis (SVA) and report the results of a study in which we compared the presence of content criteria in the statements of alleged sexual abuse victims in four age groups. The comparison was made using criteria-based content analysis (CBCA), one of the components of the SVA procedure.

Dutch Agencies

Offices of the Confidential Doctors

Although child abuse and neglect and intrafamilial sexual abuse can be reported to the Offices of the Confidential Doctors, this organization is not authorized to take legal action. The first four Confidential Doctors were appointed in 1972, primarily to help medical doctors deal with cases of child maltreatment without breaking their oath of confidentiality. It is the task of the Confidential Doctors to receive reports from anyone, especially medical doctors, who suspects that a child is being maltreated within the family. However, only 20% of all reports are from the medical profession, including nurses and midwives; most reports come from neighbors and family members. The major tasks of the Confidential Doctors are to organize care for the child and the family, to coordinate the efforts of various agencies, to organize follow-up of all cases, and to keep a register to gain insight into the prevalence of child abuse. The Confidential Doctors do not have any statutory power, and they cannot intervene themselves. They can, but are not expected to, report cases to the Child Protection Boards (see the section on Child Protection Boards).

Given Dutch society's strong antagonistic feelings toward state intervention in "family affairs," and its views on child abuse and neglect, including the view that sexual abuse is "a family affair," the Confidential Doctors seemed to fulfill an important need. Since it was first set up in 1972, the agency has expanded and now has 11 offices throughout the country with 142 employees, most of them part-time workers (29% doctors, 35% social workers, 36% administrators; van Montfoort, 1994).

Medical System

As a rule, general practitioners, pediatricians, hospital administrators, and nurses do not report child abuse and neglect. Medical examination of alleged sexual abuse victims is rare, and even when a child is examined by a medical doctor, most of them do not report or do not follow a protocol to ensure the preservation of possible evidence. Although the Dutch health care system is known to be one of the most advanced in the world, it lacks concern for abused children. Even university hospitals do not have specialized sexual abuse units, child abuse programs, or centers for child protection (Compernolle, 1994).

Mental Health System

The mental health system is funded by the government and organized around regional centers for outpatient mental health care. These centers provide diagnosis and therapy, as well as referrals to more specialized centers. Cases of child abuse and neglect, including child sexual abuse, usually are labeled as "child-rearing problems" or "family problems." Reporting to the Offices of the Confidential Doctors or the Child Protection Boards is not favored; reporting to the police is hardly ever done. Even when mental health professionals suspect sexual abuse, legal action is rarely taken. In practice, most of the suspicions of child sexual abuse, especially of young children, are not dealt with at all (Eeland & Woelinga, 1991).

Child Protection Boards

The Dutch Child Protection Boards are the counterpart of Child Protective Services in the United States or Social Service Departments in the United Kingdom. It is a public service under the control of the Ministry of Justice. The boards receive reports from mental health agencies, schools, the Confidential Doctors, the police, and so on and investigate whether the rights of the child are being violated and how that violation influences the child's normal development. They also seek to determine the causes of the violation and the measures necessary to restore the rights of the child (Veldkamp, 1993). Investigations are carried out by social workers, but contrary to usual practice in the United States and the United Kingdom, the social workers of the Child Protection Boards usually do not interview a child about alleged sexual abuse. Within the Child Protection Boards, as in the mental health system, most abuse cases are classified as child-rearing problems, family problems, or neglect. Only severe cases of child abuse are classified as child abuse. The Child Protection Boards do not keep a child abuse register.

Criminal Justice System

The police also receive reports of child maltreatment, but the majority of cases of physical abuse and/or neglect are not treated as criminal acts. Because the police do not keep registers of these cases, it is unknown how many cases of physical abuse and neglect they handle each year. Sexual abuse is handled by the police more often than is physical abuse. In criminal cases, the child is interviewed by a police officer or a court-appointed expert. In contrast to the United States trial procedure, the Dutch trial procedure is not based on an adversarial process, and there are no jury trials. In criminal cases, the judge presides over the courtroom proceedings and interrogates the defendant, the witnesses, and any expert witnesses. The defendant and the witnesses can be questioned afterward by the two other members of the trial court (i.e., the prosecuting attorney and the defendant and/or the defendant's counsel). An expert witness is appointed by the court and receives a statutory fee fixed by the court and paid out of public funds. As an unwritten rule, children under 12 do not appear in court in criminal proceedings, and by law, children under 16 are not placed under oath. The Dutch judicial system does not permit plea bargaining. Suing a perpetrator is not profitable. Confessions in child sexual abuse cases are infrequent. When a defendant confesses to the crime as charged, it is still necessary to prove all of the facts in formal courtroom proceedings. The statement of a child in itself is not enough for conviction; corroborating evidence is essential. The corroboration requirement is carefully observed.

The judicial interview of the child victim/witness is done outside the court by qualified and specially trained police officers or professionals (expert witnesses/psychologists). All interviews are audio- and video-recorded, and the videotape can be used as support during courtroom proceedings. The videotape, however, is not accepted as proof. Rather, the minutes of an interview taken down by the police officer who interviewed the child are considered the true record. The minutes include the transcripts of the parts of the interview that are relevant to the alleged offense as well as to argumentation. This procedure was developed in 1989 with the main objective of reducing repeated interviewing. The aim is to interview the child only once, as efficiently and extensively as possible. Also in 1989, a training course for police officers was developed. The aim of the course was to improve the knowledge and the skills necessary for interviewing children so as to ensure results that can be used in the judicial process (Oost & Jans, 1989). At the same time, several interview rooms were built, either inside police stations or in the neighborhood of stations. The interview rooms were designed to accommodate the child witness and are equipped with sophisticated video and audio equipment. At present, 70 police officers have been trained for interviewing young witnesses/ victims, and 10 interview rooms are in operation.

The Netherlands, in contrast to several other countries, has seen hardly any debate on strategies for improving or reinforcing the position of child witnesses or on considerations for changes in legislation. As mentioned before, children do not appear in court and cannot take the oath. Sometimes, but not always, the police officer or the expert witness who has interviewed the child has to appear in court to testify. Debate in the Netherlands has centered on the expert witness, the suggestibility of children, the use of anatomical dolls, the influence of questioning before formal interviewing, the alleged rate of false accusations during divorce procedures, and other familiar topics.

Child Abuse in the Netherlands: Some Data

In 1993, the Offices of the Confidential Doctors received 13,500 reports on intrafamilial child maltreatment; the offices were unable to substantiate 19% of the reports received. A case is considered to be verified if two independent professionals concurred that it was very likely that a child was maltreated. Most (54%) of the verified reports were of neglect, 20% were of physical abuse, and 16% were of sexual abuse (Landelijke Stichting Buro's Vertrouwensartsen inzake Kindermishandeling; LSBVK, 1994). No statistics are available regarding children who were sexually abused by someone outside of the home, and government statistics on actual child sexual abuse are virtually nonexistent.

As noted previously, within the Child Protection Boards only severe cases are classified as child abuse or incest. Research showed that in 1992, only 6% of all cases (total number of reports = 9,799) reported to the Child Protection Boards were classified as physical child abuse, and 5% as incest (van Montfoort, 1993, p. 36). A study of 2,690 Dutch children who were inpatients of residential or day treatment facilities revealed that 939 (35%) were victims of child maltreatment, including sexual abuse (Noordhoek-van Staay, 1992).

Between May 1989 and February 1992, 695 children (34% male, 66% female) were interviewed by specially trained police officers. Thirty-two percent of the witnesses were 6 years of age and under, 56% were between 6 and 12, and 12% were 12 years of age and older. Most (91%) of these witnesses were alleged victims of child sexual abuse. Statistics for 1993 showed a huge increase in child interviews: 547 children were interviewed, mostly about alleged child sexual abuse. It is assumed that this increase is mostly due to the fact that the new interview procedure is now more widely known among both judicial and laypeople (A. van der Elskamp, head of the College for Investigation and Crime Control at Zutphen, personal communication, November 1, 1995).

According to a study by van Montfoort (1993), 52% of all reported cases were investigated, and 49% of those cases were dropped between police investigations and court proceedings. Cases were more likely to be investigated when the defendant was not a member of the complainant's family or household. In 26% of all cases reported to the police, the offender was convicted for the crimes as charged. Conviction cases were more likely than nonconviction cases to involve children older than 12. Because of the absence of research (due to lack of money and to lack of interest by officials), it is unknown how the interviews with the child witnesses were valued during the criminal process.

Research on Statement Validity Analysis

Scientific interest in the testimony of child witnesses is not high in the Netherlands. Compared to the United States, for instance, research on this topic is still rare. To our knowledge, only two research projects on child sexual abuse are being carried out at this moment, one by Slurink at the Wilhelmina Children's Hospital in Utrecht and one by Lamers-Winkelman at the Free University of Amsterdam. Both studies examine children's testimony in actual cases and are thus field based. In this section, we focus on a portion of findings from the Lamers-Winkelman research project. Specifically, we present data from our use of SVA to examine children's allegations of sexual abuse.

"Statement validity analysis is a method of structuring an assessment of child sexual abuse complaints by systematically collecting and examining information from children's interviews and other relevant case facts" (Steller & Boychuk, 1992, p. 48). The method includes CBCA and the evaluation of other data, such as psychological characteristics, interview characteristics, behavioral indicators, motives to report, the context of original disclosure or report, pressures to report falsely, the relationship between the child and the alleged perpetrator, the history of the statement, and biographical information (all of which are addressed in the SVA's Validity Checklist).

The method originated in Germany and Sweden approximately four decades ago. In 1954, Undeutsch described certain relatively exact, definable, descriptive criteria that form a key tool to determine the truthfulness of a statement. Based on these criteria, Undeutsch developed a procedure called *statement reality analysis,* first described in English in 1982. Steller and Köhnken (1989) organized and systematized Undeutsch's work into specific criteria that are referred to as *content criteria,* used to assess the content of a statement. The criteria are grouped into five major categories, from broad to specific aspects of the statement (see categories introduced in Table 3.1). General characteristics, the first major category, requires examination of the entire statement. When the different details in a statement independently describe the same course of events, or when the statement "makes sense," Criterion 1 (logical structure) can be rated as present. When a statement appears somewhat chaotic, with digressions and shifts of focus scattered throughout it, Criterion 2 (unstructured production) is fulfilled. Details about time, place, persons, actions, and objects are necessary for the fulfillment of Criterion 3 (quantity of details).

The second and third major categories (specific contents and peculiarities of content) refer to more specific contents of the statement. The criteria in these categories are applied while asking the question, "Would a child be able to make up an allegation with qualities such as those described by the criteria?" (Steller, 1989, p. 138). For example, contextual embedding refers to the placing of the alleged sexual abuse in the context of the child's routine life experiences. The fourth category of criteria (motivation-related contents) refers to contents related to the possible reasons for the

TABLE 3.1 Percentage of CBCA Criteria Present in Each Age Group

	Age Group			
Criterion	2–3 (n = 17)	4–5 (n = 39)	6–8 (n = 26)	9–11 (n = 21)
General characteristics				
1. Logical structure	71	72	92	95
2. Unstructured production	29	41	46	62
3. Quantity of details	100	100	100	100
Specific contents				
4. Contextual embedding**	18	21	54	71
5. Descriptions of interactions**	6	13	46	67
6. Reproduction of conversation**	6	21	46	62
7. Unexpected complications	6	5	23	33
Peculiarities of content				
8. Unusual details	18	18	23	38
9. Superfluous details**	0	8	35	52
10. Misunderstood details	6	0	0	10
11. Related external associations	12	26	46	91
12. Accounts of subjective mental state	65	69	85	100
13. Attribution of perpetrator's mental state	0	13	15	29
Motivation-related contents				
14. Spontaneous corrections	6	15	23	43
15. Admitting lack of memory*	24	39	62	76
16. Raising doubts about one's own testimony	0	0	4	14
17. Self-deprecation	0	0	12	0
18. Pardoning the perpetrator	53	64	81	67
Offense-specific elements				
19. Characteristic details*	35	62	73	100

*$p < .01$; **$p < .001$.

child to make a false allegation. These criteria are applied while considering the question, "Would a child mention details that tend to be unfavorable to him- or herself if the child were fabricating an account?" (Steller, 1989, p. 138). The last category (offense-specific elements) refers to elements in the statement that relate to the pattern of the alleged offense. For example, a single-incident stranger assault typically is committed in a different manner than is an incestuous act. Detailed descriptions of the 19 criteria can be found in Steller and Boychuk (1992) and Yuille (1988).

The method has been applied to thousands of sexual abuse cases in Germany; 43,000 statements were analyzed at the Bochumer Institut für

Gerichtspsychologie (Arntzen, 1993), and Undeutsch (1982) reported having analyzed more than 1,500 cases. However, despite the fact that this method has a high degree of face validity, little empirical analysis has been conducted to assess its validity and reliability. Moreover, it is important to underline that research has been dedicated to only one part of the SVA, namely, CBCA. In the forensic context, a final judgment as to the credibility of a given statement cannot be reached on the basis of CBCA alone. The evaluator needs to consider other information (i.e., the Validity Checklist) and has to take into account "any additional considerations which may be of importance to the case under investigation and which have not yet been covered by the content analysis or the validity check" (Steller, 1989, p. 141). Two basic approaches—an experimental approach (simulation studies) and a field study approach—have been taken in studying the validity of the method.

Simulation Studies

The first simulation study was carried out by Köhnken and Wegener (1982). The statements of a group of female adolescents, 16 and 17 years of age, were analyzed with regard to three content criteria: quantity of details, unstructured production, and consistency of the content over repeated questioning. Half of the participants were shown a film, and the remaining half received a verbal description of the contents of this film. The participants were interviewed immediately after seeing the film and again 3 weeks later. Their transcribed statements were evaluated by five trained raters, who were unaware of the purpose of the experiment and the experimental condition of the participants. Participants who actually saw the film produced significantly more details. Unstructured production was found significantly more frequently in the group who received only the verbal description. Consistency of the content over repeated questioning did not differ between the two groups.

Yuille (1988) instructed 49 children, 6 to 9 years old, to tell a true and a false story about a chosen topic. The participants were interviewed 2 days later by an interviewer, who was unaware of which story was true and which was false. Two evaluators, who were unaware of the study's purpose, used CBCA to classify the stories as either truthful or fabricated. The evaluators agreed on 96% of their classifications; Yuille found an overall level of correct classifications of 90.9% for the true stories and of 74.4% for the false ones.

Steller (1989) argued that simulation studies relevant to the forensic application of statement analysis must use events that would contain basic psychological variables that characterize the experience of sexual abuse: direct involvement of the reporting person in the event, a predominantly negative emotional tone of the event, and an extensive loss of control. Many situations in which children receive medical treatment, and non-medical events such as being attacked by a dog and being beaten up by another child, incorporate these variables (Steller, Wellershaus, & Wolfe, 1988). Steller et al. (1988) asked 6- and 10-year-old children to tell two stories about one of the aforementioned experiences, one based on a real event and the other based on a fictitious one. Raters received standardized training in the use of reality criteria. Nine of 16 criteria were rated significantly higher in truthful as opposed to fabricated statements.

Joffe and Yuille (1992) examined whether CBCA could differentiate accounts based on experience from those based on coaching. One hundred and forty-two second- and fourth-grade children were tested in three conditions: (a) participants witnessed and were involved in a staged event, (b) heavily coached children received a detailed description and were provided with features characteristic of a number of CBCA criteria, and (c) lightly coached children were given only a brief account of the staged event. For fourth-grade children, CBCA distinguished between true reports and lightly coached reports. However, the raters could not distinguish between truthful reports and heavily coached reports. For second-grade children, no significant differences were found for the accounts of the three groups.

Honts, Peters, Devitt, and Amato (1992) examined whether CBCA could discriminate truthful from deceptive children. Seventeen children (4 to 10 years old) and one parent of each child took part in the experiment. The participants were tested in three conditions: (a) participants witnessed the stealing of a book by an unknown person and were asked not to tell about it; (b) the book disappeared, but the participants never saw anyone take the book; and (c) the parent took the book, told the child that this was their secret, and that if the child told anyone about the theft, the parent would get in trouble. When the theft was discovered, the parent was accused of the theft by one of the researchers. Later, when the parent and child were left alone, the parent instructed the child to accuse another researcher. The children were interviewed by a confederate who introduced herself as a member of the police force. Honts et al. (1992) found that CBCA significantly discriminated truthful from deceptive children.

Landry and Brigham (1992) used 14 of the 19 criteria for the analysis of true and false statements of adults. Twelve criteria differed significantly between the true and false statements. Höfer, Köhnken, Hanewinkel, and Bruhn (1993) and Köhnken, Schimossek, Aschermann, and Höfer (1995) also found that CBCA criteria distinguished significantly between truthful and distorted or fabricated statements of adults.

However, all of the aforementioned studies lack external validity; that is, they do not capture the circumstances of child witnesses in alleged sexual abuse cases. In response, Steller et al. (1988) called for "field studies actually using statements of children in sexual abuse cases" (p. 14).

Field Studies

Esplin, Boychuk, and Raskin (1988) conducted the first field study of CBCA. Forty statements obtained from alleged child victims aged 3 to 15 years were examined using CBCA. Twenty statements were considered to be confirmed because the case from which they came met at least two of the following criteria: (a) perpetrator confession prior to plea bargain, (b) extreme physical evidence, (c) one or more witnesses to the event, and (d) deceptive polygraph of the accused. Twenty highly doubtful statements came from cases that met at least three of the following criteria: (a) no confession by the accused, (b) no corroborating evidence, (c) nondeceptive polygraphs of the accused, (d) recantation of the allegation, and (e) specific finding by the court that no abuse had occurred. Esplin et al. (1988) found (a) a high mean CBCA score for the confirmed group and (b) a significantly lower mean CBCA score for the highly doubtful group. It was suggested that age could not account for the difference between the two groups.

Using a similarly defined population of confirmed and highly doubtful cases, Boychuk (1991) also found a significant difference between the presence of the 19 criteria in the two groups. However, she found an influence of age on the fulfillment of four criteria (admitting lack of memory, descriptions of interactions, attribution of perpetrator's mental state, and self-deprecation). Anson, Golding, and Gully (1993), also using statements of children in sexual abuse cases, found that age at the time of the interview correlated significantly with 6 of the 19 CBCA criteria (logical structure, contextual embedding, descriptions of interactions, reproduction of conversation, pardoning the perpetrator, and details characteristic of the offense) and with the total CBCA score.

The Boychuk (1991) and Anson et al. (1993) studies suggest that age is an important factor in relation to CBCA. The present study was designed to gain more insight into the relation between age and the presence of CBCA criteria in the statements of alleged sexual abuse victims in four different age groups.

The Present Study

The aim of our study was to compare the degree of CBCA criteria fulfilled in the statements of alleged sexual abuse victims in four different age groups. Children, 2 to 12 years old, were interviewed after allegations of sexual abuse in the course of a full-assessment procedure. Slightly more than half of the allegations (52%) originated from parents, 29% from mental health agencies, 6% from schools, and 13% from several other sources (e.g., grandparents, neighbors). The assessment procedure was initiated by either a mental health agency (42%), a Child Protection Board (15%), or a criminal justice agency (43%).

Sample

The sample contained 178 alleged sexual abuse victims. The majority of the alleged victims were female (71%). Their average age at the time of the interview was 6.5 years. With respect to the relationship of the alleged offender to the child, 65% were members of the victim's nuclear family or household, and 34% were acquaintances or members of the extended family. One percent of the children could not name a perpetrator. Nearly half (49%) of the alleged perpetrators were accused of abusing at least two children; 20% had a previous record for one or more sexual offenses, mostly child sexual abuse. The children allegedly were exposed to a wide variety of sexual behaviors: oral, vaginal, and/or anal penetration with penis, digits, or objects (59%); masturbating, fondling, and attempted intercourse (41%). The mean number of sexual behaviors to which the child was exposed was 3.7. Physical violence and/or verbal threats were mentioned by 57% of the children.

Method

In conducting the interviews, child interviewers (trained psychologists and expert witnesses) followed the guidelines recommended by Steller (1989). After rapport was established, the interviewers attempted to obtain as much free narrative as possible. Because detailed free recall is rare in young children (Saywitz, Goodman, & Meyers, 1990), open-ended questions were asked to help the younger children.

Seventy-five children did not disclose sexual abuse during the interview, leaving 103 transcriptions of interviews available for review in the study. All 103 cases were analyzed using CBCA. Data on the Validity Checklist, and on the relation between CBCA and the Validity Checklist for the present sample are contained in Lamers-Winkelman (1995).

The 103 interviews were transcribed into written statements that were rated by two professionals who had received extensive training in CBCA. The kappa coefficient for CBCA interrater reliability, based on 17 practice interviews, was .83.

To compare the rates of CBCA criteria in the statements of different age groups, the sample was divided into four groups (ages 2-3, $n = 17$; ages 4-5, $n = 39$; ages 6-8, $n = 26$; ages 9-11, $n = 21$), and chi-square analyses were performed to test for differences among the groups.

Results

The percentages present for the CBCA criteria in the four age groups are shown in Table 3.1. As expected, several criteria were not fulfilled for the very young witnesses. Four criteria (superfluous details, attribution of perpetrator's mental state, raising doubts about one's own testimony, and self-deprecation) were not at all present for the 2- to 3-year-olds. Five criteria (descriptions of interactions, reproduction of conversation, unexpected complications, misunderstood details, and spontaneous corrections) were present less than 10% of the time for the 2- and 3-year-olds. Descriptions of interactions, as well as reproduction of conversation, require complex verbal and cognitive skills and are rare in children before the concrete operational stage of development. Although it is often suggested that younger children may try to please the interviewer by responding to questions even if they do not know the answer (e.g., Ceci, Ross, & Toglia, 1987), 24% of the 2-to 3-year-olds and 39% of the 4- to 5-year-olds were able to tell the interviewer that they did not know (admitting lack of memory). This may be due to the fact that at the beginning of the interview all children were told to say "I do not know," if appropriate. Nevertheless, the youngest children fulfilled this criterion significantly less than the older children. Older children may admit to a lack of memory as a means of avoiding an embarrassing topic. Moreover, the statements of children who had been questioned several times previously revealed such admissions to be a means of expressing their irritation: "I've already said this a hundred times. Don't they believe me?"

With age, the number of criteria not fulfilled decreased. The 4- to 5-year-olds did not fulfill three criteria at all. For the two oldest age groups (6-8 and 9-11), only one of the criteria (although a different one for each group) was not present at all.

Discussion

Despite instructions to take age into account, and despite the fact that both raters had some experience in interviewing young children, in the present study age correlated significantly with six CBCA criteria. Our sample also contained very young children, which may account for our finding more criteria correlating with age than did Boychuk (1991). However, the two criteria correlating with age in the Boychuk study also correlated with age in our study (admitting lack of memory and descriptions of interactions). Five of the criteria associated with age in our study also were found in the Anson et al. (1993) study. The results of these three studies taken together suggest that the following criteria are dependent on age: contextual embedding, descriptions of interactions, reproduction of conversation, admitting lack of memory, and details characteristic of the offense.

The criteria not present and hardly present in the statements of the two youngest age groups are congruent with the developmental phase of these children. Given the limited language capacity of these young children, descriptions of sexual abuse in this age group are limited. Although 4- and 5-year-olds can be expected to describe experiences of sexual abuse in a more comprehensive way than can younger children, they still are egocentric and more oriented to action and play than to talking. Their perspective taking is limited, as is their concept of time, and one hardly can expect them to describe, for instance, a perpetrator's mental state. Complex verbal and cognitive skills are needed for descriptions of actions and reproduction of conversation and are limited in younger children. Our findings are in accordance with these developmental characteristics.

With age, the number of criteria fulfilled and the percentage present for each of the criteria increased. This indicates that younger, less verbal children are at a disadvantage. Anson et al. (1993) suggested that the frequencies of certain criteria should be compared with age-appropriate norms. However, age is not the only important factor; large-scale analyses that also take into account type of abuse, chronicity of abuse, physical force and/or verbal threats, the number of times a child has been interviewed, and cultural factors are needed before SVA can be used as a scientifically validated instrument.

Conclusion

In the Netherlands, mental health agencies, the Child Protection Boards, and the Offices of the Confidential Doctors are supposed to deal with cases of child sexual abuse. However, these agencies are mostly family oriented, so cases of extrafamilial sexual abuse often are overlooked or not dealt with at all. Furthermore, even intrafamilial sexual abuse is usually classified as child-rearing problems, family problems, or neglect.

If child sexual abuse is reported, the alleged victims usually are interviewed by specially trained police officers or court-appointed expert witnesses. For some years, Dutch professionals have used SVA as a method of assessing child sexual abuse complaints. Despite its widespread use in Germany, research on SVA began only relatively recently. Simulation and field studies indicate that some of the criteria of the SVA's CBCA differ significantly between true and false statements. Even so, the method still lacks formalized application rules; for example, it is unknown how evaluators using SVA should take age into account. In our research, we used SVA to evaluate statements given by alleged sexual abuse victims and found a significant positive relationship between age and the presence of several

CBCA criteria. Thus, age-related norms for applying CBCA are much needed if we are to draw accurate conclusions from SVA regarding the validity of alleged child abuse victims' statements.

References

Anson, D. A., Golding, S. L., & Gully, K. J. (1993). Child sexual abuse allegations: Reliability of criteria-based content analysis. *Law and Human Behavior, 17,* 331-341.

Arntzen, F. (1993). *Psychologie der Zeugenaussage. System der Glaubwürdigkeitsmerkmale* [Psychology of witness statements: The system of reality criteria]. Munich: C. H. Beck'sche Verlagsbuchhandlung.

Boychuk, T. (1991). *Criteria-based content analysis of children's statements about sexual abuse.* Unpublished doctoral dissertation, Arizona State University, Tempe.

Ceci, S. J., Ross, D. F., & Toglia, M. P. (1987). Age differences in suggestibility: Narrowing the uncertainties. In S. J. Ceci, M. P. Toglia, & D. F. Ross (Eds.), *Children's eyewitness memory* (pp. 79-91). New York: Springer-Verlag.

Compernolle, T. (1994). Het struisarts syndrom [The struisarts syndrome]. *VKM-Magazine, 8*(4), 11.

Eeland, K., & Woelinga, H. (1991). *Praktische richtlijnen voor de hulpverlening bij seksueel misbruik van kinderen* [Practical guidelines for the management of child sexual abuse in mental health agencies]. Amsterdam: VU Uitgeverij.

Esplin, P. W., Boychuk, T., & Raskin, D. C. (1988, June). *A field validity study of criteria-based content analysis of children's statements in sexual abuse cases.* Paper presented at the NATO Advanced Study Institute on Credibility Assessment, Maratea, Italy.

Höfer, E., Köhnken, G., Hanewinkel, R., & Bruhn, C. (1993). *Diagnostik und attribution von glaubwürdigkeit* [Assessment and attribution of credibility]. Kiel, Germany: Universität Kiel.

Honts, C. R., Peters, D. P., Devitt, M. K., & Amato, S. L. (1992, May). *Detecting children's lies with statement validity assessment: A pilot study of a laboratory paradigm.* Paper presented at the NATO Advanced Study Institute on the Child Witness in Context: Cognitive, Social, and Legal Perspectives, Lucca, Italy.

Joffe, R., & Yuille, J. C. (1992, May). *Criteria-based content analysis: An experimental investigation.* Poster presented at the NATO Advanced Study Institute on the Child Witness in Context: Cognitive, Social, and Legal Perspectives, Lucca, Italy.

Köhnken, G., Schimossek, E., Aschermann, E., & Höfer, E. (1995). *The cognitive interview and the assessment of the credibility of adult's statements.* Manuscript submitted for publication.

Köhnken, G., & Wegener, H. (1982). Zur glaubwürdigkeit von zeugenaussagen: Experimentelle ueberprüfung ausgewählter glaubwürdigkeitskriterien [Credibility of witness statements: Experimental examination of selected reality criteria]. *Zeitschrift für Experimentelle und Angewandte Psychologie, 29,* 92-111.

Lamers-Winkelman, F. (1995). *Seksueel misbruik van jonge kinderen* [Sexual abuse of young children]. Amsterdam: VU Uitgeverij.

Landelijke Stichting Buro's Vertrouwensartsen inzake Kindermishandeling. (LSBVK) (1994). *Jaarverslag 1993* [Annual report 1993]. Utrecht, the Netherlands: Author.

Landry, K. L., & Brigham, J. C. (1992). The effect of training in criteria-based content analysis on the ability to detect deception in adults. *Law and Human Behavior, 16,* 663-676.

van Montfoort, A. (1993). *Kindermishandeling en justitie* [Child abuse and the judicial system]. Amsterdam: VU Uitgeverij.

van Montfoort, A. (1994). The protection of children in the Netherlands: Between justice and welfare. In H. Ferguson, R. Giuigan, & R. Torode (Eds.) *Surviving childhood adversity: Issues for policy and practice* (pp. 53-64). Dublin, Ireland: Social Studies Press.

Noordhoek-van Staay, J. (1992). *De prevalentie van kindermishandeling bij kinderen met sociale, gedrags, en emotionele problematiek* [The prevalence of child abuse in children with social, behavioral, and emotional problems]. Amsterdam: Vrije Universtiteit.

Oost, J., & Jans, J. (1989). Anders omgaan met jonge getuigen of slachtoffers: Training voor horen van kinderen [Another way of dealing with young children: Training for interviewing young witnesses]. *Algemeen Politieblad, 5,* 99-101.

Saywitz, K. J., Goodman, G. S., & Meyers, J. E. B. (1990). Can children provide accurate eyewitness reports? *Violence Update, 1*(1), 1, 4, 10, 11.

Steller, M. (1989). Recent developments in statement analysis. In J. C. Yuille (Ed.), *Credibility assessment* (pp. 135-154). Dordrecht, the Netherlands: Kluwer.

Steller, M., & Boychuk, T. (1992). Children as witnesses in sexual abuse cases: Investigative interview and assessment techniques. In H. Dent & R. Flin (Eds.), *Children as witnesses* (pp. 47-71). Chichester, England: Wiley.

Steller, M., & Köhnken, G. (1989). Criteria-based statement analysis. In D. C. Raskin (Ed.), *Psychological methods in criminal investigation and evidence* (pp. 217-245). New York: Springer.

Steller, M., Wellershaus, P., & Wolf, T. (1988, June). *Empirical validation of criteria-based content analysis.* Paper presented at the NATO Advanced Study Institute on Credibility Assessment, Maratea, Italy.

Undeutsch, U. (1954). Die Entwicklung der gerichtspsychologischen gutachtertätigkeit [The development of the activity of psychological experts in court]. In *Bericht über den XIX. Kongress der Deutschen Gesellschaft für Psychologie* [Report on the XIX Congress of the German Psychological Association] (pp. 132-154). Göttingen, Germany: Hogrefe.

Undeutsch, U. (1982). Statement reality analysis. In A. Trankell (Ed.), *Reconstructing the past* (pp. 27-56). Deventer, the Netherlands: Kluwer.

Veldkamp, T. (1993). De toekomst van de kinderbescherming [The future of child protection]. In A. Groen & A. van Montfoort (Eds.), *Kinderen beschermen en jeugd hulp verlenen* [Protecting and helping children] (pp. 93-113). Arnhem, the Netherlands: Gouda Quint.

Yuille, J. C. (1988). The systematic assessment of children's testimony. *Canadian Psychology, 29,* 247-262.

4

Child Sexual Abuse Investigations in Israel
Evaluating Innovative Practices

KATHLEEN J. STERNBERG
MICHAEL E. LAMB
IRIT HERSHKOWITZ

Concerned about the potentially damaging effects of testifying on young children, scholars have recommended changes to legal and judicial procedures in the United States that would protect defendants' rights while doing less harm to young victims and witnesses. In evaluating such proposals, perhaps much can be learned by analyzing and exploring practices, procedures, and controversies in countries that have different legal histories, precedents, and social policies. By examining innovative reforms that have taken place in countries such as Sweden, Germany, and Israel, for example, it may be possible to develop novel pretrial procedures and alternative means of obtaining testimony from young children. The purpose of this chapter is to describe the Israeli system for investigating child

This chapter is reprinted with permission from *Criminal Justice and Behavior,* Vol. 23 No. 2, June 1996 322-337. © 1996 American Association for Correctional Psychology.

sex crimes and to extract lessons from 40 years of experience with a system designed to protect children from the perceived trauma of testifying in court. It evaluates the success of Israeli attempts to protect child witnesses and highlight some of the problems that arose in efforts to balance the rights of children and the rights of defendants. It shows that the Israeli system has provided unique opportunities to conduct empirical research on children's accounts of sexual abuse and reviews our own program of research on the investigation of children's testimony in Israel.

The chapter begins with a review of the Israeli system for the investigation of child sex crimes. Next, it discusses proposals for reform of the system and concerns regarding the responsibilities and skills of the professionals authorized to interview alleged victims and witnesses. In a final section, it summarizes a program of research made possible by features of the system.

In Israel, special procedures for obtaining and evaluating the testimony of young witnesses were spelled out in the Law of Evidence Revision Protection of Children (LER-PC), which was passed by the Israeli Knesset (Parliament) in 1955. This law established uniform procedures regulating the manner in which information was to be obtained from children under the age of 15 who were alleged victims, witnesses, or perpetrators of sex crimes. The passage of this law was prompted by a belief that testifying in court, particularly against family members, could cause "irreversible harm" to children because so testifying might force children to reexperience traumatic events (Harnon, 1989; Horowitz & Hovav, 1993; Melamed, 1993; Reifen, 1973). Although the number of reported cases of sexual abuse was quite low at the time (there were 503 reports in 1958 compared to 1,612 in 1993), and sex crimes against children were not believed to represent a major social problem (Reifen, 1973), several judges were concerned about the aggressive cross-examinations of children (Harnon, 1989; Nizan, 1988; Reifen, 1973). There also was widespread concern that parents were reluctant to report possible incidents of child sexual abuse to the police for fear that their children would be interrogated and asked to testify in court (Nizan, 1988) and that many charges were prematurely dismissed without prosecution because alleged victims were deemed poor witnesses. Therefore, as Harnon (1989) noted,

> The aim . . . was to find an arrangement that would protect the mental well-being of these young victims and at the same time not disrupt the administration of justice which called for bringing these criminals to court. (p. 83)

The resulting revision of the Law of Evidence transferred responsibility for investigating juvenile sex crimes from the police to a new class of professionals (termed *youth investigators*) who were given extensive power to investigate child sex crimes and a major role in any trials that followed. The law delegated to youth investigators the sole authority to interview all alleged victims, witnesses, and suspects under 15 years of age and decide whether alleged victims should (a) be allowed to undergo medical examinations, (b) be asked to identify their alleged perpetrators, (c) participate in procedures designed to reconstruct the abusive events, and/or (d) testify in court. Furthermore, when youth investigators conclude that it is not in the best interests of children to testify in court, they are authorized to testify in their place and to evaluate the truthfulness of the children's allegations.

Social workers, police officers, health care providers, and other professionals are required to refer all allegations of child abuse to youth investigators and are not permitted to conduct any interviews themselves. If other minors are involved (as alleged victims, witnesses, or suspects) the police ask youth investigators to interview them; and if they feel it is necessary to conduct supplementary interviews or have children visit the scene of alleged crimes, the police must ask the youth investigators to do so. Children are routinely interviewed once, with an occasional supplementary interview if additional information is requested by the police. Different youth investigators interview alleged victims and juvenile suspects associated with the same incidents. Since 1991, youth investigators have been required to conduct audiotaped interviews of alleged victims within 72 hours of the reports. Although allegations of sexual abuse are prosecuted within the criminal court system, child protective service workers and youth investigators work together to ensure the safety and well-being of children.

After interviewing alleged victims, juvenile witnesses, or juvenile suspects, youth investigators submit written reports (accompanied since 1991 by audiotaped records of their interviews) to the police, who, in turn, forward all material to the prosecutors' office. Prosecutors decide whether to try the case before a judge, negotiate pleas, or drop charges against the suspects. Although no official statistics are available, youth investigators estimate that fewer than 10% of the allegations are prosecuted even though most are deemed credible.

The small number of prosecutions is almost certainly attributable to a Supreme Court belief that the rights of defendants are compromised by provisions of the LER-PC (Harnon, 1989). Because judges are denied the opportunity to formulate informed impressions of alleged victims and witnesses who do not testify directly, independent corroboration of the alleged events and of the perpetrator's identity are required before a defendant can be convicted (Harnon, 1989; Horowitz & Hovav, 1993; Libai, 1969; Nizan, 1988). The number of children qualified to testify by the youth investigators declined from 28% in 1984 (Eden, 1984) to 6.8% in 1993 (Hochman & Karniel, 1994).

Although the LER-PC has been very successful in protecting children from repeated investigative interviews and has shielded children from the potential trauma of testifying in court, it also has hindered the prosecution of alleged perpetrators. Because fewer than 10% of the alleged victims are permitted to testify in court, the demand for corroboration has a substantial effect on prosecution and conviction rates. According to Nizan (1988), 40% to 60% of the cases investigated are closed because corroborative evidence is lacking. Given the private nature of sex crimes, corroborating evidence is extremely hard to obtain, and as a result, many allegations are dismissed without prosecution.

Libai (1969) once harshly criticized prosecutors in the United States for negotiating plea bargains with offenders:

> The practice of the negotiated guilty plea is thus wholly unacceptable as a means of protecting child victims of sex offenses. It provides no care for children who are called to testify in courtrooms, and it mocks the constitutional rights of defendants, tempting them to yield to the instruments and pressures promoting the negotiated guilty plea. Thus the practice falls short of accommodating the conflicting interests of the accused and the victims. Still the pattern of "bargains" does remind the legal system that it ignores the child victim's welfare and that child witnesses deserve real and effective protection as witnesses. (p. 1007)

Ironically, Libai now finds himself, as Minister of Justice, supervising a system in which plea bargains remain the primary means of ensuring at least some punishment for child molesters.

Formal criticisms of the system are summarized in the next section, and concerns regarding the qualifications and responsibilities of the youth investigators are described in the section that follows. Ironically, however, no serious attention has been paid to the premise motivating the LER-PC, the presumption that it is psychologically harmful for children to testify in court, particularly when the suspect is not known to the child. As Harnon (1988) and Cohen (1993) observed, the effects of testifying are implicitly considered more damaging than continued exposure to unpunished perpetrators and more harmful than leaving perpetrators free to victimize other children. In fact, much remains to be learned about the effects of testifying. Scholars in the United States and United Kingdom have debated this issue. Some (e.g., Goodman et al., 1992; Tedesco & Schnell, 1987) argue that the circumstances surrounding the legal proceedings, as well as the experience of testifying per se, are stressful. Others (e.g., Berliner & Barbieri, 1984; Runyan, Everson, Edelsohn, Hunter, & Coulter, 1988) believe that testifying can have positive effects on children. At the very least, the various costs and benefits of preventing children from testifying deserve reexamination in the Israeli system.

Formal Evaluations of the Law of Evidence

The Melamed Committee was appointed by the Minister of Justice in 1985 to consider criticisms of the LER-PC from lawyers, jurists, and mental health professionals and recommend further revisions of the law. The complaints summarized for the Melamed Committee were numerous. Police officers criticized the quality of evidence obtained by youth investigators, blaming this for reductions in the number of arrests and convictions (Harnon, 1988). Some legal scholars worried that the rights of defendants were so seriously compromised that they were not allowed fair trials, and child advocates argued that the failure to punish child molesters left other children at continued risk of maltreatment. Judges complained that they were denied opportunities to form direct impressions of alleged victims or witnesses and thus had to demand independent corroborative evidence (Harnon, 1989; Horowitz & Hovav, 1993). Although judges commended youth investigators when their evaluation of the alleged victims' credibility were well articulated, they also criticized investigators for (a) evaluations that lacked objectivity, (b) the presence of others during interviews, (c) extensive delays in scheduling interviews and/or medical examinations, (d) nonsystematic investigations, (e) the failure to consider alternative investigative hypotheses, and (f) the use of leading questions (Horowitz & Hovav, 1993).

Not surprisingly, the members of the Melamed Committee heard many recommendations for changes that would allow judges to formulate their own impressions of young witnesses. These included a proposal that all interviews conducted by youth investigators be videotaped and that judges be permitted to interview children (in their chambers, but in the presence of youth investigators, prosecutors, and defense attorneys) whenever the youth investigators had recommended that the children not testify in court. In the proposed system, defense attorneys and prosecutors could provide judges with their questions in advance but would not be permitted to question the children directly. Judges could decide whether defendants should be present. Advocates of this reform argued that it would allow judges the opportunity to formulate their own impressions of witnesses, spare children from the effects of testifying in court, and permit relaxation of the need for corroborative evidence because the evidence would no longer be hearsay. They further suggested that special judges should be trained to play this unique role and that they should interview children in this fashion no more than 3 months after the initial investigation. Others proposed that juvenile court judges should review the interviews conducted by the youth investigators, and then interview the children themselves, perhaps in the presence of prosecutors and defense attorneys, and decide whether the children should testify in criminal court. This reform would thus transfer some of the youth investigators' power to judges, based on the assumption that their skills and objectivity would be greater than those of youth investigators. Such reforms would modify the existing practices quite drastically, but also would reduce the need for corroborating evidence.

After considering recommendations such as these, the Melamed Committee surprised many by deciding not to recommend any changes to the LER-PC and instead to extol its virtues. Apparently, the committee members feared that parliamentary debate of so controversial a law might lead to abandonment of all the special procedures that were designed to protect children. Instead, Nizan (1988) suggested that the reforms described in the preceeding paragraph could be made without amending the existing law. Both the national coordinator of the youth investigators and the police supervisor of juvenile investigation agreed that these changes could facilitate fact-finding and reduce the traumatic effects of testifying without further jeopardizing defendants' rights. To date, however, the Melamed Committee report has led only to a requirement that all interviews be audiotaped.

Qualifications and Responsibilities of Youth Investigators

The LER-PC envisioned a well-coordinated system in which the police, child protective service workers, and youth investigators would together investigate juvenile sex crimes efficiently while attempting to protect the emotional and physical well-being of the children involved (see Hovav, 1993, for a detailed description). In reality, however, the daily work of the youth investigators is fraught with conflict between their roles as probation officers and youth investigators, as well as with conflict between their desire to provide therapy while conducting investigative interviews. Although the LER-PC did not specify the qualifications of youth investigators, legislators made clear at the time that they needed to be professionals who had both legal knowledge and experience in caring for and evaluating children. In practice, most youth investigators have bachelor's degrees in social work or education and have received training as juvenile probation officers rather than as forensic investigators (Harnon, 1989; Reifen, 1973). Administratively, the youth investigators have been under the auspices of the Division of Correctional Services and Services for Youth in Distress in the Ministry of Labor and Social Affairs since 1985, and the majority of the youth investigators spend most of their time supervising juvenile offenders on probation.

It is somewhat unclear why the responsibility for investigating child sex crimes was assigned to the unit responsible for juvenile probation, and questions about the appropriateness of this assignment have become more numerous (e.g., Eigelstein, 1993; Kadman, 1993), particularly as the majority of youth investigators would prefer to work as probation officers, the primary role for which they were trained. As the number of reports has increased, these officers have been required to interview growing numbers of children, and the magnitude of the demand for investigative interviews was further exacerbated in 1989 when the youth investigators were given responsibility for interviewing victims of physical abuse as well. Recent increases in the number of youth investigators have not been sufficient to keep pace with the growing demand, and because the youth investigators consider it more difficult and complicated to investigate allegations of physical than sexual abuse, the latter reports are often referred to less experienced investigators (Dash, 1994). Youth investigators are not adequately trained in forensic investigation and must therefore learn the necessary skills "on the job" (Harnon, 1989; Melamed, 1993).

Kadman (1993) emphasized a clash between the professional values and goals of probation and forensic investigation, noting that probation workers regard the investigation of juvenile sex crimes as a marginal aspect of their job, for which they are not properly rewarded. This criticism is reinforced by the results of two surveys (Eigelstein, 1991, 1993). After surveying all youth investigators who had been employed for at least 6 months ($N = 97$), Eigelstein (1991) found that most did not identify with their roles as youth investigators, viewed themselves primarily as therapists, and found it difficult to perform investigative interviews. In a later survey of 87 youth investigators, Eigelstein (1993) further explored the potential conflict between the demands of investigative and probationary work. Again, the youth investigators reported that the demands of their two roles were professionally incompatible and claimed that this was a primary reason for staff turnover. Such responses led Eigelstein to recommend that juvenile sex crimes should not be investigated by probation officers, and that a new office should be created to supervise and conduct these investigations.

Although the LER-PC did not assign youth investigators responsibility for providing therapy, a therapeutic orientation is frequently mentioned in official documents (e.g., Eden, 1987; Karniel, 1993; Melamed, 1987) and is perceived by youth investigators as an important part of their job (Eigelstein, 1991, 1993). Therapeutic and investigative roles need to be differentiated, however: The primary goal of forensic investigation is to obtain full and accurate accounts of alleged incidents, whereas therapists focus on the feelings related to, and effect of, the clients' experiences (Lamb, Sternberg, & Esplin, 1994; Raskin & Esplin, 1991). In the current system, the forensic aspects of the investigation are often compromised by attempts at therapeutic intervention (Harnon, 1989).

Although the LER-PC described the unique qualifications, training, and compensation that should characterize youth investigators (Libai, 1969), youth investigators are, in reality, overworked, undertrained, and poorly compensated (Harnon, 1989; Melamed, 1993). In the words of an experienced youth investigator (David, 1989):

> The Law gave birth to a new and unique professional creature—the youth interrogator—who became a central figure invested with enormous powers, privileges, and responsibilities. The youth interrogator is indeed almost next to God. The good or bad functioning of this Law depends mainly on the professional abilities of the youth interrogator. (p. 99)

Unfortunately, it is difficult to investigate children's allegations of abuse competently, and youth investigators generally have not had sufficient training in forensic interviewing so that they can exercise their extraordinary powers to best effect. Without improvement in the quality of training, encouragement to specialize in forensic interviewing, reductions in their caseloads, and elimination of the conflicting professional responsibilities of youth investigators, the "unique professional creature" described by David may well disappear.

Research on Young Witnesses in Israel

Regardless of its advantages and disadvantages, implementation of the LER-PC, with the central investigative role played by youth investigators, its provisions for mandatory audiorecording, centralization, and restrictions on the number of interviews to which children are subjected, has provided us with excellent opportunities for studying children's allegations of sexual abuse. In the United States, children are interviewed routinely by a number of professionals, and these interviews are not always recorded. Because repeated investigation can contaminate children's accounts (Ceci & Bruck, 1993) or induce fatigue, it is often difficult to evaluate information provided in the 5th, 6th, or even 20th professional interview. Furthermore, because investigative procedures vary widely both across and within jurisdictions, it is difficult to obtain random samples for research purposes and to collect relevant information from diverse, often competing, agencies.

By contrast, because the investigation of juvenile sex crimes is centrally conducted in Israel, and all of interviews are recorded, we have been able to obtain for research purposes a random sample of all of the interviews conducted over a 2-year period. Furthermore, the LER-PC prohibits other professionals from interviewing children, and thus all of the interviews we study are "front line" interviews. Finally, because youth investigators also interview alleged perpetrators and witnesses under the age of 15, we have been able to obtain transcripts of many forensic interviews with perpetrators and witnesses. These detailed confessions, denials, and reports supplement the accounts provided by alleged victims and improve our capacity to explore the richness and accuracy of children's accounts. In this section, we briefly describe our ongoing program of research in Israel, undertaken in collaboration with the Division of Correctional Services and Services for Youth in Distress.

Our major focus has been on the development and evaluation of techniques for examining the validity and completeness of children's allegations in a field setting. Despite the growing number of allegations, professionals around the world lack reliable and accepted techniques for evaluating children's allegations (Lamb et al., 1994). Accordingly, the objective of one study in Israel is to evaluate and improve on statement reality analysis (SRA), a system designed by Undeutsch (1982, 1989) to evaluate the credibility of children's allegations (see also Lamers-Winkelman & Buffing, 1996 [this volume]). Undeutsch proposed that true events are reported in richer detail and with clearer links to other real-world events than events that have been fabricated. Although SRA has been used in the German courtroom for more than 30 years, researchers only recently have begun to evaluate the validity and reliability of the system. Criteria-based content analysis (CBCA) is the product of such efforts to quantify and operationalize Undeutsch's conceptual framework (Raskin & Esplin, 1992; Steller & Köhnken, 1989). Many of the 19 CBCA criteria should be present in descriptions of events that actually happened, and two field studies have supported this prediction (Boychuk, 1991; Raskin & Esplin, 1992). However, these studies were limited to unrepresentative samples of highly probable and highly dubious allegations, whereas our collaboration has permitted us to conduct research using a more representative sample of cases. Furthermore, we are able to use investigative evidence independent of the children's statements (e.g., confessions, witness statements, medical and material evidence) to determine how likely it is that the alleged incidents took place. We focus special attention on children under 5 years of age, who routinely provide briefer and less detailed accounts of experienced events than do older children.

No systematic research using the CBCA system has heretofore focused on such young children, and it probably would be difficult to obtain a large sample of well-validated cases anywhere else.

One of our series of studies has been concerned with the effects of interview style on the quality and quantity of information obtained from children in investigative interviews. Although many researchers have advocated the use of open-ended questions and have cautioned against the use of leading and suggestive questions (Jones & McQuiston, 1988; Lamb et al., 1994; Raskin & Yuille, 1989), there had been no systematic field research on the association between type of question and informativeness of response in investigative interviews. Therefore, the goal of our first study was to examine whether open-ended invitations would yield longer and richer responses from children than directive, leading, and suggestive questions (Lamb et al., in press).

We selected 22 interviews, conducted in Hebrew by 12 different interviewers, of victims who ranged in age from 5 to 11 years. In other respects, the selected transcripts represented a random sampling from the universe of sexual abuse allegations investigated throughout the country between 1991 and 1992. Detailed psycholinguistic coding was conducted on these transcripts to examine the relationship between five types of interviewer utterances—open-ended or invitational, facilitative (nonsuggestive encouragements to continue talking), directive (in which the children's attention was refocused on something they had mentioned earlier), leading (in which the children's attention was directed to something they had not mentioned previously), and suggestive (those that hinted at an expected response) utterances—and on the length and richness of the children's responses to these utterances. A procedure developed by Yuille and Cutshall (1986, 1989; Cutshall & Yuille, 1990) was used to tabulate the number of new details provided by the children in each of their utterances.

As predicted, invitational utterances yielded responses that were approximately three times longer and up to three times richer than responses to any of the three types of utterances that focused the children's attention (i.e., directive, leading, or suggestive). Fortunately, most of the interviewers' focused questions were directive rather than leading or suggestive. Because they involve refocusing the child's attention on previously mentioned details, directive utterances are less likely to shape the child's response than are leading or suggestive questions. Unfortunately, interviewers asked very few (2.2%) invitational questions, even though each open-ended question yielded more information than the average specific question. We do not know how much information might have been obtained if open-ended invitations had been employed more extensively.

We also designed a quasi-experimental field study to determine whether the style (open-ended or direct) of the introductory (rapport-building) phase of the interview influences the quality and quantity of information provided in subsequent phases (Sternberg et al., 1995). Forensic interviews constitute novel situations for children, and the introductory portion of the interview may be used to train children to provide interviewers with as much information as possible (Saywitz, Geiselman, & Bornstein, 1992). In our study, investigators were trained to open their interviews following either of two defined scripts focused on similar content areas—the child's family, school or kindergarten activities, and a recent holiday—obtained using either open-ended probes ("Tell me about your family") or more focused probes ("How many brothers and sisters do you have?") to elicit information. In both conditions, youth investigators asked the child the following question after completing the introductory phase of the interview: "I understand that something may have happened to you. Can you tell what happened from the very beginning to the very end?"

Children exposed to the open-ended rapport-building condition provided almost three times as many details as children who experienced the direct rapport-building technique. This trend persisted throughout the substantive portion of the interview, with children in the open-ended condition providing more details than those in the direct condition. Such findings suggest that the rapport-building phase of the interview can be used to practice a response style that leads informants to provide more complete descriptions of abusive experiences.

This ongoing study also will permit us to compare children's accounts of meaningful but nonstressful events with incidents of sexual abuse, because the scripted phase includes questions (either direct or invitational) about a recent important holiday. Many questions have been raised about the effect of stressful events on children's memorial and descriptive capacities (see Lamb et al., 1994, and Lamb, Sternberg, & Esplin, 1995, for a more extensive discussion of this issue), and in this study children's descriptions of the recent celebration will be compared with their reports of abusive events.

Conclusion

The LER-PC clearly spelled out the roles and responsibilities of the various agencies involved in the investigation of child abuse, allocating broad powers to youth investigators in both the investigative and testimonial phases of this process. Although these provisions have been very successful in protecting children from repeated investigations by multiple authorities and have shielded children from the presumed trauma of testifying in court, they appear to have impeded the prosecution of alleged perpetrators. The unique role of the youth investigator has proven to be both the greatest asset and the greatest hindrance to the system. Because children rarely are permitted by youth investigators to testify, the demand for corroborative evidence has reduced the number of prosecutions, resulting in concerns about the release of alleged perpetrators and about the potential for revictimization. Furthermore, youth investigators appear to lack the training and conditions necessary to conduct skilled investigations of child abuse.

Unless issues involving the training, workload, and potential conflict between the therapeutic and forensic roles played by youth investigators are addressed, it is unlikely that this system will endure. The LER-PC was clearly revolutionary at the time it was enacted, but recent criticisms highlight the need for major revision in its implementation. Unfortunately, although the legislation grants youth investigators discretion to implement alternative procedures, few attempts have been made to do so.

References

Berliner, L., & Barbieri, M. K. (1984). The testimony of child victims of sexual assault. *Journal of Social Issues, 40,* 125-137.

Boychuk, T. D. (1991). *Criteria-based content analysis of children's statements about sexual abuse: A field-based validation study.* Unpublished doctoral dissertation, Arizona State University, Tempe.

Cohen, N. (1993). The youth investigators' reasons for prohibiting or permitting children to testify in court. In M. Hovav (Ed.), *Sexual offenses against children: The law, the investigator, and the court* (pp. 84-94). Tel Aviv, Israel: Shirikova. (in Hebrew)

Cutshall, J. L., & Yuille, J. C. (1990). Field studies of eyewitness memory of actual crimes. In D. C. Raskin (Ed.), *Psychological methods for investigation and evidence* (pp. 97-124). New York: Springer.

David, H. (1989). The role of the youth interrogator. In J. R. Spencer, G. Nicholson, R. Flin, & R. Bull (Eds.), *Children's evidence in legal proceedings: An international perspective* (pp. 97-103). Cambridge, England: Cambridge Law Faculty.

Eden, L. (1984). Sexual offenses against minors. In L. Eden & P. Rudick (Eds.), *Moral offenses against children*. Jerusalem: Ministry of Labor and Welfare. (in Hebrew)

Eden, L. (1987, November). *Investigation and treatment of children involved in moral offenses*. Paper presented at the Regional Congress of the World Association of Social Psychiatry, Budapest, Hungary.

Eigelstein, S. (1991). *A survey of youth investigators*. Jerusalem: Ministry of Labor and Welfare. (in Hebrew)

Eigelstein, S. (1993). *A survey of youth investigators: Second and third time*. Jerusalem: Ministry of Labor and Welfare. (in Hebrew)

Goodman, G. S., Taub, E. P., Jones, D. P. H., England, P., Port, L. K., Rudy, L., & Prado, L. (1992). Testifying in criminal court. *Monographs of the Society for Research in Child Development, 57* (5, Serial No. 229).

Harnon, E. (1988). Examination of children in sexual offenses: The Israeli law and practice. *Criminal Law Review*, pp. 263-274.

Harnon, E. (1989). Children's evidence in the Israeli criminal justice system with special emphasis on sexual offenses. In J. R. Spencer, G. Nicholson, R. Flin, & R. Bull (Eds.), *Children's evidence in legal proceedings: An international perspective* (pp. 81-96). Cambridge, England: Cambridge Law Faculty.

Hochman, I., & Karniel, I. (1994). *Investigations with children: Victims, witnesses, and suspects involved in sexual offenses and physical offenses by their parents* (Annual report, 1993). Jerusalem: Ministry of Labor and Welfare. (in Hebrew)

Horowitz, D., & Hovav, M. (1993). The youth investigator in the eyes of the court. In M. Hovav (Ed.), *Sexual abuse of children: The law, the investigator, and the court* (pp. 133-256). Tel Aviv, Israel: Shirikova. (in Hebrew)

Hovav, M. (Ed.). (1993). *Sexual abuse of children: The law, the investigator, and the court*. Tel Aviv, Israel: Shirikova. (in Hebrew)

Jones, D. P. H., & McQuiston, M. G. (1988). *Interviewing the sexually abused child*. London: Gaskell.

Kadman, I. (1993). The law and its punishment: The correction to the law of evidence and its application: A critical view. In M. Hovav (Ed.), *Sexual offenses against children: The law, the investigator, and the court* (pp. 95-108). Tel Aviv, Israel: Shirikova. (in Hebrew)

Karniel, I. (1993). The work of the youth investigator: Professional, ethical, and personal conflicts. In M. Hovav (Ed.), *Sexual offenses against children: The law, the investigator, and the court* (pp. 73-83). Tel Aviv, Israel: Shirikova. (in Hebrew)

Lamb, M. E., Hershkowitz, I., Sternberg, K. J., Esplin, P. W., Hovav, M., Manor, T., & Yudilevitch, L. (in press). Effects of investigative utterance types on Israeli children's responses. *International Journal of Behavioral Development*.

Lamb, M. E., Sternberg, K. J., & Esplin, P. W. (1994). Factors influencing the reliability and validity of statements made by young victims of sexual maltreatment. *Journal of Applied Developmental Psychology, 15*, 255-280.

Lamb, M. E., Sternberg, K. J., & Esplin, P. W. (1995). Making children into competent witnesses: Reactions to the amicus brief *In re* Michaels. *Psychology, Public Policy and Law, 1*, 438-449.

Lamers-Winkelman, F., & Buffing, F. (1996). Children's testimony in the Netherlands: A study of statement validity analysis. In B. L. Bottoms & G. S. Goodman (Eds.), *International Perspec-*

tives on Child Abuse and Children's Testimony: Psychological Research and Law (pp. 304-321). Thousand Oaks, CA: Sage.

Libai, D. (1969). The protection of the child victim of a sexual offense in the criminal justice system. *Wayne State Law Review, 15,* 977-1032.

Melamed, A. (1987). *Report by the Committee on Sexual Offenses Against Minors.* Jerusalem: Committee on Sexual Offenses Against Minors. (in Hebrew)

Melamed, A. (1993). The role of the youth investigator as perceived by legislators, judges, and the public. In M. Hovav (Ed.), *Sexual abuse of children: The law, the investigator, and the court* (pp. 28-59). Tel Aviv, Israel: Shirikova. (in Hebrew)

Nizan, Y. (1988). Children as witnesses in child sex crimes: Revisiting the issues. *Law, 18,* 297-336. (in Hebrew)

Raskin, D. C., & Esplin, P. W. (1991). Statement validity assessment: Interview procedures and content analysis of children's statements of sexual abuse. *Behavioral Assessment, 13,* 265-291.

Raskin, D. C., & Esplin, P. W. (1992). Assessments of children's statements of sexual abuse. In. J. Doris (Ed.), *The suggestibility of children's recollections: Implications for eyewitness testimony* (pp. 153-164). Washington, DC: American Psychological Association.

Raskin, D., & Yuille, J. C. (1989). Problems of evaluating interviews of children in sexual abuse cases. In S. J. Ceci, D. F. Ross, & M. P. Toglia (Eds.), *Perspectives on children's testimony* (pp. 184-207). New York: Springer-Verlag.

Reifen, D. (1973). *The juvenile court in a changing society: Young offenders in Israel.* Jerusalem: Keter.

Runyon, D. R., Everson, M. D., Edelsohn, C. A., Hunter, W. M., & Coulter, M. L. (1988). Impact of legal intervention on sexually abused children. *Journal of Pediatrics, 113,* 647-653.

Saywitz, K. J., Geiselman, R. E., & Bornstein, G. K. (1992). Effects of cognitive interviewing and practice on children's recall performance. *Journal of Applied Psychology, 77,* 744-756.

Steller, M., & Köhnken, G. (1989). Criteria-based statement analysis. In D. C. Raskin (Ed.), *Psychological methods in criminal investigation and evidence* (pp. 217-245). New York: Springer.

Sternberg, K. J., Lamb, M. E., Hershkowitz, I., Yudilevitch, L., Orbach, Y., Esplin, P. W., & Hovav, M. (1995). *Effects of rapport-building style on children's abilities to describe experiences of sexual abuse.* Manuscript in preparation.

Tedesco, J. F., & Schnell, S. V. (1987). Children's responses to sex abuse investigation and litigation. *Child Abuse & Neglect, 11,* 267-272.

Undeutsch, U. (1982). Statement reality analysis. In A. Trankell (Ed.), *Reconstructing the past: The role of psychologists in criminal trials* (pp. 27-56). Stockholm: Norstedt.

Undeutsch, U. (1989). The development of statement reality analysis. In A. Trankel (Ed.), *Reconstructing the past: The role of psychologists in criminal trials* (pp. 27-56). Stockholm: Novsteat.

Yuille, J. C., & Cutshall, J. L. (1986). A case study of eyewitness memory of a crime. *Journal of Applied Psychology, 71,* 291-301.

Yuille, J. C., & Cutshall, J. L. (1989). Analysis of the statements of victims, witnesses, and suspects. In J. C. Yuille (Ed.), *Credibility assessment* (pp. 175-191). Norwell, MA: Kluwer Academic.

5

Children and the Courts in Canada

LOUISE DEZWIREK SAS
DAVID A. WOLFE
KEVIN GOWDEY

Until the early 1980s, child sexual abuse in Canada was almost an invisible social problem. Child protection agencies did not identify child sexual abuse as a significant feature of their protection cases, police filed charges of child sexual abuse infrequently, and criminal prosecution of child sexual abuse cases occupied very little time on the court dockets across the country (Badgley, 1984; Biesenthal & Clement, 1992). However, despite the infrequent reporting of child sexual abuse prior to the 1980s, there were cases from time to time that challenged the notion that child sexual abuse was a rare event. Increasingly, over a 10- to 15-year period beginning in the late 1970s, more and more professionals were uncovering cases of child sexual abuse in their clinical practices. The reality that sexual abuse was much more prevalent than was ever before imagined brought forth the demand that the problem be more formally investigated.

This chapter is reprinted with permission from *Criminal Justice and Behavior,* Vol. 23 No. 2, June 1996 338-357. © 1996 American Association for Correctional Psychology.

In 1981, in response to widespread concern about protecting Canadian children from sexual abuse and exploitation, the Canadian government established the Committee on Sexual Offenses against Children and Youth. This committee, which became known as the Badgley Commission, had a 3-year mandate to conduct extensive research on the incidence and prevalence of sexual offenses against children in Canada and on the response to the problem by both the child welfare and criminal justice systems. Their findings were shocking and served to mobilize significant changes in the handling of child sexual abuse in Canada. The Badgley Commission made more than 52 recommendations, ranging from programs to increase public awareness of the social problem to specific amendments of Canadian Criminal Law (Badgley, 1984).

Identified Problems With the
Legal Response to Child Sexual Abuse

The Badgley Commission noted that the laws of evidence were premised largely on the idea that children were inherently unreliable as witnesses. Obstacles to the reception of their evidence existed in two forms: a corroboration requirement for unsworn testimony given by children under 14 years of age, and an emphasis on the ability of children to swear an oath to give their statement. A further example of the courts' reluctance to hear children's accounts of sexual abuse and convict on their testimony was reflected in the warnings that judges were required to give to jurors concerning the frailties of children and the dangers of convicting an adult on a child's testimony (Bala, 1993).

According to the Badgley Commission, and supported by the experiences of many professionals working with child sexual abuse victims, young children were not being protected adequately by the existing laws because their testimonies were for the most part barred from the courtroom. Advocates reasoned that the younger the child, the less responsive the criminal justice system was to his or her victimization. In consultation with parents, survivors, and professionals, it was determined by the Badgley Commission that there was indeed a lack of responsiveness by the legal system to child sexual abuse cases.

The legal system as a whole, but especially the criminal justice system, was seen as contributing to the perception that child sexual abuse was not a widespread problem in Canada and indeed that many of the cases reported were unfounded (Bala, 1993). The Badgley Commission found that when matters were brought before the courts, judges frequently dismissed the evidence of children as unreliable and made it difficult for crown prosecutors to introduce other evidence in support of the children's allegations. Furthermore, expert testimony was rarely even contemplated in child abuse cases and corroborative testimony of other children under age 14 who witnessed an abusive event was equally difficult to relay because of the traditional rules. Convictions in child sexual abuse cases were difficult to achieve, in part because of the clandestine nature of the acts but also because of the legal obstacles governing the reception of children's testimony. As a result, the Badgley Commission recommended revisions to the Criminal Code (CCC, federal legislation that applies to all provinces) and to the Canada Evidence Act (which defines the manner in which evidence is admissible in court) to reflect the reality of what was happening to Canadian children, and the commission suggested fundamental changes to the law to allow children to speak directly for themselves at legal proceedings.

Recent Legislative Reforms:
Bills C-15 and C-126

In response to the Badgley Commission's recommendations, two sets of amendments to the CCC and to the Canada Evidence Act were approved by Parliament (Bill C-15 in 1988 and Bill C-126 in 1993). The intent of these amendments was to modify the existing rules of criminal evidence, so that (a) more successful prosecutions of child sexual abuse cases would result, (b) the experiences of child victims and witnesses would be improved, (c) better protection would be provided to child sexual abuse victims and witnesses, and (d) sentencing would be brought in line with the severity of the offenses (Standing Committee on Justice and the Solicitor General, 1993).

Changes to the CCC

Defining who is a victim. Philosophically, three of the new amendments to the CCC served to alter the prevailing view of children as victims. Even up to 1988, the CCC had sections creating the offense of sexual intercourse with a female person between the ages of 14 and 16 who was not the accused's wife and who was of previously chaste character, the offense of seduction of a female passenger on a ship, and the offense of sexual intercourse with a stepdaughter, foster daughter, or female ward. The latter offense was punishable by only a maximum sentence of 2 years in jail (in contrast with life imprisonment for breaking and entering a residence). It was lawful to have sexual intercourse with a female person under the age of 14 if the accused and the female person were married. Bill C-15 extended protection to children under 14 years of age by voiding their consent to any kind of sexual activity whatsoever with an adult. It eliminated the archaic sections that on occasion provided a defense where there was an inherently coercive relationship of sex between a child and an adult caretaker. This change has had particular significance for intrafamilial cases of sexual abuse and cases where a person in charge of the child such as teacher or counselor is involved. The statement from the Canadian Parliament to the courts was clearly that evidence of a child victim's prior sexual behavior was not a defense for child sexual abuse.

Removing the statute of limitations. Bill C-15 also expanded the ability of the courts to prosecute abusers and abusive behavior by removing the 1-year limitation for the prosecution of certain sexual offenses. These were all seldom-used offenses where a trust relationship was used for a sexual purpose. They included the seduction of a female person of previously chaste character between the ages of 16 and 18 and the seduction under promise of marriage. Time limits were all but eliminated in the new legislation in response to available research on the frequency of delayed disclosures in cases of child sexual abuse.

Expanded definition of abusive behavior. In addition, the creation of three new offenses expanded the court's ability to prosecute child sexual abuse (Standing Committee on Justice and the Solicitor General, 1993). These new gender-neutral offense categories were (a) sexual interference (touching a person under the age of 14 for a sexual purpose), (b) invitation to sexual touching (requesting that a child perform sexual acts), and (c) sexual exploitation (sexual touching or invitation to touch of children over 14 but under 18 by a person in a position of trust or authority). These offenses were important additions because they addressed the full range of sexually abusive situations involving children and, in particular, took into consideration the inherent power imbalance and vulnerability of the child victim of a caretaker.

Changes to the Canada Evidence Act

Abrogating the need for corroboration. Probably the most crucial amendments in Bill C-15 with respect to child witnesses are those that eliminated the necessity for corroboration. The amended Canada Evidence Act abrogated all rules that required corroboration to obtain a conviction in sexual offenses committed on children or adults. Notably, the Canada Evidence Act (1987) was changed to eliminate the requirement of corroboration for the testimony of children under age 14 who could not swear an oath. Prior to Bill C-15, very young children had little hope of testifying in court. Most child victims under the age of 6 or 7 were simply unable to satisfy the courts that they understood the oath. Cases involving children of this age were dismissed or not brought before the courts because of the lack of corroboration. These amendments have been the most critical to the prosecution of child sexual abuse cases, because they have essentially opened the courts to the testimony of younger children.

Qualifications of children as witnesses. Relative to other legal issues involved in child sexual abuse, Canada has shown considerable preoccupation with the question of children's ability to tell the truth (Wilson, 1989). Historically, judges have had discretionary powers to determine whether children could give sworn testimony and, barring that, to decide if they at least understood their duty to speak the truth. This inquiry typically has been carried out by means of rather complex questions about the nature and consequences of the oath (Bala, 1993). In *Regina v. Fletcher* (1982), the court rejected the notion that a child had to have a religious understanding to swear an oath. Gradually, a more flexible approach to both sworn and unsworn testimony has been developing in the courts, although questions by judges continue to vary greatly in type and difficulty. In general, Bill C-15 amendments to the Canada Evidence Act have reinforced the trend toward accepting the unsworn testimony of children. For example, one provision allows a child who cannot swear an oath, but who is able to communicate the evidence, to testify on a "promise to tell the truth."

Abrogating judges' duty to warn. Common law rule of practice for many years has involved the requirement that the judge warn the jury of the frailties of the evidence of a child, even under oath (*Regina v. Kendall,* 1962). This rule, which became known as the Kendall warning, governed practice in most courtrooms. As a result, judges routinely warned juries about the dangers of convicting solely on the evidence of a child. Following Bill C-15, the reception of unsworn testimony became more frequent, but many judges continued to draw distinctions between the evidence of children and adults. In recent decisions, the Supreme Court of Canada has rejected the traditional approach in favor of the view that every person giving testimony in court must be assessed by looking at mental development, understanding, and ability to communicate. Although children may not be able to testify with the same clarity as adults, that does not mean they are inherently unable to describe what happened and who did it. In case there was any doubt, the most recent amendment to the CCC, contained in Bill C-126, abrogated the duty to warn. Judges were directed by the new legislation not to make assumptions about the reliability of evidence because of a witness's age, and not to warn juries that children's testimonies are frail, unreliable, or should be viewed with skepticism.

In addition to the controversy over whether children can give reliable evidence is the issue of how children's evidence should be received. There are two different philosophical approaches to this issue. One approach is that of accommodation, which aims to bring children into courtrooms and have their testimony heard by the judge while taking steps to accommodate their needs and reduce their fears. The other approach is that of substitution, which criticizes the adversarial system as inappropriate and potentially harmful and seeks to keep children off the witness stand, using evidence on videotape or hearsay from third-party witnesses (Ministry of the Attorney General of Ontario, 1993). Generally, the reforms contained in Bill C-15 and Bill C-126 reflect a combination of both approaches.

Modifications to Court Procedure
Reflecting an Accommodation Approach

Recognition that testifying in court can be a frightening experience for many children and can inhibit their ability to give their testimony has led to much-needed reforms to court procedure. Similar to legislative reform in other countries, such as England and Wales (Davies & Noon, 1991) and

Australia (Cashmore, 1992), several modifications to court process were codified to allow special procedural rules for the giving of testimony by child victims of sexual assault.

Specific sections of Bill C-15 allow the child to testify behind a screen in the courtroom or to testify using a closed-circuit television link-up outside the courtroom if the judge is satisfied that the child cannot give a full and candid account of the sexual assault on the witness stand. The standard of proof for this application has been applied variably across the country, with some judges requiring expert testimony and others a less rigid evidentiary basis such as the testimony of a parent or investigating police officer regarding the child's ability to communicate in the courtroom. The Supreme Court of Canada recently upheld the constitutionality (under the Canadian Charter of Rights and Freedoms) of the screen for victims, basing its decision on the premise set out in the legislation "to better get at the truth by young victims." It was determined by the court that this provision did not infringe on the rights of the accused and that it could contribute to the administration of justice by increasing the possibility that a child would be able to give a full and candid account in court. This new provision in the law, and the position taken by the Supreme Court of Canada with respect to it, reflects the increasing awareness on the part of the judiciary of existing social science research concerning the potential harm to child victims who testify.

Two other recent legislative reforms contained in Bill C-126 provide further examples of the understanding by the criminal justice system of child witnesses' vulnerability and special needs. Children under 14 are now permitted to have a neutral support person accompany them to the witness stand, and children under 14 can no longer be cross-examined by an accused who chooses not to be represented by a defense counsel. In general, present state of the law shows a willingness to deviate from traditional procedures to accommodate children's needs.

Modifications Reflecting a Substitution
Approach to Receiving Evidence

Hearsay provisions expanded. In most court proceedings, the only admissible evidence is direct evidence from a witness about what he or she experienced, did, or knows. In child sexual abuse cases, however, there are three major reasons why the admission of hearsay evidence regarding children is important. First, the initial disclosure of sexual abuse by a young child to a parent is often the most graphic and complete account and directly supports the allegations of sexual abuse that have led to the charge. Second, it may be the only evidence available if the child cannot or will not testify. Third, it may be more reliable than the live testimony of the child for a variety of reasons (e.g., fear of the accused, child's lack of understanding of court process).

Canadian judges have begun to display a more developmentally sensitive attitude toward the admissibility of hearsay in child sexual abuse cases through the development of common law rules governing the admission of prior out-of-court statements of children, expert evidence, and the evidence of prior incidents of abuse by an accused. In a recent Supreme Court of Canada decision (*Regina v. Khan*, 1990), the need for increased flexibility in the interpretation of the hearsay rule to permit the admission in evidence of statements made by children to others about sexual abuse was recognized. Two conditions were set as part of the test to allow hearsay evidence in court: necessity and reliability. Because the facts of one case may not apply to cases that follow, there has been some judicial inconsistency in the application of the *Khan* decision. The law does appear to be evolving in a way that will allow courts to hear more of this type of relevant and probative evidence without making the automatic assumption that because it was something that the child said to someone else it should automatically be disregarded. The courts are in the early stages of accepting the evidence of out-of-court statements of children where their reliability has not been affected by the opportunity of others to influence. However, this acceptance is slow and erratic. For younger child victims, the *Khan* decision could increase the likelihood of a successful prosecution.

Videotaped testimony. When mandated child welfare agencies receive disclosures of sexual abuse by children, it is now common practice for many of them to videotape the disclosure interview. The original reason for using videotapes was to prevent the routine occurrence of multiple interrogations during the investigative process. Bill C-15 contains a provision for the admissibility of videotaped interviews of child complainants of sexual abuse as long as the child accepts the contents of the tape on the witness stand, and the tape has been made within a reasonable length of time after the offense. The constitutionality of a videotaped statement was recently upheld in the Supreme Court of Canada (*Regina v. Laramee,* 1993).

The reality, however, is that in many communities crown prosecutors are reluctant to use existing videotapes. They believe that videotapes do little to prevent the child's trauma of having to testify in court, because the child must accept the contents of the tape on the witness stand and be subject to the identical cross-examination by defense counsel that would have taken place had the videotape not been used. Crown attorneys also are concerned about the quality of the videotaped interviews and defense lawyers' ability to challenge the content and interview procedures if leading questions are used.

On the other hand, videotapes are clearly valuable when they can preserve the evidence of a child while getting as much information as possible in a nonleading, less stressful manner.

Four-Year Review of Bill C-15 Implementation

A decade ago, it was determined that a disturbing proportion of sexual offenses known to the criminal justice system involved children as victims (Badgley, 1984). Recent statistics indicate that of every 10 sexual assault victims known to the police, 4 are teenagers and 4 are under age 12 (Biesenthal & Clement, 1992; Statistics Canada, 1992). Moreover, it has been found that one third of federally incarcerated sex offenders are convicted for victimizing children and one third for victimizing adolescents (Correctional Service of Canada, 1991). Without a doubt, children have been found to be victims of sexual violence in Canada. A crucial question is whether the changes to legislation are making any difference in the prosecution of child sexual abuse.

In 1993, the Canadian Department of Justice undertook an evaluation of Bill C-15 to determine whether it was being successfully implemented. Overall, the research (Beisenthal & Clement, 1992) demonstrated that more police charges of child sexual abuse were being filed, in part because the new laws covered a broader range of inappropriate sexual behavior involving children, and in part because police were more aware of the issues and willing to file charges. It also found that more cases involving younger complainants (4-9 years old) were being prosecuted and that more younger complainants are being allowed to testify in courts across the country. These findings suggest that judges are being exposed to a more realistic profile of child victims of sexual assault.

The review further found that modifications to court procedures outlined in the legislation were being used very sparingly across the country, with the screen employed more frequently than were closed-circuit television links (Schmolka, 1992). Substitution approaches to having the child testify, such as the use of hearsay evidence regarding children's allegations (i.e., *Khan* application) also have been applied sparingly. Implementation of modification procedures has been slow largely due to lack of funding to retrofit courtrooms with video equipment. Thus, crown attorneys have been unable to take advantage of the legislation. In addition, the test in the application that must be met in court to enable the child to obtain the screen has been very stringent.

With respect to the admission of hearsay evidence on behalf of a child victim, the test has also often been too stringent, and there has been little training for crown attorneys in mounting a successful *Khan* application.

It is encouraging that changes brought about by Bills C-15 and C-126 reflect a significant shift in the Canadian criminal justice system's approach to prosecuting child sexual abuse cases. Inherent in these changes has been the underlying acceptance of children as potentially credible witnesses. However, just because the law recognizes that children's needs are different from those of adults and that accommodations made for children can ensure that they are good witnesses, it does not mean that the judiciary, crown attorneys, and defense lawyers necessarily act in accordance with those principles. Opening the doors of the courtroom to child complainants carries an ethical responsibility to avoid further victimization of children.

More education and an increased awareness of the problem of child sexual abuse on the part of the judiciary is crucial if the legislation is going to have the desired effect. The National Judicial Institute recently developed a training program for all federally appointed judges on many issues related to child sexual abuse. By the number of attendants at the training sessions, it appears that judges are willing to participate in formal training programs and are not as concerned that the training will interfere with their judicial independence. As well, Canadian courts are wrestling with the issue of receiving evidence from experts on such topics as child sexual abuse symptomatology, reliability of allegations of abuse, patterns of disclosure and recantation, competency of children to testify in court, suggestibility, and memory for abusive incidents.

The extent to which a judge can rely on an opinion of an expert on the witness stand whose decision is based on unproven hearsay is a matter before the courts. A recent Supreme Court of Canada ruling (*Regina v. Marquard,* 1993) concerning the issue of expert testimony concluded that (a) the only requirement for the admission of expert opinion is that the expert witness possess special knowledge and experience going beyond that of the trier of fact, and (b) the ultimate conclusion regarding the credibility or truthfulness of a particular witness is for the trier of fact and is not the proper subject of expert opinion. The *Marquard* decision, as well as others before it, clearly has recognized that there is a place in our courts for experts to assist in interpreting the behaviors of children, both before and after disclosures of sexual abuse.

As more children testify in court, there is the potential that many of them will be traumatized by their court experience. A need for adequate court preparation has been identified by professionals involved with child victims. In response to this need, a number of different approaches have developed across the country. The following section describes an innovative approach to preparing children to testify in court.

The London Family Court Clinic Child Witness Project

The past decade saw an increasing number of studies dealing with the potential trauma of court testimony for children (e.g., Berliner & Barbieri, 1984; Bulkley, 1982; Jaffe, Wilson, & Sas, 1987; Lusk & Waterman, 1986; Wells, 1986; Whitcomb, Shapiro, & Stellwagen, 1985; Wolfe, Sas, & Wilson, 1987). These studies generally have found that the trauma of these children resembles that of adult female rape victims who have testified in court (Veronen & Kilpatrick, 1983). Furthermore, research has indicated that children express many fears about testifying and that for some children it is very distressing (Avery, 1983; Goodman et al., 1992; Runyan, Everson, Edelsohn, Hunter, & Coulter, 1988; Sas, Hurley, Hatch, Malla, & Dick, 1993; Whitcomb, Runyan, DeVos, & Hunter, 1991). Stressors associated with the legal system, combined with the emotional sequelae related to the abuse itself, often result in overwhelming problems faced by the children—a factor that can affect their ability to provide competent and compelling evidence in a court of law (Sas, Austin, Wolfe, & Hurley, 1991).

Overview of Court Preparation

The Child Witness Project (CWP) was set up in 1988 with the goal of reducing the traumatization of child witnesses in the criminal justice system. In designing the CWP, the most frequently occurring stressors faced by children in the criminal justice system were targeted: lengthy delays, public exposure in the courtroom, facing the accused while testifying, understanding complex procedures, interacting with many professionals around the abuse, changing crown attorneys, undergoing difficult cross-examination by defense lawyers, testifying without the benefit of family support due to the mandatory exclusion of witnesses, and coping with negative disclosure aftermath such as apprehension and placement outside of the home or emotional abandonment by the family (Sas et al., 1991). To help child witnesses cope with these stressors, a court preparation protocol was developed with the goals of (a) demystifying the courtroom through education, (b) reducing the fear and anxiety related to testifying through stress reduction, and (c) empowering the children through emotional support and system advocacy.

The underlying philosophy guiding the choice of components for the court preparation protocol was based on the belief that children, due to their inherent vulnerability caused by their tender years, limited social awareness, lack of life experiences, and naive understanding of the criminal justice system, are generally ill prepared for the demands made of witnesses in a court of law. Moreover, many have been seriously traumatized by their victimization and therefore remain emotionally fragile. Their lack of knowledge about the court process, along with their obvious anxiety, confusion, and ignorance of legal terms and concepts, could interact with their fears of facing the accused in court. Accordingly, it was proposed that empowering the child victim through education and stress reduction would readjust the imbalance that exists in court between the accused and the child complainant by providing support for and advocacy on behalf of the child witness.

The CWP was set up primarily to work with child witnesses on an individual basis. As a result, considerable effort is spent in assessing the individual needs of child witnesses with respect to court preparation and in designing an intervention that will meet those needs. Together with background information, the therapist then determines which factors are operating to either enhance or interfere with each child's ability to testify, and the therapist tailors the two major components of the court preparation accordingly. The child witness court preparation protocol requires an average of five sessions (ranging from three to eight individual sessions). Parents are included in sessions as needed, or seen individually if necessary, but the majority of the work is carried out with the child alone.

Educational Component

The purpose of the protocol's educational component is to prepare the child witness in such areas as court procedures and etiquette, legal terminology, the oath, and the processes of the criminal justice system. These areas previously had been left to police officers and crown attorneys, who by virtue of ever-increasing responsibilities rarely were able to give it proper attention. Innovative equipment and aids are used in the preparation to teach the child about the criminal justice system in a creative and nondirective manner. Table 5.1 provides a summary of these educational objectives and methods.

Stress Reduction Component

The decision to include a stress reduction component in the preparation was based on our clinical findings that the majority of child victims expressed much fear and anxiety concerning their court dates and, in particular, concerning their participation in the hearings and trials as key witnesses. The five most salient fears documented in the study sample (Sas et al., 1993) were (a) facing the accused person, (b) being hurt by the accused in the courtroom or outside, (c) being on the stand or crying on the stand, (d) being sent to jail, and (e) not understanding the questions. These fears often were evidenced by the child having difficulty relaxing, falling asleep, or concentrating at school. Many children felt powerless to control their fears about testifying. Indeed, an examination of a subset of

TABLE 5.1 Summary of Educational Components

Objective	Medium
Teach child courtroom procedures and roles of key persons	Court tour Courtroom model Booklets Review checklist terms Role-play scenes (judge's gown)
Familiarize child with legal terms and concepts	Repetition and review Homework assignments Activity book Court tour
Teach child meaning of oath taking	Review terms Generate vignettes Provide real-life examples Homework assignments
Develop in child good techniques of testifying	Role-play practices Speaking loudly Answering yes or no Speaking slowly Clear articulation
Help child understand adversarial nature of criminal justice system	Provide explanation of system
Explain court outcomes to child	Review "reasonable doubt" and range of dispositions
Make child comfortable with physical layout of courtroom	Court tours

90 children from the original study sample who had completed all test questionnaires showed that 48% of them evidenced posttraumatic stress disorder symptomatology (Wolfe, Sas, & Wekerle, 1994).

The stress reduction component can involve a combination of techniques: (a) deep breathing exercises, (b) deep muscle relaxation, (c) development of a fear hierarchy, (d) cognitive restructuring and empowerment, and (g) systematic desensitization, if needed. All children are taught to employ deep breathing relaxation exercises as a basic strategy for managing their anxiety and nervousness in court. Frequent practice of this technique is encouraged. Depending on the degree of stress, the other techniques are introduced. Table 5.2 provides a summary of these stress

TABLE 5.2 Stress Reduction Components

Audience	Objective	Medium
All child witnesses	Breathing relaxation exercises	Instruction: Script of technique—to be used in court while on the stand
All children who present with significant fears	Deep muscle relaxation training	Imagery-based relaxation script (ages 5-10) Regular deep muscle relaxation script (ages 11-17)
All child witnesses	Development of fear hierarchy	Five most salient fears—least to most anxiety-provoking generated by child
All child witnesses	Cognitive restructuring and empowerment	Positive reasons for attending court List of strengths Concept of a team going to court
Child witnesses with extreme fears who are able to use imagination	Systematic desensitization	Pairing of fears with deep muscle relaxation exercises
All child witnesses	Therapeutic support	Words of encouragement Advocacy

reduction components and methods. Full details of the protocol, design, and training of therapists, as well as evaluation results from a sample of 120 children, is provided in Sas et al. (1991).

Effects of Court Preparation

Several findings from the program evaluation (Sas et al., 1991) and 3-year follow-up warrant discussion (Sas et al. 1993). First, it was found (Sas et al. 1991) that court preparation benefited child witnesses in four distinct ways: (a) by educating them about court procedures, (b) by helping them deal with their stress and anxieties related to the abuse and to testifying, (c) by helping them give full evidence on the stand, and (d) by providing an advocacy role on their behalf with the other mandated agencies in the criminal justice system. Second, findings related to the educative component of the preparation protocol indicated that child witnesses in both conditions learned much necessary information about the court system. The standard services to child witnesses previously in place (i.e., the Victim/Witness Assistance Program tour of the courtroom and explanation) served to increase child witnesses' knowledge with respect to court procedures and legal terms. However, child witnesses who received the individual court preparation learned significantly more about court. This finding was particularly important in light of studies showing that a major difficulty that child witnesses experience in the court system is their lack of knowledge and overall lack of understanding (Peterson-Badali & Abramovitch, 1992). In particular, young children may be more easily intimidated and confused by the criminal justice system because of their ignorance (Saywitz, Nathanson, Snyder, & Lamphear, 1993).

Third, benefits of the stress reduction component were also demonstrated. Children who received stress reduction evidenced significantly fewer generalized fears and specific abuse-related fears (such as revictimization) than did the control group at the time of court testimony. Additionally, parents rated the stress reduction component received by their children very highly, saying that it reduced their children's fears and provided support and individual attention. Through self-report measures, children also described this component favorably, indicating that they felt understood by their therapist, felt less afraid, believed they knew more about how the system worked, and felt they would be good witnesses.

The results of the 3-year follow-up study (Sas et al., 1993) on the social and psychological effect of court involvement suggested that in general, negative court outcome was associated with significantly more emotional distress and poorer adjustment in child witnesses. Additionally, cases in which the abuser was a father figure also were more likely to result in poorer emotional adjustment by the child witnesses. The most significant protective variable identified for child witnesses was the availability of a supportive mother, who from the moment of disclosure was able to protect and support the child.

Conclusions

Based on our evaluation findings and ongoing follow-up of these children, we have drawn the following conclusions:

1. It is unfair to expect children to testify in a court of law without adequate preparation. All child witnesses require court preparation that educates them about the court process and prepares them for their roles as witnesses. In addition, many children, due to their pronounced fears and anxieties, require stress management techniques to help them cope with what is usually an ordeal. Advocating for modifications to court procedures for anxious, traumatized child victims, demanding increased sensitivity to child victims on the part of crown attorneys and police officers, and ensuring support for children to help them deal with the disclosure aftermath and their involvement with the criminal justice system are a necessary part of any child witness protocol.

2. Handling intrafamilial abuse in the criminal justice system is particularly difficult. These cases require extra support and added sensitivity for the victim and the family. For these child victims, the personal cost of testifying is the greatest, and every effort must be put into reducing the child's emotional pain and strengthening the mother-child bond as a protective factor (Goodman et al., 1992; Sas et al., 1993; Whitcomb et al., 1991).

3. All sexual abuse cases involving child victims must be expedited. Lengthy delays are unbearable for children and can have a deleterious effect on a child witness's testimony at trial.

4. Expert testimony on issues related to the psychological symptoms of abused children, recantation, delayed disclosure, the need for the screen or closed-circuit presentation, suggestibility, and memory in children should be offered as much as possible to the court as part of the prosecutor's case against an accused.

5. Testimonial aids such as the screen or closed-circuit television should be readily available to children who are not able to testify in front of an accused in court. The child should be allowed to sit in a witness-only waiting room, with a segregated area of the courtroom specially designated for child victim-witnesses services.

6. Hearsay testimony by individuals who have received a sexual abuse disclosure from a child should be admissible in court, weighed for its probative value.

In summary, child sexual abuse victims involved in the criminal justice system require coordination among prosecutors, police, child protective service workers, and when available, victim/witness assistance program staff to ensure that cases are dealt with in an integrated and child-focused manner from the moment of disclosure through sentencing and beyond. Canada's Bills C-15 and C-126 are progressive modifications of the criminal law that have brought about important changes for children and the courts. We await further continued efforts to design and implement procedures that protect children from harsh treatment and increase their ability to assist Canadian courts of law.

References

An Act to Amend the Criminal Code of Canada and the Canada Evidence Act, S.C. 1986-87, c. C-15, R.S.C. 1985 (3rd Supp.) (Bill C-15).

An Act to Amend the Criminal Code of Canada and the Young Offenders Act, S.C. 1993, c. 45 (Bill C-126).

Avery, M. (1983). The child abuse witness: Potential for secondary victimization. *Criminal Justice Journal, 7,* 1-48.

Badgley, C. R. (1984). *Child sexual abuse in Canada: Further analysis of the 1983 National Survey.* Ottawa, Canada: National Health & Welfare Canada.

Bala, N. (1993, July). *Child sexual abuse prosecutions: Children in the courts.* Paper presented at the Canadian Judicial Council Seminar, Aylmer, Quebec.

Biesenthal, L., & Clement, J. (1992). *Canadian statistics on child sexual abuse.* Ottawa, Canada: Canada Department of Justice.

Berliner, L., & Barbieri, M. (1984). The testimony of the child victim of sexual assault. *Journal of Social Issues, 40,* 125-137.

Bulkley, J. (1982). *Recommendations for improving legal intervention in intrafamilial child sexual abuse cases.* Washington, DC: American Bar Association.

Canada Evidence Act. R.S.C. 1987, c. 24, s.16(1).

Cashmore, J. (1992). *The use of closed-circuit TV for child witnesses in the court.* Sydney, Australia: Australia Law Reform Commission.

Correctional Service of Canada. (1991). Everything you wanted to know about Canadian federal sex offenders and more. *Forum on Corrections Research, 3,* 3-6.

Davies, G., & Noon, E. (1991). *An evaluation of the live link for child witnesses.* London: Home Office.

Goodman, G. S., Pyle-Taub, E., Jones, D. P. H., England, P., Port, L. K., Rudy, L., & Prado, L. (1992). Testifying in criminal court: The effects on child sexual assault victims. *Monographs of the Society for Research in Child Development, 57* (5, Serial No. 229).

Jaffe, P., Wilson, S., & Sas, L. (1987). Court testimony of child sexual abuse victims: Emerging issues in clinical assessments. *Canadian Psychology, 28,* 291-295.

Lusk, R., & Waterman, J. (1986). Effects of sexual abuse on children. In K. MacFarlane & J. Waterman (Eds.), *Sexual abuse of young children.* New York: Guilford.

Ministry of the Attorney General of Ontario. (1993). *Consultation paper: Evidence Act reforms for child and vulnerable adult witnesses.* Queens Park, Canada: Author.

Peterson-Badali, M., & Abramovitch, R. (1992). Children's knowledge of the legal system: Are they competent to instruct legal counsel? *Canadian Journal of Criminology, 34,* 139-160.

Regina v. Fletcher, 7 C.C.C. (3rd) 370 at 380 (Ont. C.A.) (1982).

Regina v. Kendall, 132 C.C.C. 216, at 220 (S.C.C.) (1962).

Regina v. Khan, 79 C.R. (3rd) 1 (1990).

Regina v. Laramee, 6 C.R. (4th) 277 (Manitoba Court of Appeal) (1993).

Regina v. Marquard, 25 C.R. (3rd) 1 S.C.C. (1993).

Runyan, D., Everson, M., Edelsohn, G., Hunter, W., & Coulter, M. (1988). Impact of legal intervention on sexually abused children. *Journal of Pediatrics, 113,* 647-653.

Sas, L., Austin, G., Wolfe, D., & Hurley, P. (1991). *Reducing the system-induced trauma for child sexual abuse victims through court preparation, assessment, and follow-up.* Ottawa: Health and Welfare Canada, National Welfare Grants Division.

Sas, L., Hurley, P., Hatch, A., Malla, S., & Dick, T. (1993). *Three years after the verdict: A longitudinal study of the social and psychological adjustment of child witnesses referred to the child witness project.* Ottawa: Health and Welfare Canada, Family Violence Prevention Division.

Saywitz, K., Nathanson, R., Snyder, L., & Lamphear, V. (1993). *Preparing children for the investigative and judicial process: Improving communication, memory and emotional resiliency* (Final report to the National Center on Child Abuse and Neglect, Grant No. 90CA1179).

Schmolka, V. (1992). *Is Bill C-15 working? An overview of the research on the effects of the 1988 child sexual abuse amendments.* Ottawa: Department of Justice, Canada, Communications and Consultation Branch.

Standing Committee on Justice and the Solicitor General. (1993). *Four-year review of the child sexual abuse provisions of the Criminal Code and the Canada Evidence Act* (Formerly Bill C-15). Ottawa: Supplies and Services Canada.

Statistics Canada. (1992). Teenage victims of violent crime. *Juristat Service Bulletin, 12.* Ottawa: Supplies and Services Canada.

Veronen, L., & Kilpatrick, D. (1983). Stress management for rape victims. In D. Meichenbaum & M. E. Jaremko (Eds.), *Stress reduction and prevention* (pp. 341-374). New York: Plenum.

Wells, M. (1986). Court as a catalyst for treatment. *Vis-a-Vis, 4,* 3.

Whitcomb, D., Runyan, D., DeVos, E., & Hunter, W.. (1991). *Final report: Child victim as witness research.* Washington, DC: U.S. Department of Justice, Office of Juvenile Justice and Delinquency Prevention.

Whitcomb, D., Shapiro, E., & Stellwagen, L. (1985). *When the victim is a child: Issues for judges and prosecutors.* Washington, DC: U.S. Department of Justice.

Wilson, J. (1989). Children's evidence in legal proceedings: A perspective on the Canadian position. *Law Society of Upper Canada Gazette, 23,* 281.

Wolfe, D. A., Sas, L., & Wekerle, C. (1994). Factors associated with the development of posttraumatic stress disorder among child victims of sexual abuse. *Child Abuse & Neglect, 18,* 37-50.

Wolfe, V. V., Sas, L., & Wilson, S. K. (1987). Some issues in preparing sexually abused children for courtroom testimony. *Behavior Therapist, 10,* 107-113.

The Effect of Child Witness
Research on Legislation in Great Britain

RAY BULL

GRAHAM DAVIES

In the summer of 1994, one of the longest ever criminal trials involving child witnesses in England and Wales came to a conclusion.

> Child-sex gang is convicted after £8 million trial. (*Daily Telegraph,* June 13, 1994)

> The jurors were told details of how terrified children were subjected to systematic abuse after being taken to isolated barns and sheds. Knives and shotguns were used to ensure the victims' silence. Interviews by social workers uncovered a picture of weeping and humiliated children being passed around members of the gang. (*Times,* June 13, 1994)

The trial, which lasted 8 months, resulted in five men being found guilty by a jury that took 5 days to deliberate on the verdicts. The defendants had denied the children's allegations. One of their defense lawyers described the children's horrific stories as "pure fantasy." However, the police and social services claimed that they had conducted a "model enquiry" in keeping with the existing guidelines. Ten of the children gave their evidence via live video links, and videorecordings of earlier interviews were shown. One 11-year-old "endured six days of cross examination and frequently broke down in tears" (*Daily Telegraph,* June 13, 1994). D. Evans, Director of Social Services said, "This case shows that children can disclose abuse and be believed" (*Daily Telegraph,* June 13, 1994).

Although the outcome of this trial does suggest that the evidence of child witnesses can make a meaningful contribution to criminal proceedings, this has not always been the case. Spencer and Flin (1993) noted that only a few years ago an English lawyer provided (in a textbook on evidence) a summary of reasons adduced to justify the then legal suspicion concerning children's testimony. Heydon (1984) stated:

> First, a child's powers of observation and memory are less reliable than an adult's. Secondly, children are prone to live in a make-believe world, so that they magnify incidents which happen to them or invent them completely. Thirdly, they are also very egocentric, so that details seemingly unrelated to their own world are quickly forgotten by them. Fourthly, because of their immaturity they are very suggestible and can easily be influenced by adults and other children. One lying child may influence others to lie; anxious parents may take a child through a story again and again so that it becomes drilled in untruths. Most dangerously, a policeman taking a statement from a child may without ill will use leading questions so that the child tends to confuse what actually happened with the answer suggested implicitly by the question. A fifth danger is that children often have little notion of the duty to speak the truth, and they may fail to realize how important their evidence is in a case and how important it is for it to be accurate. Finally, children sometimes behave in a way evil beyond their years. They may consent to sexual offences against themselves and then deny consent. They may completely invent sexual offences. Some children know that the adult world regards such matters in a serious and peculiar way, and they enjoy investigating this mystery or revenging themselves by making false accusations. (p. 84)

Such views as Heydon's made it difficult for criminal courts to hear the testimony of children, especially young ones. (For more on this, see the excellent 1993 book by Spencer and Flin.) However, since 1984, when Heydon made such claims, psychologists' scientific research has produced replicated results that are contrary to his views. On the basis of this research, laws and procedures relating to child witnesses in various countries have recently been changed or are being changed. In addition, recent and ongoing research by psychologists has been directed toward helping the interviewers of child witnesses to increase their interviewing skills and related knowledge.

In October 1992, a report was published on behalf of the secretary of state for Scotland by Lord Clyde concerning his inquiry into the removal of children from their homes in Orkney in 1991 (Clyde, 1992). In this report, the skills of those who interviewed the alleged child victims of sexual abuse were described as inadequate and deficient. In the *Independent,* it was stated that "a Scottish Office spokesman said it was widely accepted that this was a difficult area. 'What we *don't* know about interviewing children would fill books' he said" (Braid & Mackinnon, 1992). Among the recommendations in Lord Clyde's report were several concerning the interviewing of children.

In 1990, Sue White argued that "until relatively recently, suspected victims of child sexual abuse did not receive much special consideration with reference to how they should be interviewed" (p. 368). She suggested that "techniques for interviewing these young children have been based on practical experiences and are only now beginning to receive any research attention" (p. 369). She pointed out that although "a number of authors have made detailed suggestions of how best to interact with a child suspected of being a victim of sexual abuse . . . interviewers have been forced to discover clinical techniques which work best in their particular situation" (p. 369). She believed that "the first goal in investigatory interviewing must be the gathering of data which are as true as possible a representation of the child's experiences and which are not subject to charges of being contaminated" (p. 370).

Psychologists' research in the past decade has found (contrary to what the English lawyer Heydon, 1984, claimed) that children are usually able to provide a worthwhile oral account of what has happened to them, if they are interviewed properly (Bull, 1994a, 1995a). The results of such research have had a positive effect, in several countries, in terms of influencing recent legislative changes that aim to make it more likely that courts will hear evidence from children. However, this psychological research has also clearly demonstrated that inappropriate interviewing/questioning can bias children's accounts.

Recent years have seen important changes in the law about the evidence of children in criminal proceedings in England and Wales. Until recently, the competency requirement was interpreted as making it impossible to hear evidence from a child under the age of 6 years. In 1990, the Court of

Appeal ruled that a child of any age could give evidence, provided the judge thought him or her sufficiently intelligent and able to understand the duty of speaking the truth. The Criminal Justice Act of 1991 went much further and attempted to abolish the competency requirement altogether (Bull & Spencer, 1992).

At the same time, the corroboration rules have been greatly attenuated. The statutory ban on convicting on the uncorroborated evidence of unsworn children was abolished in 1988 and with it, the duty to warn the jury of the danger of accepting the evidence of a child. Until recently, the judge was still obliged to warn of the danger of believing sexual complaints (whether child or adult), but abolition of this requirement was embodied in the 1993 Criminal Justice and Public Order Act, as was a sentence making it absolutely clear (as was intended by the 1991 act) that "a child's evidence shall be received unless it appears that the child is incapable of giving intelligible testimony."

Steps have also been taken to make it less stressful for children to give their evidence in court. The Court of Appeal has approved the practice of allowing children to give evidence from behind screens, and the Criminal Justice Act of 1988 introduced the live video link, enabling children to testify live at trial via a closed-circuit television from a private room away from the defendant.

In 1988, the Home Office (the relevant government department) set up a committee chaired by the distinguished Judge Mr. Justice Pigot. This committee recommended radical changes that went beyond those just described. The committee's report proposed a new scheme under which the evidence of children would routinely be taken in advance of trial and recorded on videotape. A videotape of the initial interview would replace the child's evidence-in-chief (testimony presented by a prosecution witness during the main part of the trial) at court, and a videotape of a cross-examination held in chambers (with the defendant physically absent but able to watch through closed-circuit television) would replace live cross-examination at trial. The main arguments for this innovation were two: First, the court would get a fresher and fuller account of the incident from the child, and second, the procedure would enable the child to drop out of the proceedings once the second interview had taken place.

This proposal attracted widespread support from judges and practicing lawyers, as well as from professionals concerned with child care matters. It was too radical for the Home Office, however, which settled for a more limited scheme, that of creating a new exception to the hearsay rule whereby a videotape recording of an earlier interview with a child can be used to supplement the evidence-in-chief a child gives live at trial. The big difference between this and the Pigot scheme, of course, is that the child must attend the trial and undergo a live cross-examination, probably via a live video link. The new hearsay exception came into operation in October 1992.

Under the provisions of the Criminal Justice Act of 1991, the judge has discretion to exclude all or part of the videotape of an interview that he or she considers to have been unfairly conducted. In the hope of ensuring that interviews are conducted properly—and also to give judges a basis for the exercise of discretion—the Home Office in 1992 published the *Memorandum of Good Practice on Video Recorded Interviews With Child Witnesses for Criminal Proceedings* (see Bull, 1992).

The *Memorandum of Good Practice*

In 1991, the *Times* noted:

> Law reforms to stop children having to give live evidence in abuse cases were urged yesterday after the "black magic" trial collapsed because the prosecution could no longer rely on the child's evidence.
>
> The Government has brought in some reforms to make it easier for children to give evidence. But . . . a reform under the Criminal Justice Act of 1991, allowing the video-taped evidence does not come into effect until next Autumn.

The recent legislative changes described in this chapter's introduction will probably eventuate in more children than before (especially younger ones) testifying in criminal trials. In light of these developments, a Home Office minister announced in the House of Commons in 1991 that his department would be producing a memorandum of good practice on videorecorded interviews with child witnesses for use in criminal trials. The videorecording of interviews will enable much closer scrutiny of the interviewing techniques employed. To obtain worthwhile evidence from children in a reliable way that can stand up to such scrutiny, the Home Office felt that many interviewers (whether police, social workers, lawyers, or others) would welcome guidance designed to assist them, especially because such videorecorded interviews should usually be of the first investigative interviews conducted with the child.

Although following the guidance offered in the *Memorandum of Good Practice* is voluntary, questions are regularly asked in criminal trials (and in the stages preceding such trials) concerning the extent to which interviewers followed such guidance. (The authors of this chapter are often asked, usually by the defense, to comment on the extent to which particular videorecorded interviews have been conducted along the lines recommended in the *Memorandum.*)

The Home Office made considerable effort to ensure that the *Memorandum* was as useful as possible. Together with Di Birch (Professor of Law at Nottingham University), the first author was asked by the Home Office to produce, by July 1991, a working draft memorandum. This initial draft was then revised by the Home Office, particularly with regard to its organization. The Home Office set up a Policy Steering Group that consisted of a representative from each of a considerable number of relevant bodies (e.g., police, social workers, lawyers, psychologists, psychiatrists, child welfare organizations). The first revision of the document was sent for comment to each member of the Policy Steering Group (plus others knowledgeable on the topic). The Policy Steering Group then met at the Home Office (with the first author and Di Birch being present, as was the second author representing the British Psychological Society) to discuss revisions and to make suggestions for improvement. A second revision was then produced by the Home Office, which went through a similar procedure as, subsequently, did a third revision. A fourth revision was produced in January 1992. This version was used in a Home Office pilot study to see if police officers and social workers in three towns were able to understand and implement its recommendations. In the light of the outcome of this pilot study, and of further comment from experts, a final revised version of the *Memorandum* was published in August 1992.

The *Memorandum* covers a very wide range of issues. Advice on the legal conditions about which a criminal court may wish to be satisfied before admitting a videorecording are included, as is guidance on the legal rules to be observed in producing an evidential recording acceptable to criminal courts (see Birch, 1992). It gives guidance on what to do prior to an interview, including when and where to conduct a videorecording. Guidance is also offered on the equipment to use. An essential component gives advice on conducting the interviews so that children can give as full an account as possible without undue influence taking place. The *Memo-*

randum also provides recommendations about postinterview issues such as the storage, custody, and disposal of such videorecordings. The section on conducting interviews recommends a phased approach (Jones & McQuiston, 1988; Yuille, Hunter, Jaffe, & Zaparniuk, 1993) that follows the sequence of (a) rapport, (b) free recall, (c) questioning, and (d) closure. The *Memorandum* outlines, in its questioning phase, that question types vary in how suggestive/leading they are, and it recommends that certain question types (e.g., open-ended questions) should precede other types (e.g., leading questions).

Most of the content of the *Memorandum* was based closely on the research available at the time (Bull, 1992). The professional opinions of interviewers with considerable experience also made a contribution, as did the views of the Home Office (and the Department of Health). The *Memorandum* is often described by the first author as being "on how to do the easy ones." That is, it is based on research with children who do wish to tell the interviewer what happened. Extremely little research existed prior to the publication of the *Memorandum,* or exists today, on the interviewing of children who (for various reasons) do not wish to tell or who have been threatened not to tell. Similarly, there is a dearth of research on the interviewing of children with communication difficulties (Bull, 1995b).

The Use of Videotaped Evidence in Trials

The 1991 Criminal Justice Act permits prosecutors in England and Wales to substitute a child's videotaped interview for that child's live examination at court by the prosecutor. Like the use of closed-circuit television (see the following section), this concession is limited to children under 14 years in physical assault cases and 17 years for offenses of a sexual nature and is subject to the agreement of the presiding judge. The video interview must be conducted as soon as is feasible subsequent to a child making an allegation. It will usually be conducted by a police officer or social worker, who will normally follow the precepts of the *Memorandum* for the conduct of such interviews.

The rationale for the 1991 Act reflected a mixture of child welfare and prosecution-led concerns. On the welfare side, the Act was seen as further limiting the exposure of the child to the courtroom (although the child was still to be available for live cross-examination at trial, which is usually done via the live link) and permitting therapy for traumatized children, who might otherwise have to await the trial for fear of the defense alleging contamination of evidence. Law enforcement personnel saw the act as likely to produce more complete, vivid, and spontaneous testimony than was normally available from the child on the witness stand and to open the way for much younger children to give evidence in the criminal courts.

Prior to the implementation of the Act in October 1992, the Home Office commissioned the second author to conduct an evaluation of its effect, both within the legal system as a whole and on the child witnesses and the quality of their evidence. The methods employed have included questionnaires directed to samples of judges, barristers, court officials, police officers, and social workers that cover, first, their expectations of the Act and second, their experience with the Act in operation. Trained court observers have watched children giving their evidence both in taped interviews and live at trial, and a representative group of interviews has been assessed for the degree to which they adhere to the recommendations of the *Memorandum*. The research program is not yet completed, but there are already some indications of the likely strengths and failings of the existing legislation.

It is evident from the available statistics that the provisions of the Act have not been used as widely as might have been anticipated. Police sources quote a figure of 14,896 interviews having been conducted by officers in the first 9 months of the Act, but of these only 3,652 (24.5%) led to a recommendation to the Crown Prosecution Service (CPS) that prosecution should take place. Other statistics from the Lord Chancellor's Department suggest that the CPS in turn has chosen to pursue only a small minority of cases. In the whole of 1993, there were only 340 applications to show video interviews at trial of which presiding judges turned down just 11 for technical or evidential failings. Some of these cases in turn resulted in late guilty pleas, leaving just 116 videos being shown to juries in the whole of England and Wales, the great majority in cases of alleged sexual abuse. Complete figures on conviction rates in video cases are not yet available, but statistics for the first half year show 38% of the defendants pleaded guilty to all or part of the indictment, a further 24% were found guilty at trial, 32% were found not guilty, and the remaining 6% resulted in retrial or bench warrant (where the accused had jumped bail) (Butler, 1993).

The major discrepancy between the number of interviews conducted and those actually used in court proceedings has inevitably led to allegations that a large procedural hammer has been fashioned to crack a small judicial nut. Social workers in particular have charged that the sensitive process of investigative interviewing has been hijacked by the evidential demands of the police (Bilton, 1994). Certainly, marked differences of opinion emerged among the various professional groups when asked in the preliminary questionnaire whether the act would work to the benefit of justice and of children. Judges took a generally positive view of videotaping on both counts, whereas social workers and police officers were uncertain of its effect on justice and were deeply skeptical as to its value for children.

However, the same questionnaire revealed overwhelming support for the value of the *Memorandum* among all professional groups. The idea of the staged interview, the avoidance of inappropriate questioning procedures, and the importance of a preliminary planning meeting prior to the interview (Bull, 1992) have met with widespread acceptance (Davies & Wilson, 1994). Some of the problems arising from the need to combine evidential and investigatory interviews have been voiced by Wattam (1992). Her interviews with children who had themselves been the subject of formal police interviews suggested that the children frequently had a distorted view of the nature and purpose of such interviews. This bewilderment was not helped by legal constraints that prevent interviewers from being the first to mention the name of the accused or the nature of the alleged offense (Bilton, 1994). Requests for the detail demanded by the court such as places, dates, and context may be viewed by the child as skepticism or outright disbelief (Westcott & Davies, in press).

A second problem identified by Wattam (1992) concerns an alleged mismatch between the ideals of the *Memorandum* for a single 1-hour interview and the dynamics of disclosure of familial abuse. The latter may involve a gradual process of building up trust over several interviews with minimal disclosures gradually being replaced by more serious allegations. The Act allows more than one videotaped interview to be submitted as evidence, but clearly, the defense in these circumstances would seize on any discrepancies between what the child alleged in one interview and in a second. Clearly, the question of when to tape is quite crucial. A recent police survey underlined the fact that there is as yet no consistent policy on these matters, with some forces routinely videotaping all child witness interviews and others being far more selective. The proportion of interviews submitted to CPS for prosecution varied from 7.9% in one force to 64% in another (Butler, 1993). Guidance on these and other matters should form the central part of any revision to the *Memorandum.*

Clearly, police, social workers, and the courts are still learning to live with the provisions of the 1991 Act. If its effect to date has been less than some had hoped, it would be premature to dismiss it as a unsuccessful. The number of videotape cases coming to the courts has risen steadily in each of the Lord Chancellor's Department's quarterly returns. The number of police and social work personnel trained in *Memorandum* interviewing is also on the increase, although the absence of nationally agreed-on training standards and awards (Bull, 1994b) continues to be a concern. Home Office spokespersons have ruled out any further changes to the law until the results of the current research evaluation have been digested. These results will also contain full figures on the proportion of tapes that lead to convictions at court, which should enable a judgment to be made on the effect of live, as opposed to taped, testimony. Even if the figures are no better than under the old legislation, any beneficial effect on the well-being of the child witnesses themselves could more than justify the direction of change. Similarly, improvements in interviewers' skills, occasioned by their interviews now routinely being videorecorded and therefore open to scrutiny, will benefit children.

Closed-Circuit Television in the Courtroom

Unlike the United States, English law confers no right of confrontation between a witness and an accused. Since the case of *R. v. Smellie* (1919), English courts have recognized that the conventions of open court can be set aside if there is a risk of the child witness being unable to testify in the presence of the accused (Spencer & Flin, 1993). An interview study by Flin, Davies, and Tarrant (1988) confirmed that fear of the sight of the accused and giving evidence in the novel and sometimes alien atmosphere of the courtroom were major sources of stress for child witnesses. In an effort to obviate such concerns, closed-circuit television (or the live link as it is known in Britain) was introduced into British courts on a trial basis in 1989 and is now available in 36 of the 72 crown court centres in England and Wales. Unlike the United States and other countries wedded to the confrontation principle, the English legislation embodied in the 1988 Criminal Justice Act incorporates a presumption of need, and access to the link is normally routinely granted by the judge on application from the attorney (the barrister). Liberal use of the link has meant that English and Welsh courts have amassed a great deal of practical experience of the system and can provide a test bed for many of the arguments surrounding its introduction in other judiciaries.

The configuration of closed-circuit television in courts in England and Wales differs markedly from procedures used in North America. In the English system, the child is in a room adjacent to the court but alone except for a support person, typically a court usher, whose role it is to ensure the child's privacy and to offer social support during periods of waiting. Judge, prosecution, and defense attorney are all situated in court and communicate with the child via electronic workstations that both send and receive pictures. In addition to the workstations, large monitors are set up in the courtroom for the benefit of the defendant, the jury, and the general public. The cameras, which form part of the workstations, are normally voice activated, so the child sees whoever is speaking to her or him while the court always sees the child. (Defendants are not allowed to represent themselves.) The facility is available to children appearing as victim or bystander witnesses in cases involving violence or sexual assault (with age limits on use of 14 and 17, respectively).

When the system was introduced in October 1989, the second author was commissioned by the Home Office to carry out an evaluation covering its acceptance and use by the courts and its effect on the quality of children's testimony (Davies & Noon, 1991; Noon & Davies, 1993). In the first 23 months of its availability, some 544 applications were made for use of the live-link facility, of which all but 3% were allowed by the presiding judge. Outcomes were known in some 468 cases, of which 36% resulted in late guilty pleas by the accused to part or the whole of the indictment. Of the trials that went ahead, 28% led to a conviction, 26% to an acquittal, and in a further 3% of cases, the defendant was discharged. The remaining 7% of cases resulted in retrials or bench warrants. No comparable figures are available for the period prior to the introduction of the live link, but the conviction rates appear broadly in line with those for similar offenses in judiciaries that adhere to the traditions of open-court testimony (Davies & Noon, in press).

Opinions on the benefits and drawbacks of live-link testimony were solicited from some 50 judges, 78 barristers, and 13 court administrators who had practical experience with the link. When asked to identify the benefits of evidence given via the live link, rather similar points were made by all three groups, and those of the judges can be considered representative. One advantage mentioned by 38% of the judges reflected the original motive for the introduction of the live link, namely, the protection it provides from the oppressive atmosphere of the courtroom and in particular, from the physical presence of the accused. However, the most frequently cited advantage mentioned by 48% of those questioned was the perceived reduction in stress displayed by the witness that, according to 20% of the sample, led to an improvement in the quality and amount of evidence provided.

There was some support for these observations from the results of observational ratings made by trained observers who watched 154 children testify in 100 separate trials. Over 40% of the children observed were rated as either "confident" or "very confident" in giving their evidence via the live link, and over 85% were "relatively" or "very" fluent under examination and cross-examination. The absence of data from the same courts prior to the 1988 Act makes a comparison difficult with the behavior of children giving evidence in open courts. However, some parallel rating data were kindly made available by Flin, Bull, Boon, and Knox (1990, 1993), who had observed children giving evidence in open court in Scotland. Comparison of the two samples suggested that the English children giving evidence via the live link were more fluent, more audible, and less unhappy under cross-examination than their Scottish counterparts and more likely to give consistent testimony.

Although differences in the characteristics of these two samples make any comparison inevitably tentative, the results are consistent with the judges' observations. They are also congruent with the recent experimental studies of Saywitz and Nathanson (1993) that demonstrate that children aged 8-10 years show lower levels of recall and greater vulnerability to leading questions when questioned in a courtroom as opposed to a more familiar and less alien setting.

The survey of legal personnel also uncovered some criticisms of the live link, chief of which was a potential loss of impact of testimony. In all, 44% of judges agreed that live-link evidence had less effect on the jury than open-court testimony, with 34% disagreeing and 22% undecided. Some limited support for the impact factor comes from a series of experimental studies conducted by Clifford, Davies, Westcott, and Garratt (1992) that compared mock juror assessments of live versus live-link testimony provided by children. Although in most instances no differences in ratings were found, one study produced higher assessments of witness confidence for the same testimony given live as opposed to via a link, and a second study found a similar effect on rated attractiveness (see also Tobey, Goodman, Batterman-Faunce, Orcutt, & Sachsenmaier, 1995).

Nonetheless, for the court personnel surveyed in the Home Office project, the advantages of the link outweighed the disadvantages. By the conclusion of the study, some 74% of the judges, 83% of the barristers, and 12 of the 13 court administrators had formed either a "favorable" or "very favorable" view of the scheme. However, it seems that the assumed disadvantages weigh heavily among Crown Prosecution Service staff who have a key role in initiating requests for the live link for prosecution witnesses. Prosecutors can be accused of sometimes giving a greater priority to gaining a conviction than to the welfare of the child (Plotnikoff & Woolfson, 1994). However, it is important to keep in mind that improvements in the quality and quantity of children's testimony will frequently outweigh any loss of immediacy in the eyes of the jury (Davies, 1994).

Recent Research on Enhancing
Methods of Interviewing Children

In the few years since the *Memorandum* was written, a considerable amount of research has been undertaken on increasing further our knowledge about how best to interview child witnesses. The fruits of such research may well be incorporated into an expanded, updated, and revised *Memorandum*. In England, some research has recently been conducted on the use of the cognitive interview, of the felt board, and of children hearing a recording of their recall.

The Cognitive Interview

A considerable number of studies in the United States and in Germany (Köhnken, Milne, Memon, & Bull, 1994) have found that the cognitive interview (Memon & Bull, 1991; Memon & Köhnken, 1992) helps adult witnesses to recall correctly more of a witnessed event. However, its usefulness with young children is not so well established. In Britain, Milne, Bull, Köhnken, and Memon (1994) studied the effectiveness of their revised version of the cognitive interview (CI) for children aged 8 to

10 years. They found that use of the CI resulted in over 20% more correct information being recalled of an event witnessed 1 day earlier (compared to a structured interview, SI, which only differed from the CI in terms of the special CI techniques). This extra correct recall did not occur in the (initial) free-recall phase of the interview, but only in the subsequent questioning phase, which focused on items already mentioned in the child's free recall. This extra recall was largely concerned with the recall categories of "person" and "action" information. Although across all recall categories combined there was no significant error difference between the CI and SI interviews, the CI children's recall of "person" information contained significantly more (a) incorrect recall and (b) confabulations. However, the overall proportion of what the children said that was correct was very similar for the CI and SI groups (at 80.7% and 79.6%, respectively). Milne et al. (1994) further found that use of the CI reduced the effects of subsequent suggestive questioning. This worthwhile effect applied both to suggestive questions that misled the children away from the correct answer and to those that led the children toward the correct answer.

Wark, Memon, Holley, Köhnken, and Bull (1994) also found in a separate British study that their version of the CI (i.e., as used by Milne et al., 1994) also helped 8- and 9-year-old children correctly to remember significantly more of an event witnessed 2 days before. Wark et al. (1996) also found (as did Milne et al.) that the CI children had more incorrect recall of "person" information. As in Milne et al.'s study, the positive effect of the CI on correct recall was found only in the open-ended question phase (that was based entirely on what each individual child mentioned in his or her free recall). The extra recall was for "person" and "object" information. However, when interviewed 11 days after the witnessed event, Wark et al. found no differences between the CI and SI children (whether or not they were also interviewed 2 days after the event). In the Milne et al. study and the Wark et al. study, the children's ratings of their interview experience did not favor the CI, thus ruling out a simple "motivational" explanation of the better recall using CI.

Use of the Felt Board and of
Children Hearing Their Accounts

Some young children assume that adults know everything (Fielding & Conroy, 1992; McGurk & Glachan, 1988; Menig-Peterson, 1975), and therefore they may not realize the need that interviewers have for full accounts from child witnesses. The felt board was devised by Poole (1992) as a procedure for helping such children realize what is required of them in investigative interviews. On the felt board is drawn the outline of a child's head and of an adult's head. Initially, a large number of felt triangles (of a different color from the board) are all located in the child's head. The interviewer explains to the child that these represent what the child knows of the incident (in question), and that initially, the adult's head is empty because the adult (i.e., the interviewer) does not know what happened. During the interview, as the child proceeds to give an account of the incident the interviewer moves triangles from the child's head to the adult's head. Poole found this procedure to result in children giving accounts of longer duration. Sattar and Bull (1994) have recently found in a pilot study that use of the felt board occasioned from young children longer accounts (in number of words) of a live, staged incident (compared to a control group), but these longer accounts did not contain significantly greater correct recall.

Poole (1992) also suggested that playing back to a child witness an audio-recording of the child's (first) recall attempt might aid an immediate, subsequent attempt at "Can you remember any more?" Sattar and Bull (1994) found this procedure to increase significantly the extra correct recall achieved compared to a control group who were asked to "remember more" (but who did not hear a recording). Therefore, playing back to a child a tape recording (either audio or video) of his or her account may well enable a child to remember validly more of an event.

Conclusion

This chapter has overviewed recent, significant developments in England and Wales regarding the criminal law and procedures relevant to child witnesses and victims. Psychological research worldwide has made a very meaningful contribution to these changes (e.g., that young children are no longer deemed to be incompetent as witnesses merely because of their age). The introduction of the live-video-link apparatus in many criminal courts, and the nationwide installation of several dozen child-appropriate videorecording interview suites by police and social services, demonstrates how seriously this issue is taken, especially because both types of video facilities are rather costly. The courts, the Home Office, and the Lord

Chancellor's Department (i.e., the relevant government departments) have responded, and are responding well to the results of psychological research. This relates not only to such research informing legislation and practice but also to government departments' using psychologists to evaluate the effectiveness of new procedures and to produce guidelines for the interviewing of child witnesses.

However, in England and Wales some problems remain:

- Not being able to videorecord cross-examination
- The need to develop procedures to allow children who have "communication disability" (Bull, 1995b) to give evidence of what has happened to them, especially because these children may be at greater risk of abuse
- The belief among many people (especially some lawyers) that the criminal justice system may be more important than the welfare of particular children
- The English/Welsh emphasis on protecting children from some of the aspects of criminal proceedings contrasting with the emphasis in the United States on preparing children to testify (Westcott & Davies, 1993), resulting in a British lack of research on the latter

Although some problems remain, we trust that this chapter has demonstrated that recently there have taken place in England and Wales a number of very significant developments concerning children's testimony. These include provisions in criminal trials for the routine use of closed-circuit television so that children need not give their live evidence from within the courtroom, the use of previously videorecorded interviews with children as their evidence-in-chief, and the government's publication of the *Memorandum* for the conducting of such interviews. Developments such as these have been informed by relevant research, and they have played a role in the administration of justice as exemplified by the disturbing 1994 criminal trial with which this chapter began.

References

Bilton, K. (1994). *Child protection practice and the "Memorandum of Good Practice on Video Recorded Interviews With Children": A discussion paper.* London: British Association of Social Workers.

Birch, D. (1992, April). Children's evidence. *Criminal Law Review,* pp. 262-276.

Braid, M., & Mackinnon, I. (1992, October 28). Orkney report calls for 194 reforms. *Independent,* p. 8.

Bull, R. (1992). Obtaining evidence expertly: The reliability of interviews with child witnesses. *Expert Evidence, 1,* 5-12.

Bull, R. (1994a). Good practice for video recorded interviews with child witnesses for use in criminal proceedings. In G. Davies, S. Lloyd-Bostock, M. McMurran, & C. Wilson (Eds.), *Law and psychology* (pp. 100-117). Berlin: de Gruyter.

Bull, R. (1994b, June 10). Child interviewers' expertise: Accreditation [Letter to the editor]. *Police Review,* p. 14.

Bull, R. (1995a). Innovative techniques for the questioning of child witnesses, especially those who are young and those with learning disability. In M. S. Zaragoza, J. R. Graham, G. C. N. Hall, R. Hirschman, & Y. S. Ben-Porath (Eds.), *Memory and testimony in the child witness* (pp. 179-194). Thousand Oaks, CA: Sage.

Bull, R. (1995b). Interviewing people with communication disabilities. In R. Bull & D. Carson (Eds.), *Handbook of psychology in legal contexts* (pp. 247-260). Chichester, England: Wiley.

Bull, R., & Spencer, J. (1992). England's changes in child witness laws, procedures and a code of good practice. *Violence Update, 3,* 3.

Butler, A. (1993, December). Spare the child. *Police Review,* pp. 14-15.

Clifford, B. R., Davies, G., Westcott, H., & Garratt, K. (1992). *Videotechnology and the child witness* (Final report to the Police Foundation). London: University of East London.

Clyde, J. (1992). *The report of the inquiry into the removal of children from Orkney in February 1991.* Edinburgh, Scotland: Her Majesty's Stationery Office.

Davies, G. M. (1994). Live links: Understanding the message of the medium. *Journal of Forensic Psychiatry, 5,* 225-227.

Davies, G. M., & Noon, E. (1991). *An evaluation of the live link for child witnesses.* London: Home Office.

Davies, G. M. & Noon, E. (in press). The impact of CCTV on children's court testimony. In D. Peters (Ed.), *The child in context: Cognitive, social and legal perspectives.* Dordrecht, the Netherlands: Nijhoff.

Davies, G. M., & Wilson, C. (1994). The videotaping of children's evidence: Issues of research and practice. *Practitioner's Child Law Bulletin,* pp. 68-70.

Fielding, N., & Conroy, S. (1992). Interviewing child victims: Police and social work investigations of child sexual abuse. *Sociology, 26,* 103-124.

Flin, R., Bull, R. H. C., Boon, J. C. W., & Knox, A. (1990). *Child witnesses in Scottish criminal proceedings* (Report to the Scottish Home and Health Department). Glasgow, Scotland: Glasgow College.

Flin, R., Bull, R., Boon, J., & Knox, A. (1993). Child witnesses in Scottish criminal trials. *International Review of Victimology, 2,* 309-329.

Flin, R., Davies, G., & Tarrant, A. (1988). *The child witness* (Final report to the Scottish Home and Health Department). Aberdeen, Scotland: Robert Gordon Institute.

Heydon, J. (1984). *Evidence, cases and materials.* London: Butterworths.

Home Office and Department of Health. (1992). *Memorandum of good practice on video recorded interviews with child witnesses for criminal proceedings.* London: HMSO.

Jones, D., & McQuiston, M. (1988). *Interviewing the sexually abused child.* London: Gaskell.

Köhnken, G., Milne, R., Memon, A., & Bull, R. (1994, March). *Recall in cognitive interviews and standard interviews: A meta-analysis.* Paper presented at the biennial meeting of the American Psychology-Law Society, Sante Fe, NM.

McGurk, H., & Glachan, M. (1988). Children's conversation with adults. *Children and Society, 2,* 20-34.

Memon, A., & Bull, R. (1991). The cognitive interview: Its origins empirical support, evaluation and practical implications. *Journal of Community and Applied Social Psychology, 1,* 291-307.

Memon, A., & Köhnken, G. (1992). Helping witnesses to remember more: The cognitive interview: *Expert Evidence, 1,* 39-48.

Menig-Peterson, C. (1975). The modification of communicative behaviour in pre-school children as a function of the listener's perspective. *Child Development, 46,* 1015-1018.

Milne, R., Bull, R., Köhnken, G., & Memon, A. (1994, April). *The cognitive interview and suggestibility.* Paper presented at the Fourth European Conference of Law and Psychology, Barcelona.

Noon, E., & Davies, G. M. (1993). Child witnesses and the "live link." *Expert Evidence, 2,* 11-12.

Plotnikoff, J., & Woolfson, R. (1994). *The pace of child abuse prosecutions* (Report to the Nuffield Foundation). Hitchin, Herts: Woolfson-Plotnikoff Consultants.

Poole, D. (1992, May). *Eliciting information from children with non-suggestive visual and auditory feedback.* Paper presented at the NATO Advanced Studies Institute on the Child Witness in Context, Italy.

R. v. Smellie, 14 Cr. App. R. 128 (1919).

Sattar, G., & Bull, R. (1994). *The effects of the felt board and auditory feedback on young children's recall of a live event.* Paper presented at the annual conference of the British Psychological Society's Division of Criminological and Legal Psychology, Rugby.

Saywitz, K. J., & Nathanson, R. (1993). Children's testimony and their perceptions of stress in and out of the courtroom. *Child Abuse & Neglect, 17,* 613-622.

Spencer, J., & Flin, R. (1993). *The evidence of children: The law and the psychology* (2nd ed.). Chichester, England: Wiley.

Tobey, A. E., Goodman, G. S., Batterman-Faunce, J. M., Orcutt, H. K., & Sachsenmaier, T. (1995). Balancing the rights of children and defendants: Effects of closed-circuit television on children's accuracy and jurors' perceptions. In M. S. Zaragoza, J. R. Graham, G. C. N. Hall, R. Hirschman, & Y. S. Ben-Porath (Eds.), *Memory and testimony in the child witness* (pp. 214-239). Thousand Oaks, CA: Sage.

Wark, L., Memon, A., Holley, A., Köhnken, G., & Bull, R. (1994, April). *Children's memory for a magic show: Use of the cognitive interview.* Paper presented at the Fourth European Conference on Law and Psychology, Barcelona.

Wattam, C. (1992). *Making a case in child protection.* London: Longman.

Westcott, H., & Davies, G. M. (1993). Children's welfare in the courtroom: Preparation and protection of the child witness. *Children and Society, 7,* 388-396.

Westcott, H., & Davies, G. M. (in press). Sexually abused children's and young people's perspectives on investigative interviews. *British Journal of Social Work.*

White, S. (1990). The investigatory interview with suspected victims of child sexual abuse. In A. La Greca (Ed.), *Through the eyes of a child* (pp. 368-394). Boston: Allyn and Bacon.

Yuille, J., Hunter, R., Joffe, R., & Zaparniuk, J. (1993). Interviewing children in sexual abuse cases. In G. Goodman & B. Bottoms (Eds.), *Child victims, child witnesses: Understanding and improving testimony.* New York: Guilford.

7

Children's Evidence
Scottish Research and Law

RHONA FLIN
BRIAN KEARNEY
KATHLEEN MURRAY

The English proverb that children should be seen and not heard has never applied in the Scottish courts, where young children traditionally have been admitted as witnesses. In this chapter, we present a brief outline of recent concern regarding children's ability to act as witnesses, a summary of the Scottish rules of evidence governing children's testimony in both criminal and civil cases, and the main findings from a program of psychological research into children's evidence in criminal cases funded by the Scottish Home and Health Department.

Until very recently, child witnesses in Scottish criminal courts were examined and cross-examined in open court, in the same way as an adult (providing they had been admitted as a competent witness). For some

This chapter is reprinted with permission from *Criminal Justice and Behavior,* Vol. 23 No. 2, June 1996 358-376. © 1996 American Association for Correctional Psychology.

children, this was a very difficult and stressful experience, especially where the allegations concerned sexual abuse. Scottish lawyers were not insensitive to the problems in these trials. More than 50 years ago, a barrister wrote, "Not only counsel, but all concerned are harassed almost beyond endurance. It is as if all in court were in conspiracy to rape the child again" (Crawford, 1938, p. 127). His expression of concern appears to have fallen on deaf ears; 30 years later the same problem was discussed again, this time by the Thomson Committee (Scottish Home and Health Department and Crown Office, 1975) who considered whether children who have been the victims of sexual offenses should be required to give evidence in court. They concluded that although

> the present procedure is not ideal and children are inevitably caused a certain amount of distress by having to give evidence in court, we are not aware of any alternative procedure that would satisfy the interests of justice and be fair to accused persons. (p. 165)

Again, no formal changes ensued. It was another 10 years before the plight of the child witness was taken more seriously, when the media began to publicize the concern that was being expressed by social workers and psychologists across the United Kingdom about the procedures used to hear and test children's testimony, particularly in sexual abuse cases.

In England and Wales, the position was even worse than in Scotland. Some of their abuse cases were almost impossible to prosecute because their criminal courts were not prepared to listen to child witnesses unless they were at least 7 or 8 years of age. Younger children generally were regarded as incompetent witnesses—a situation that prompted one English lawyer to describe their rules of evidence as a child molester's charter (Spencer & Flin, 1993).

By the late 1980s, many other countries had begun to assess carefully their procedures for hearing children's testimony, and psychologists in Australia, Canada, the United States, and mainland Europe were studying common problems and considering possible solutions (Loesel, Bender, & Bliesner, 1992; Spencer, Nicholson, Flin, & Bull, 1990; Zaragoza, Graham, Hall, Hirschman, & Ben-Porath, 1995). In 1985, the Royal Scottish Society for the Prevention of Cruelty to Children was so worried about the problems observed when children were giving evidence in court that it organized a conference in Edinburgh titled The Child: Victim of the

Legal Process? This was well attended by lawyers, social workers, police officers, and psychologists, and there was little doubt by the end of the day that many professionals were seriously concerned about the welfare of child witnesses at the hands of our legal system. It could not, however, be said that this was a unanimous opinion. A senior Scottish judge, Lord McCluskey, was reported as saying at the conference that he "could find no clear evidence that the child suffered unnecessary trauma and distress other than of a temporary nature and what one would normally expect of a witness before a court. His verdict on whether the child was a victim of the legal process was one of not proven" (Irvine & Dunning, 1985, p. 265).

Fortunately, the matter was not laid to rest. In 1986, psychologists at Aberdeen University were awarded funding by the Scottish Home and Health Department to study child witnesses in criminal trials (see the section, Research on Children's Evidence in Scotland). Two years later, the Scottish Law Commission (1988) issued a discussion paper on the evidence of children and other potentially vulnerable witnesses, and they also commissioned Murray (1988) to carry out a study of the alternatives to in-court testimony being used in the United States. In its subsequent report, the Scottish Law Commission (1990) recommended minor procedural changes, as well as more radical proposals for reform, which are reviewed below.

The Legal Background

There has never been an age limit below which a child's evidence may not be received by the courts in Scotland. The classic 19th-century work (Dickson, 1887) on the Law of Evidence in Scotland tells us that in 1837 a 3-year-old appeared before the judges of the High Court of Justiciary (Scotland's supreme criminal court) in Edinburgh to testify, it was hoped, in relation to a charge of theft of clothing. The little girl, when she appeared before the judges in their wigs and red robes may well have been terrified. In the event, "she could not be induced to speak" (Dickson, 1887, para. 1554, note b). Had she been able to utter and had the judges been satisfied by examining her that she understood the difference between truth and falsehood, and the obligation to tell the truth, then her evidence would have been admissible for what it was worth. It would have been capable, if the jury were satisfied as to its weight, of equaling in value the evidence of an adult.

In Scots law, then as now, a person accused of a crime in the criminal courts could not be convicted on the evidence of one witness alone. Corroboration was and, with some statutory exceptions, still is, required. The evidence of the 3-year-old girl, therefore, would accordingly have had to be corroborated before the accused could have been convicted, but so would the evidence of an adult. There has never been a rule in Scots law that evidence required corroboration simply because it derives from a child who has not formally taken the oath. (Until recently, this was a requirement in England and Wales.)

This fundamental position has changed little. A child, typically defined as under 14 years (Walker & Walker, 1964; Wilkinson, 1986), usually is regarded as being too young to testify unless the court is satisfied that he or she is a competent witness, in the sense of understanding the nature of truth and falsehood and the obligation to tell the truth (*Rees v. Lowe,* 1990). The judge may, however, hear evidence from sources other than the child that the child is or is not a competent witness (*M. v. Kennedy,* 1993). This can have important consequences for those cases when it is sought to admit hearsay evidence of a child (see the section, Hearsay Evidence).

Legal Procedures

The cases in which the evidence of children figures most largely are those in which the child is involved either as an alleged offender or as a child who, by reason of being offended against (i.e., sexually or otherwise abused) is thought to be in need of special measures of care. Since 1971, when the Social Work Act of 1968 came into force, such children generally are not dealt with in the ordinary courts but are referred to the Children's Hearings system (Bissett-Johnson, 1995; Kearney, 1987; Wilkinson & Norrie, 1993).

Admission to the Children's Hearings system is dependent on one or more statutory "grounds of referral" being admitted by the child and parents or, if not admitted, proved. The grounds of referral include being beyond control of parents, being in moral danger, being subject to such lack of parental care as is likely seriously to impair health or development, being subject to abuse (sexual or otherwise), truanting, and the commission by the child of an offense.

The tribunal of the Children's Hearings system consists of three trained laypersons, Children's Panel members, among whom both men and women must be represented. The child's case is brought to a hearing by an official known as the reporter to the Children's Panel or the Children's reporter. If the child and parent do not accept the grounds of referral or if the child does not understand them, the hearing may direct the Children's reporter to take the case before the sheriff. In Scotland, the sheriff is the local professional judge, who has a very extensive civil and criminal jurisdiction. The proceedings before the sheriff have been described as "civil proceedings sui generis" (*McGregor v. D.*, 1977)—that is, in a class of their own. The Children's reporter lays before the sheriff the testimony of witnesses, who may be cross-examined by the child's attorney. The child's attorney, if he or she thinks it advisable, can present testimony on behalf of the child. The decision of the sheriff is subject to appeal on point of law to the Court of Session, Scotland's supreme civil court.

The protection of children from abuse is largely accomplished by establishing the abuse within the Children's Hearings system and separating the abuser from the child, if necessary, by receiving the child into care, rather than by prosecuting the alleged offender. The hearings system has no sanction that it can directly impose on the abuser. Nevertheless, prosecution of abusing adults, especially where the abuse is serious, is still necessary from time to time, and the law has developed so as to facilitate the giving of evidence by children while ensuring that the alleged offender is accorded the due process insisted on by our criminal law. Prosecutions of adults on allegations of child neglect and/or cruelty still take place before the sheriff, sitting without a jury. The more serious cases of child physical abuse and child sexual abuse generally involve prosecution before a High Court judge and a jury or before a sheriff and a jury.

Receiving Evidence From Child Witnesses

In 1990, Lord Justice General Hope (Scotland's most senior judge), following a recommendation of the Scottish Law Commission, issued a memorandum (see Nicholson & Murray, 1992) suggesting, as good practice, possible measures that a judge might, at his or her discretion, take to reduce formality when children are giving evidence. These measures include removing wigs and gowns, positioning of the child at a table rather than in the witness box, allowing the presence of a relative or other supportive person, and clearing the court.

Screens. A child who is likely to be afraid of giving evidence because of the presence in court of the alleged abuser may, when the judge allows, be protected from confronting the alleged abuser by the latter's being concealed by a screen (Prisoners and Criminal Proceedings Act, 1993). When this is done, arrangements must be put in place to enable the accused to hear and see the witness. This may be accomplished by the use of a camera and television monitor.

Closed-circuit television. The most radical measure to protect children from confrontation with the alleged offender is the use of closed-circuit television, frequently referred to as the "live link" ("Protection of Child Witnesses," 1993). A court may authorize the use of the live link if there are indications (based on the child's age, the nature of the alleged offense, and the nature of the evidence and the relationship, if any, between the child and the accused) that the child will be better able to give evidence in this way rather than in the normal way (Law Reform Act, 1990).

In the case of *H. M. Advocate v. Birkett* (1992), it was alleged that the accused attempted to murder a 3-year-old by assaulting (e.g., throwing a knife) at him. The Crown applied to the High Court for permission to use the live link to receive the evidence of the alleged victim and four other child witnesses, aged from 4 to 8 years. Two of these children were said to be quiet and hesitant witnesses and better able to give evidence regarding the traumatic event outside of the accused's presence. The defense did not object to use of the live link for the 3-year-old complainer (who was said to be frightened of the accused) but did object to its use for the other children, arguing that there was no indication that these children were frightened, age alone did not justify the use of the live link, and that the charges did not concern sexual abuse. The petition was argued in front of a senior judge (Lord Ross), who accepted the defense arguments and granted the application only for the 3-year-old complainer. However, he reserved the possibility of use of the live link for the other children at trial, depending on the decision of the trial judge. This case illustrates that to secure use of the live link, it will not be sufficient to argue that testifying may be traumatic for children. The case is also of interest in that it demonstrates the court's flexibility in interpreting the legislation.

Identification of offenders. Scots law always has attached great importance to personal identification of an accused by a witness in court, with the consequent necessity for confrontation. When evidence involving the use of screens or by live link has been authorized and the child gives evidence that he or she recalls having identified the accused previously, then evidence by others as to the previous identification is admissible, thus avoiding the need for confrontation (Law Reform Act, 1990). The case of *Brotherston v. H. M. Advocate* (1995) established that the child could competently identify the accused by way of the live link. This case also established that where a child's evidence was given by way of the live link "the jury were entitled if they thought fit, to attach the same value to the evidence given by this means as to evidence given in court by the other witnesses."

Evidence by videorecording. Since 1994, it has been possible for the prosecution and the defense to ask the court to allow evidence by the child to be taken in private before a commissioner (Prisoners and Criminal Proceedings Act, 1993). The judge has the discretion as to whether to grant such an application, taking into account the child's age and maturity, the nature of the alleged offense, the nature of the evidence, and any relationship between the child and the accused person. When the evidence is thus taken by videorecording, the accused person and the Crown are represented and able to examine and cross-examine. Once completed, the videotape record of the evidence can be admitted in place of the child's live testimony.

Hearsay evidence. In cases of alleged sexual abuse heard before a sheriff in the context of the Children's Hearings system (but not before a hearing by the Children's Panel), hearsay is now admissible. The requirement that the child be competent still exists. In a case where the child did not communicate at all in court and where there was no question of evidence from any other source as to the child's competency, hearsay evidence was held to be inadmissible (*F. v. Kennedy,* 1992). However, in a remarkable case wherein the child uttered no sounds when giving evidence in court (because of a condition of being an elective mute), the sheriff conducted an examination of the witness by means of written notes, nods, and shakes of the head and satisfied himself that the child was a competent witness (*M. v. Kennedy,* 1993). In this case, it also was observed by the court that evidence concerning competence might be obtained from a source independent of the child, such as a psychologist who had examined the child.

Once the child's competence to give evidence has been established, the allowance of hearsay has remarkable consequences. For example, in a 1992 case, the court had before it both the child's oral evidence and admissible hearsay evidence of what she had said previously. In her earlier evidence, she had incriminated the alleged offender of sexual abuse. In her oral evidence she retracted this. The sheriff did not accept the retraction but preferred the earlier hearsay evidence; his decision was upheld on appeal (*K. v. Kennedy,* 1992).

For further details of the law of evidence in Scotland as it relates to children, see Spencer and Flin (1993), Flin and Spencer (1995), and Wilkinson (1986). The following sections review the program of research into child witnesses that has been undertaken in Scotland during the past 10 years.

Research on Children's Evidence in Scotland

In 1985, Flin and Davies successfully applied to the Scottish Home and Health Department's Criminological Research Branch for research funding to examine some of the more controversial issues relating to children's evidence. The project plan included experimental studies of child witness memory, a tracking survey of child witnesses in criminal trials in Aberdeen, and interviews with child witnesses and their parents (Flin, Davies, & Tarrant, 1988). In the experimental studies of children's ability to remember and recount witnessed events, they found that younger children (6-8 years) could be useful witnesses (Davies, Stevenson, & Flin, 1988), but that the style of questioning was very important, especially where it concerned photographic identifications (Davies, Tarrant, & Flin, 1989). These findings concurred with the results being produced by other researchers, particularly from North America. Since that time, the problems of pretrial interviews with child witnesses have been well documented in both Scotland (Bissett-Johnson, 1993; Hutcheson, Baxter, Telfer, & Warden, 1995) and the United States (Montoya, 1993). In Strathclyde (the largest region in Scotland), new guidelines for investigative interviewing of children have been developed (Strathclyde Social Work Department, 1993), and the *Memorandum of Good Practice on Video*

Recorded Interviews With Child Witnesses for Criminal Proceedings (Home Office, 1992) does provide sound advice based on psychological research.

The main part of the first study (Flin et al., 1988) involved the identification and tracking of child witnesses called to give evidence in the criminal courts. The researchers logged all the criminal prosecution cases in Aberdeen that involved child witnesses (226 in one year), and for a number of these cases interviewed children and their parents on the morning of the trial. Their results showed that many of the children were unhappy about the prospect of giving evidence in court and that two of the main sources of stress for child witnesses were (a) the long delays between witnessing an alleged incident and the trial and (b) the children's very limited knowledge of court procedures.

In an attempt to provide some stronger evidence to support the above claim that lack of knowledge appeared to be causing child witnesses stress, Flin, Stevenson, and Davies (1989) carried out a study to examine children's knowledge of criminal proceedings in Scotland. Ninety schoolchildren (age 6-10 years) and 15 adults were interviewed. The results showed very clearly that children were ignorant of trial procedures and the role that they would play if they were called to court as a witness. These research findings provided useful ammunition for child care professionals and lawyers who believed that child witnesses were entitled to be given the necessary information to enable them to understand the format and purpose of court proceedings. A number of improvements have now been made to prepare child witnesses for a court appearance, and all child witnesses in Scotland are sent a colorful booklet that explains who they will meet at court and what is expected of them when they are called to give evidence (Crown Office, 1989). A new research study has just been commissioned (September 1995) that will look in more depth at the preparation of child witnesses for a court appearance.

In a subsequent project, Flin, Bull, Boon, and Knox (1993) recorded observations of 89 child witnesses' behavior when testifying in open court in Glasgow. This study showed that although many children apparently could cope with the examination process, some children did demonstrate signs of anxiety or difficulty communicating with the lawyers. The researchers also tracked a sample of 1,800 cases in a 15-month period and found that child witnesses were waiting on average 6.5 months between the alleged incident and the trial. There was little relevant research on the effects of long delays on children's memory, so to investigate this problem, an experimental study was designed to test the effects of a 5-month delay on children's and adults' eyewitness memory. The results indicated that although younger children (6-8 years) could remember an incident 5 months later, their recall was less complete than that of older children and adults (Flin, Boon, Knox, & Bull, 1992). The problem of delays in the legal system is not peculiar to Scotland, as evidenced by a recent study in England (Plotnikoff & Woolfson, 1995).

The psychological research to date has helped to reveal the main difficulties for children giving evidence in Scottish courts. These have included the more obvious stressors, such as the pretrial interviews (Hutcheson et al., 1995) and confronting the accused (Montoya, 1995) or being cross-examined (McGough, 1994; Myers, 1992), and the research has also identified some of the less salient stress factors relating to lack of knowledge (Mellor & Dent, 1994) and the effect of long delays. The most recent research on children's testimony in Scotland was designed to assess the value of one of the new reforms—the use of televised evidence, which enables the child to testify at the trial but outside of the courtroom. In the next section, we describe an evaluation of this new system.

Evaluation of the Live Television Link

When the live television link was first introduced in Scotland in 1991, the findings of recent research on its use in other countries were available. An English evaluation (Davies & Noon, 1991) had found that live link successfully reduced stress on child witnesses and improved the quality of their evidence. An Australian evaluation (Cashmore & De Haas, 1992) reported that "children's observed emotional state was influenced more by whether they were able to use closed-circuit television when they wanted to than by whether they did or did not use it" (p. 135). Favorable impressions of the television procedure also were reported in the findings of small pilot studies in Perth, Australia (Western Australia Department of Community Services, 1990), and New Zealand (Whitney & Cook, 1990).

The Form of Live Television Link in Scotland

In Scotland, the child's testimony is relayed by live television link to the court from a room adjacent to the courtroom. The child is accompanied by a support person and sometimes also by a court officer. A small television monitor in front of the child displays an image of the person in the courtroom who is talking to the child. The child's image is transmitted to the courtroom from a small camera mounted on top of the monitor. In the courtroom itself, there are similar monitors on the judge's bench and on the bar table, each displaying an image of the child and also an image of the questioner in a small insert at the top right-hand side of the screen. Larger monitors displaying an image of the child are in front of the jury; these are viewed also by the accused and other persons in the courtroom. A picture of the whole of the room occupied by the child is relayed from a fish-eye camera to independent monitors on the judge's bench and on the bar table. This ensures that the judge and legal counsel can check that no one is prompting the child. The judge controls the picture and sound from a remote handset that allows him or her to switch from one questioner to another, to have discreet personal communication with the child, and to switch the equipment on and off.

The use of live television link in the Scottish criminal courts was monitored and evaluated over the 2-year introductory period (Murray, 1995a, 1995b). The purpose was to identify factors influencing the decision to authorize use of the procedure. The evaluation also investigated the effect of live television link on child witnesses and on the quality of their evidence. To provide a basis for comparison, the study included a sample of children who testified in the traditional way. The performance of the two groups of witnesses was compared on a number of child and legal system variables. Because the attitudes and expectations of all who figure in the case may have a bearing on how the live television system is used, the research also explored the views of the judges and lawyers, the adults accompanying the child witnesses in court, and the accused persons. The research design and the interview and court observation schedules were adapted from those used in the Australian and English evaluations (Cashmore & De Haas, 1992; Davies & Noon, 1991).

The Use Made of Live Television Link and Other Measures

In Scotland between October 1991 and December 1993, applications were made to allow 144 child witnesses cited in 70 indictments to give their evidence by live television link; all but one came from the prosecution. Applications were refused to 16 children. No application was made for the other 37 child witnesses who were cited in these cases. Forty-one cases ended in a late guilty plea and one was abandoned. In the 28 cases that went to trial, 51 children gave all or part of their evidence by live television link, and 10 testified in the traditional manner.

The other measures available for child witnesses (described earlier) were used more frequently. All children who testified were permitted to have an adult support person present in the courtroom or in the adjacent television room. In all trials involving sex-related charges, the child's testimony was heard in closed court. In the majority of cases, the trial judge and legal counsel removed their wigs.

Factors Influencing the Decision to Allow Use of Live Television Link

The judge may authorize a child witness to use the live television link only after determination of its necessity. During the first year after implementation, the successful applicants demonstrated to the judge that the statutory conditions were met, taking into account the age and maturity of the child, the relationship of the child to the accused, the nature of the charge, and the kind of evidence that the child might be called on to give. Their comments on the possible effect on the child of testifying in the traditional way were based on observation of the child's reaction to the alleged abuse and of behavioral or verbal indications that the child feared testifying either in open court or in the presence of the accused. These observations also influenced the applicant's judgment as to whether the child would be better able to give evidence if removed from the formal atmosphere of the courtroom.

With increasing awareness of the new system by the legal profession, during the second year of operation, the majority of applications were supported by expert opinion as to the ability of the child to withstand the trauma of testifying in the traditional way, the likelihood of emotional harm to the child, and the likely effect on the quality of the child's testimony. Decisions about its use were made at the discretion of the judge on a case-by-case basis, guided by statutory criteria. To evaluate the possible effect on the child of testifying in the conventional manner, the judge increasingly depended on expert opinion, a requirement that made extra demands on children and families and on professional resources.

Effect of Live Television Link on Child Witnesses

Pretrial interviews with 71 parents and posttrial interviews with 37 parents and 56 children supported the findings of earlier research that before a trial, one of the principal fears of children is confronting the accused in the courtroom (Flin et al., 1988). The worst experiences for both parents and children included the long delay between the report of the most recent alleged offense and the trial (mean = 15 months, SD = 12 months), repeated interviews by a variety of professionals (mean = 5, range = 1-30), the absence of choice about use of the television system (75% parents, 72% children), limited information about how to access the procedure, and the paucity of support services available to child victims and their families. The absence of support for nonaccused fathers was particularly marked.

The news that the child was being permitted to give evidence without the presence of the accused greatly reduced the anxiety and apprehension felt by child and parent. The few children who were refused use of the television link were confused about the reasons for this decision and distressed by the prospect of in-court testimony. Although it is recognized that going to court can rarely be a stress-free experience for anyone, at least for child witnesses some of it could be alleviated by proper coordination of services and more thought being given to the needs of young witnesses and their supporting adults.

The great majority (92%) of children who testified over the live television link were very glad that they had done so. Although 57% of children said they found talking to a television screen quite strange, 73% were sure that they would have found it difficult to speak in the presence of the accused. Being at a distance from the accused was more important to them than being outside the courtroom itself. Only four children disliked the equipment. At least half of the children did not fully understand that the accused was seeing and hearing them giving their evidence, and three were visibly startled when defense lawyers drew attention to the nearby presence of the alleged abuser.

Observations at trial revealed that children who testified by means of live television link were confident and only mildly anxious, their speech was audible and fluent, they concentrated well, and they cooperated fully with both prosecution and defense lawyers. They stood up to lengthy examinations (mean length = 62 minutes), but failed to understand some of the questions and appeared to be under greater stress during cross-examination than in direct examination. Except in those cases resulting in an acquittal, the children perceived the process as fair and just. Although there were relatively few significant differences between the behaviors of children who testified via live television link and children who testified in open court, the former cried significantly less during cross-examination than did the latter.

Effect of Live Television Link on Children's Evidence

The fact that some of the younger children's evidence reached the trial at all was a significant step forward (41% were aged 7 or under). Both prosecution and defense lawyers agreed that use of the live television link enabled some children to give evidence who would otherwise have been unable to speak. Nevertheless, the evidence of the younger children often lacked consistency and gave insufficient detail to satisfy the proof requirements of the criminal trial. There were few significant differences in the quality of the children's evidence when they testified via live link versus in open court; however, the amount of detail the children provided and the children's ability to resist leading questions was actually judged to be somewhat superior in open court. In any case, to gain access to the whole of the evidence that the child might be capable of giving, more attention needs to be paid to minimizing the delay in coming to trial, improving the examiners' skill and enhancing the child's knowledge and understanding of the legal process.

The adults who accompanied the children in the television room supported the merits of the live television link. However, they drew attention to a number of practical problems, mainly concerning the poor sound quality and the need for careful selection and preparation of the child's support person.

Effect on Other Participants in the Proceedings

Whether appearing for the prosecution or the defense, the 65 lawyers who were interviewed following the various trials acknowledged that the live television link could lessen the ordeal of testifying for the child witness. They were less certain whether this was always in the interest of justice. The lawyers' reservations about use of the television procedure focused on its interference with the principle of confrontation, on the obstacles that stood in the way of effective communication with the witness, and on the interference, as they saw it, with the ability of the fact-finder to assess the witness's reliability and credibility. Each party could discern in the use of live television link some advantages for the opposite side.

Many lawyers were aware of their lack of expertise in questioning children and believed that the use of technology increased these difficulties. They were highly conscious of their need for training and experience. They were interested in experimenting with alternative options, such as putting the accused outside while the child testified in court and the use of screens to shield the witness from the accused in the courtroom. They were more guarded about the likely value of a forthcoming provision allowing a child's prerecorded evidence to be introduced at trial in lieu of the child's courtroom testimony. There was little support from the lawyers for the use of videorecorded interviews as evidence, although some thought they could be helpful at the pretrial stage and also for viewing by the judge when considering sentence.

The 20 judges and sheriffs who were interviewed remained convinced that the evidence of children is always best when elicited in the courtroom. However, 53% were favorably impressed by the technology and supported the view that some children who testified successfully over the live television link might not otherwise have done so. A fifth of the judges considered that use of the new provision was potentially unfair to the accused. They did not believe that live television link provided the ideal solution to the problems presented by the prosecution of child sexual abuse. Some wished to see the development of more imaginative and constructive ways of dealing with these cases.

The findings of the research gave rise to a number of recommendations, such as installing the equipment in additional courts across Scotland, statutory provision for use of a live television link in civil proceedings, training for judges and lawyers in questioning children, and in the provision of up-to-date information on emerging psychological knowledge about child witnesses. The study also suggested a number of topics for future research. These include the effect of the live television link on jurors' ability to evaluate a child's evidence, the effect of repeated interviews on a child's evidence, and the relative value of alternatives to in-court testimony that are now available for child witnesses in Scotland.

Conclusion

The Scots are undeniably proud of their independent legal system, and the innovative Children's Hearings procedure has attracted worldwide interest. In recent years, there have been a significant number of changes to the procedures for hearing and testing children's evidence, as we have described. Lawyers and psychologists do not always share a common view of the human psyche, but in the case of children's evidence there has been a generally fruitful, if at times challenging, working relationship. The resulting reforms will continue to be scrutinized and debated, we hope, with an underlying spirit founded on a genuine concern for children's welfare within the Scottish legal system.

References

Bissett-Johnson, A. (1993). Family violence—Investigating child abuse and learning from British mistakes. *Dalhousie Law Journal, 16,* 5-61.

Bissett-Johnson, A. (1995). Scottish Office White Paper—"Scotland's children—Proposals for child care policy and law"—A critical analysis. *Journal of Social Welfare and Family Law, 17*(1), 17-42.

Brotherston v. H. M. Advocate, SCCR 613 (1995).

Cashmore, J. , & De Haas, N. (1992). *The use of closed-circuit television for child witnesses in the ACT* (Report for the Australian Law Reform Commission and the Australian Capital Territory Magistrates Court. Sydney, Australia: Australian Law Commission.

Crawford, A. (1938). *Guilty as libelled.* London: Barker.

Crown Office. (1989). *Going to court* (Leaflet for child witnesses). Edinburgh, Scotland: Author.

Davies, G. M., & Noon, E. (1991). *An evaluation of the live link for child witnesses* (Grant report). London: Home Office.

Davies, G., Stevenson, Y., & Flin, R. (1988). Children's memory for an unexpected event. In M. Gruneberg, P. Morris, & R. Sykes (Eds.), *Practical aspects of memory* (pp. 122-127). Chichester, England: Wiley.

Davies, G., Tarrant, A., & Flin, R. (1989). Close encounters of the witness kind: Children's memory for a simulated health inspection. *British Journal of Psychology, 80,* 415-429.

Dickson, W. G. (1887). *A treatise on the law of evidence in Scotland* (3rd ed., P. J. Hamilton Grierson, Ed.). Edinburgh, Scotland: T. & T. Clark.

F. v. Kennedy, SCLR 139 (1992).

Flin, R., Boon, J., Knox, A., & Bull, R. (1992). The effects of a five-month delay on children's and adults' eyewitness memory. *British Journal of Psychology, 83,* 323-336.

Flin, R., Bull, R., Boon, J., & Knox, A. (1992). Children in the witness box. In H. Dent & R. Flin (Eds.), *Children as witnesses* (pp. 167-180). Chichester, England: Wiley.

Flin, R., Bull, R., Boon, J., & Knox, A. (1993). Child witnesses in Scottish criminal trials. *International Review of Victimology, 2,* 309-329.

Flin, R., Davies, G., & Tarrant, A. (1988). *The child witness* (Final report to the Scottish Home and Health Department, Edinburgh, Grant No. 85/9290). Edinburgh, Scotland: Scottish Home and Health Department.

Flin, R., & Spencer, J. (1995). Annotation: Children as witnesses—Legal and psychological perspectives. *Journal of Child Psychology and Psychiatry, 36,* 171-189.

Flin, R., Stevenson, Y., & Davies, G. (1989). Children's knowledge of court proceedings. *British Journal of Psychology, 80,* 285-297.

H. M. Advocate v. Birkett, SCCR 850 (1992).

Home Office. (1992). *Memorandum of good practice on video recorded interviews with child witnesses for criminal proceedings.* London: Home Office with Department of Health.

Hutcheson, G., Baxter, J., Telfer, K., & Warden, D. (1995). Child witness statement quality: Question type and errors of omission. *Law and Human Behavior, 19,* 631-648.

Irvine, R., & Dunning, N. (1985). The child and the criminal justice system. *Journal of the Law Society of Scotland, 30,* 264-266.

K. v. Kennedy (1992), SCLR 386 (1993), SLT 1281.

Kearney, B. (1987). *Children's hearings and the sheriff court.* Edinburgh, Scotland: Butterworths.

Law Reform Act (Miscellaneous provisions). (1990). Sections 56-59. (Scotland)

Loesel, F., Bender, D., & Bliesner, T. (Eds.). (1992). *Psychology and law: International perspectives.* Berlin: Walter de Gruyter.

M. v. Kennedy, SCLR 69 (1993).

McGough, L. (1994). *Fragile voices: The child witness in American courts.* New Haven, CT: Yale University Press.

McGregor v. D., SC 330 (1977).

Mellor, A., & Dent, H. (1994). Preparation of the child witness for court. *Child Abuse Review, 3,* 165-175.

Montoya, J. (1993). Something not so funny happened on the way to conviction: The pre-trial interrogation of child witnesses. *Arizona Law Review, 35,* 927-987.

Montoya, J. (1995). Lessons from Akiki and Michaels on shielding child witnesses. *Psychology, Public Policy and Law, 1,* 340-369.

Murray, K. (1988). *Research paper on evidence from children: Alternatives to in-court testimony in criminal proceedings in the United States of America.* Edinburgh, Scotland: Scottish Law Commission.

Murray, K. (1995a). *Live television link: An evaluation of its use by child witnesses in Scottish criminal trials.* Edinburgh, Scotland: Her Majesty's Stationery Office.

Murray, K. (1995b). Closed-circuit television in Scottish courts. *Journal of the Law Society of Scotland, 40,* 314-316.

Myers, J. E. B. (1992). *Legal issues in child abuse and neglect.* London: Sage.

Nicholson, G., & Murray, K. (1992). The child witness in Scotland. In H. Dent & R. Flin (Eds.), *Children as witnesses* (pp. 131-150). Chichester, England: Wiley.

Plotnikoff, J., & Woolfson, R. (1995). *Prosecuting child abuse: An evaluation of the government's speedy progress policy.* London: Blackstone.

Prisoners and Criminal Proceedings Act. (1993). Section 33-34. (Scotland)

Protection of child witnesses. (1993). *Scots Law Times,* p. 369.

Rees v. Lowe (1990), JC 96, SCCR 664 (1989).

Scottish Home and Health Department and Crown Office. (1975). *Criminal procedure in Scotland* (2nd report, Thomson Committee, Cmnd 6218). Edinburgh, Scotland: Crown Office.

Scottish Law Commission. (1988). *The evidence of children and other potentially vulnerable witnesses* (Discussion Paper No. 75) Edinburgh, Scotland: Author.

Scottish Law Commission. (1990). *Report on the evidence of children and other potentially vulnerable witnesses* (SLC No. 125) Edinburgh, Scotland: Author.

Spencer, J., & Flin, R. (1993). *The evidence of children: The law and the psychology* (2nd ed.). Chichester, England: Wiley.

Spencer, J., Nicholson, G., Flin, R., & Bull, R. (Eds.). (1990). *Children's evidence in legal proceedings. An international perspective.* Cambridge, England: Cambridge University Law Faculty.

Strathclyde Social Work Department. (1993). *Guidelines on the investigative interviewing of children.* Glasgow: Strathclyde Regional Council. (Social Work Department, 35 Church Street, Glasgow G11 5JT, Scotland)

Walker, A., & Walker, N. (1964). *The law of evidence in Scotland.* Edinburgh, Scotland: Hodge.

Western Australia Department of Community Services. (1990). *Closed-circuit television in the Perth children's court.* Perth, Australia: Department of Community Services.

Whitney, L., & Cook, A. (1990). *The use of closed-circuit television in New Zealand courts: The first six trials.* Wellington, New Zealand: Department of Justice.

Wilkinson, A. (1986). *The Scottish law of evidence.* Edinburgh: Butterworths/Law Society of Scotland.

Wilkinson, A., & Norrie, K. (1993). *The law relating to parent and child in Scotland.* Edinburgh, Scotland: Green, Sweet, and Maxwell.

Zaragoza, M. S., Graham, J. R., Hall, G. C. N., Hirschman, R., & Ben-Porath, Y. S. (Eds.). (1995). *Memory and testimony in the child witness.* Thousand Oaks, CA: Sage.

The Child Witness and
Legal Reforms in Australia

SANDRA SHRIMPTON
KIM OATES
SUSAN HAYES

This chapter begins with a discussion of some of the factors leading to an understanding of child abuse in the Australian community and the effect this has had on the judicial system. It then goes on to describe some of the Australian research that has been influential in obtaining legislative reforms. Finally, four areas of recent legal reform are discussed: competency reforms, preparation-for-court programs, closed-circuit television, and pretrial diversion.

AUTHORS' NOTE: This project was supported by grants from the Law Foundation of New South Wales and the National Health and Medical Research Council of Australia. We acknowledge the assistance of Judy Cashmore of the Social Policy Research Centre, University of New South Wales.

Background

The problem of abuse and neglect of Australian children has been recognized by legislators for over 100 years. For example, in 1865 the Queensland Parliament passed the Offences Against the Person Act. This act contained severe penalties for the crimes of child stealing, indecent assault on girls under 12 years of age, and aggravated assault on children under 14 years. Although this act recognized the need to punish those who committed offenses against children, there was little interest at the time in assessing the reliability of a child's allegations or in ensuring that the legal process acted in the child's best interests. The emphasis was on punishment rather than protection. One could assume that only the most clear-cut cases came to the attention of the court (Thearle & Gregory, 1986).

In 1965, the first report of child physical abuse appeared in an Australian medical journal (Wurfell & Maxwell, 1965). The authors described 26 cases of physical abuse, 8 of which were fatal. The next year, another eight cases of serious physical abuse were reported (Birrell & Birrell, 1966). Both of these articles recommended that model legislation should be developed that would require all child abuse cases to be reported to a central authority and that would also protect those who made reports. However, there was little response to these suggestions until the mid-1970s. This period was the time when the women's movement, child welfare groups, and some pediatricians joined forces to lobby governments and government agencies about the need for improved legislation to protect children, resulting in the introduction of mandatory notification in the state of New South Wales in 1977. Other states followed suit, although two of the Australian states have not adopted mandatory notification.

Mandatory notification had the effect of increasing the community's awareness of the seriousness and extent of child abuse because many more cases were reported. The most recent figures for Australia, with a total population of almost 17 million, show 49,721 cases reported over 12 months (Angus & Wilkinson, 1993), with 20,868 (42%) of these reports being substantiated. This gives a rate of 4.2 substantiated reports for 1,000 children. These cases were almost equally distributed among physical abuse (26%), emotional abuse (25%), neglect (25%), and sexual abuse (24%).

The increased awareness of child abuse led to increased involvement of the courts. In Australia, physical abuse has usually been dealt with in a children's or juvenile court. Here, the standard of proof is "on the balance of probability" so that it is unusual for the child to be asked to testify. It was only as sexual abuse became more widely recognized, and was dealt with in the criminal courts where the standard of proof is "beyond reasonable doubt," that concern started to be expressed about the difficulties children face in the criminal justice system (Naylor, 1985).

This concern was acknowledged by the Australian government in 1977, at the time when cases of sexual abuse first started to be recognized. The government's Royal Commission on Human Relationships recommended that in child sexual assault cases a tribunal should be established to decide whether a criminal prosecution was desirable. If there was to be a criminal prosecution, the Royal Commission recommended that trial procedures should be altered so as to minimize the risk of causing distress to children who testify. Although these recommendations were not implemented, they were the beginning of awareness of the problems for the child witness in criminal proceedings and laid the groundwork for some of the subsequent reforms. The views of the Royal Commission were consistent with the subsequent published evidence showing that although having a case heard in a juvenile court may be an innocuous, or even a positive experience (Runyan, Everson, Edelsohn, Hunter, & Coulter, 1988), the involvement of children in a criminal court may have adverse effects for the child (Dezwirek Sas, 1992; Landwirth, 1987).

Research

There is now an extensive international literature on children as witnesses, including some of the problems encountered by the child witness. Some of the Australian research in this area has been influential in obtaining legislative reforms. This includes work on delays in bringing cases involving children to court, the language used in the court, and children's perceptions of the court process.

Delays

In a study of 59 sexually abused children where 18 of the cases were committed for trial, the average time between the initial police interview and the trial was 15 months (Oates, Lynch, Stern, O'Toole, & Cooney, 1995). In a larger series of 550 cases of child sexual assault coming before the court in New South Wales in 1991-1992, Cashmore (1994) found that the average time for a charge being laid to a committal hearing was 6 months, with an average of just under 12 months from the committal to the trial. These delays are not only stressful for the children, they also fail to take into account the need that young children have for an immediate response and their different concept of time (Dezwirek Sas, 1992). Delays may be caused by lack of coordination between the police and the prosecutor, insufficient time being set aside for the hearing so that it is adjourned and heard at a later date, and by the defense using delays as a tactic to unsettle the child witness and to gain a more favorable judge. These problems led the New South Wales Child Protection Council (1994) to suggest that firm hearing dates should be set for child sexual assault matters and to ensure that adjournments are not given without good reason.

The need to reduce delays for children who have to give evidence in court is supported by our own work on memory in children (Oates & Shrimpton, 1991). We showed that children (aged 4 to 12 years) who had a blood sample taken retained an accurate memory of the event, particularly if minor cues were used, but that memory was less accurate after a longer time interval had elapsed. We also showed that the older children performed better in free recall, although what the younger children did recall was highly accurate. When errors did occur, these were more likely to be errors of omission, rather than of commission, a finding that was similar in all age groups.

The Language of the Courtroom

When the children's cases eventually do go to court, the children have to face an unfamiliar situation and may be questioned in a way that they find difficult to understand. The complex language encountered by children in Australian courts was demonstrated by Brennan and Brennan (1988). They analyzed the transcripts of 26 cases where children were witnesses. This study showed that the children had been asked questions that were multifaceted and involved double negatives and juxtapositions. Children had the greatest difficulty with multifaceted questions, which the authors described as consisting of "convoluted preambles, confused centres and rhetorical endings which invite no response." For example:

Well I know, I understand what you say. You have been talking to her today but you see, what I am asking you is this. That statement suggests that you said those things that you now say are wrong to the police. Now did you say it to the police or did you not? (Brennan & Brennan, 1988, p. 26)

Brennan and Brennan list 13 features of courtroom language that they say are outside the normal competencies of many adult users of the English language. This makes it even more difficult for young children whose concepts of language are still developing. Because Australia is multicultural, with a large, recent immigrant population, for many children English is their second language, rather than the language they use in their homes. For this substantial group of young children, the language used in the courtroom may be even more confusing. Although the complex language used in court may simply reflect the inability of some lawyers to communicate with children, others admit that they use cross-examination to exploit particular vulnerabilities of the opposing child witness, such as fear, suggestibility, and lack of good language skills (Leippe, Brigham, Cousins, & Romanczyk, 1989).

Children's and Parents' Perceptions of the Court Process

Even if there was not the problem of the language used in court, many children do not understand their role as a witness in court. They may be concerned that their inability to express themselves adequately may embarrass them or harm their case (Cashmore, 1991). Young children may know that court has something to do with punishment and may believe that they may be sent to jail as punishment if they make a mistake in court (Cashmore, 1991). It is not surprising that sometimes the young child witness may decide that it is better to remain silent.

Cashmore and Bussey (1989a) interviewed 96 Australian children aged 6-14 years and concluded that children under 10 years often do not have the minimal knowledge that would be needed for them to be effective witnesses. This included not being aware of the role of the lawyer in asking questions and not understanding the decision-making role of the jury. Some children felt that they were required to prove their own innocence in the court, some felt the trial was to decide whether they were guilty or whether the accused was guilty, and others were nervous about speaking in front of people or of being "tripped up" by the defense lawyer. Their two major concerns about the consequences of appearing in court were facing the defendant in the court and fear of later retaliation by the offender.

Taking into account these factors, it is understandable that children and parents may have negative perceptions of their court involvement. Cashmore and Bussey (personal communication, 1994) investigated the perceptions of children aged 7-14 years who were involved in care and protection hearings. Before the hearing, the children had clear expectations that the lawyer would act as their advocate. When interviewed after the hearing, they were less likely to see the lawyer as their ally, although they were generally satisfied with the way the lawyer represented them in court. This is a useful study because it gives the children's own views rather than the parents' opinions of their children's feelings. This is in contrast to a study where 21 nonoffending parents whose children's cases of sexual assault had been to court were asked to rate on a scale from 0–5, ranging from *not upset at all* to *extremely upset,* how their child felt after the court hearing (Oates & Tong, 1987). Eighteen of the 21 parents gave a rating of between 4 and 5, indicating that their child was very upset immediately after the hearing. When these parents were asked to rate how their child was an average of $2\frac{1}{2}$ years later, more than half of the parents still rated their child as being extremely upset about the court hearing. When the parents rated their own degree of satisfaction about the outcome of the court hearing, 16 (76%) rated themselves as being completely dissatisfied.

To see whether children's and parental perceptions of the court process actually influence behavior and emotions, 59 children who had been sexually abused were reviewed (Oates et al., 1995). In 32 of these cases, there was either a committal or trial. Although 55% of parents claimed that the legal system was stressful for their children, a comparison of children who testified with children who did not failed to show any significant differences on indexes of depression, self-esteem, or behavior. One possible reason for this lack of effect on the children who testified was that the majority had been involved in a preparation-for-court program.

Legislative Reforms

Australian research such as described here, along with media interest and public controversy over some child sexual abuse cases where the alleged victims were prevented from giving evidence (Parkinson, 1991), has been influential in bringing about reforms in four areas: competency reforms, preparation-for-court programs, the use of closed-circuit television, and a pretrial diversion program.

Reform of Competency Requirements

In 1989, a New South Wales magistrate decided not to allow the alleged victims of sexual abuse in a kindergarten to give evidence in what became known as the "Mr. Bubbles" case. The wording of the 1900 Oaths Act, which was the basis on which the children's evidence was excluded in the Mr. Bubbles case, shows some of the problems of the competency requirement (Parkinson, 1991). The act allowed for a child to make a declaration instead of an oath if he or she was of "sufficient intelligence to justify the reception of the evidence" and understood "the duty to tell the truth before the court." Parkinson (1991) pointed out the problems with the wording. The word *intelligence* is inappropriate because a 3-year-old might be highly intelligent, yet not have enough linguistic development to justify the reception of his or her evidence. The words *before the court* also posed a problem. Children under age 6 may be quite capable of understanding the duty to tell the truth and may be willing to do so, but may not have sufficient understanding of the significance of court proceedings (Cashmore & Bussey, 1989) to pass this strict competency test.

The public and judicial controversy over this case was influential in the New South Wales government, changing the relevant legislation to make the competency test for children less restrictive. The Oaths Amendment Act (1990) is a significant improvement. It applies to a child giving evidence in court or before any person authorized to administer an oath and covers civil as well as criminal proceedings. In court proceedings, if the child is deemed not competent to take an oath the child may make a declaration that has the same validity as an oath. The act provides for two simple conditions to be satisfied before the child may give evidence. The court must first inform the child that it is important to tell the truth. Then the child must make a declaration: "I will not tell any lies in this court." Alternatively, a statement to this effect may be obtained by question and answer.

It is possible for the child's competency to be challenged. Section 33 (3) makes provision for the child's evidence not to be allowed if the court is satisfied that the child does not understand the difference between a truth and a lie, or if the child is not able to respond rationally to questions. However, the child is presumed to be competent in terms of this test, unless the court is satisfied otherwise. This new legislation makes it much easier for children to give evidence. As Parkinson (1991) notes, the legislation has quite properly shifted the focus from the admissibility of children's evidence to the weight that should be attached to it.

Preparation-for-Court Programs

These programs are at present voluntary and have no legislative support. However, they are becoming widely used. They vary in nature and include a mixture of counseling for children and visits to courtrooms. This allows children to become familiar with the setting, the people involved, and some of the legal terms prior to a trial, helping to allay some of the fears that children may have about the court process (Cashmore & Bussey, 1989b). The programs are not available to all children. Their availability depends to a large extent on whether the counselor involved initiates this type of help. The New South Wales Department of Health's Sexual Assault Education Unit has prepared standardized material for use by sexual assault counselors in an effort to obtain some uniformity and to make this type of counseling more widely available (Swinfield, 1993).

This material is aimed at helping counselors run groups for children, their parents, and adolescents. Usually, a children's group is run concurrently with a parent group, with a separate leader conducting each group. Groups run for 1½ hours per week over 4 weeks, with participants from all groups meeting for supper after each session. The group discussions cover explanation of the function of the court, the roles of various people in the court, and the meaning of the oath (for children over 12 years) or promise (for children under 12 years) they make in court. They are given some examples of the types of questions they are likely to be asked and given help with relaxation techniques.

However, not all children receive quality programs. Sometimes they are not referred for counseling at all. At other times, counseling may not be available to family members other than the victim, and at times agencies are reluctant to take responsibility for providing this type of support (New South Wales Child Protection Council, 1994; Wilson & Collingridge, 1992). In a review of 59 cases of child sexual assault in which police laid charges against an alleged offender, it was found that 26 (44%) of these proceeded to a court hearing with just over two thirds (68%) of the children receiving some sort of preparation-for-court program (Lynch, 1993). It is likely that legislation will be necessary to ensure that all children having to testify in court will receive high-quality preparation-for-court programs.

Closed-Circuit Television

The aim of closed-circuit television is to reduce the stress on child witnesses by removing them from direct physical confrontation with the defendant. This is usually achieved by having the child in a room other than the courtroom but still able to give evidence and be questioned via closed-circuit television. In this way, it is hoped that the quality of the child's evidence will be improved without the stresses likely to be caused if the child was in the courtroom (Cashmore, 1990; Cashmore & Cahill, 1991). Legislation allowing the use of closed-circuit television for child witnesses has been enacted in most Australian states. For example, the Evidence (Closed Circuit Television) Act (1991) provides that a court may order the use of closed-circuit television if satisfied that the child is likely to suffer mental or emotional harm if required to give evidence in the ordinary way or that the facts would be better ascertained if the child's evidence is given using closed-circuit television. The legislation provides that the court is not to make an order if it considers that to do so would be unfair to any party in the proceedings. In considering whether to make an order for the use of closed-circuit television, the court may consider the age, intelligence, maturity, and any disability in the child as well as the importance of the matters on which the child is called to give evidence. It can be seen that closed-circuit television is not an automatic right, with the court needing to be satisfied in each case that its use would be an advantage over the ordinary method of testifying.

An evaluation of the use of closed-circuit television (Cashmore, 1992) compared children who did not use this with those who did. The study found that although researchers observing the testimony of the children found few observed differences between the users and nonusers in terms of stress and quality of evidence, closed-circuit television did affect the behavior of the professionals who dealt with the child in court. Lawyers were more supportive and magistrates were more likely to intervene when closed-circuit television was used. This was particularly evident when questions were clarified during cross-examination and when stressed or tired children were more likely to be offered a brief respite. The study showed that all of the children who used closed-circuit television said that it was easier to testify this way compared with seeing the defendant or being in the courtroom. The professional groups involved in the use of closed-circuit television, as well as the parents of testifying children, felt, in contrast to the observers, that the closed-circuit television reduced stress on children as they gave evidence. The general view was that the system was thought to be fair to the defendant as well as to the child.

However, the study found some problems with the system. On some occasions, closed-circuit television was not offered to the child because of decisions made by professionals involved in the case. The decisions by the court to use closed-circuit television were found to be inconsistent. There was considerable variation in the views of the magistrates as to whether a case was suitable for closed-circuit television. The study recommended that in contrast to the current situation, there should be a presumption that when children give evidence in court they be allowed to use closed-circuit television unless they do not wish to use it (Law Reform Commission, 1992). Despite this recommendation, closed-circuit television is not yet widely used. A recent study by the New South Wales Child Protection Council (1994) found that closed-circuit television, or even the use of a screen in court so that the child does not see the accused, occurred in only 13% of child sexual abuse trials. It will probably be necessary for reforms, such as suggested above by the Law Reform Commission, to be enshrined in legislation before closed-circuit television is widely used.

Pretrial Diversion

Pretrial diversion was introduced on a pilot basis in Australia in 1989. It allows for certain categories of child sexual assault offenders to be diverted from the criminal justice system into a 2-year treatment program. To be eligible for the program, the offender must be the child's parent, stepparent, or parent's common-law spouse and have had no previous conviction for sexual assault. In addition, the child sexual assault offense for which the person is being considered must not have been accompanied by any acts of violence. It must also be felt that the offender's participation in the treatment program is in the best interests of the child. The offenders must accept responsibility for their behavior and have some understanding of the effect of their behavior on the child and other family members.

The diversion occurs after charges have been filed, but before the matter proceeds to judgment. If the offender is assessed as being suitable for the program and enters an undertaking to participate, a conviction is not recorded. This provision has led to some criticism by those who feel that it is important that sexual offenders should receive criminal convictions, even if the end result is a treatment program, rather than imprisonment. During the 2-year treatment period, the offender is bound by the conditions of the program. If these conditions are breached, the offender is returned to the criminal justice system for sentencing. If the program is completed successfully, no further action against the offender takes place.

To participate, the offender signs an agreement to move out of the home where the children live, not to live where they or any other children who are under age 16 live, and to become involved in treatment. Treatment involves other members of the family as well as the offender and includes individual counseling, family therapy, and group treatment. The program has the capacity to treat 25 offenders and their families at any one time. Although no long-term evaluation of the results of the program have been undertaken, a recent review of the program (Vinson, 1992) has shown that it is cost-effective when compared with incarceration. There are some problems with this scheme. The relatively small amount of funding available to provide therapy for offenders is disproportionate to the size of the problem so that only a small proportion of suitable offenders are able to enter the scheme. Because it is a city-based program, critics point out that it is biased in favor of those living in the cities, because those dwelling in the more remote parts of Australia are unable to participate.

Conclusion

Australia has had a long awareness of the fact of child abuse. However, it is only in recent years that large numbers of children are being asked to testify in court. This change has come about for two main reasons. First, mandatory-notification legislation has brought many more cases into the open. Second, awareness and detection of sexual abuse cases has involved the criminal court, where children may be asked to testify. This is in contrast to cases of physical abuse and neglect, which have been dealt with by the juvenile courts, where children rarely testify. In parallel with this change, there has been an increased awareness among some legal professionals, medical and welfare groups, and a slowly increasing community groundswell that children do have rights, including the right to be heard in court. Considerable progress has been made, as described in this chapter, and the process of reform is continuing.

References

Angus, G., & Wilkinson, K. (1993). *Child abuse and neglect in Australia 1990-91* (Australian Institute of Health and Welfare: Child Welfare Series No. 2). Canberra, Australia: Australian Government Printing Service.

Birrell, R. G., & Birrell, J. H. W. (1966). The "maltreatment syndrome" in children. *Medical Journal of Australia, 2,* 1134-1138.

Brennan, M., & Brennan, R. (1988). *Strange language: Child victims and cross-examination.* Wagga Wagga, Australia: Riverina Murray Institute of Higher Education.

Cashmore, J. (1990). The use of video technology for child witnesses. *Monash University Law Review, 16,* 228-250.

Cashmore, J. (1991). Problems and solutions in lawyer-child communication. *Criminal Law Journal, 15,* 193-202.

Cashmore, J. (1992). *The use of closed-circuit television for child witnesses in the ACT.* Sydney, Australia: Australian Law Reform Commission.

Cashmore, J. (1994). *The perceptions of child witnesses and their parents concerning the court process* [Monograph]. Sydney, Australia: Office of the Director of Public Prosecutions.

Cashmore, J., & Bussey, K. (1989a). Child witnesses in court. *Judicial Officers' Bulletin, 14,* 3-5.

Cashmore, J., & Bussey, K. (1989b). Disclosure of child sexual abuse: Issues from a child-oriented perspective. *Australian Journal of Social Issues, 22,* 13-26.

Cashmore, J., & Cahill, R. (1991). Closed-circuit television and child witnesses: Achieving its objective? *Law Society Journal, 29,* 57-60.

Dezwirek-Sas, L. (1992). Empowering child witnesses for sexual abuse prosecution. In H. Dent & R. Flin (Eds.), *Children as witnesses* (pp. 181-199). London: Wiley.

Evidence (Closed Circuit Television) Act. (1991). (Australian Capital Territory).

Landwirth, J. (1987). Children as witnesses in child sexual abuse trials. *Pediatrics, 80,* 585-589.

Law Reform Commission. (1992). *Children's evidence: Closed-circuit T.V.* (Australian Law Reform Commission Report No. 63). Fyshwick, Australian Capital Territory, Australia: National Capital Printing.

Leippe, M. R., Brigham, J. C., Cousins, C., & Romanczyk, A. (1989). The opinions and practices of criminal attorneys regarding child eyewitnesses: A survey. In S. J. Ceci, D. F. Ross, & M. P. Toglia (Eds.), *Perspectives of children's testimony* (pp. 100-131). New York: Springer-Verlag.

Lynch, D. (1993). *Outcomes of child sexual abuse.* Doctoral thesis, University of Sydney, Australia.

Naylor, B. (1985). Sexual assault: The law and the child victim. *Legal Service Bulletin, 10,* 72-75.

New South Wales Child Protection Council. (1994). *System abuse: Problems and solutions.* Sydney, Australia: Author.

Oates, K., & Shrimpton, S. (1991). Children's memories for stressful and non-stressful events. *Medicine, Science and the Law, 31,* 4-10.

Oates, R. K., Lynch, D. L., Stern, A., O'Toole, B. I., & Cooney, G. (1995). The criminal justice system and the sexually abused child—Help or hindrance? *Medical Journal of Australia, 162,* 126-130.

Oates, R. K., & Tong, L. (1987). Sexual abuse of children: An area with room for professional reforms. *Medical Journal of Australia, 147,* 544-548.

Oaths Act 1900 (New South Wales).

Oaths (Children) Amendment Act 1990 (New South Wales).

Offences Against the Person Act 1865 (Queensland).

Parkinson, P. (1991). The future of competency testing for child witnesses. *Criminal Law Journal, 15,* 186-192.

Runyan, D. K., Everson, M. D., Edelsohn, G. A., Hunter, W. M., & Coulter, M. L. (1988). Impact of legal intervention on sexually abused children. *Journal of Pediatrics, 113,* 647-653.

Swinfield, P. (1993). *Nothing but the truth.* New South Wales, Australia: Women's Health and Sexual Assault Unit, New South Wales Department of Health.

Thearle, M. J., & Gregory, H. (1986). Oppression of the innocents. *Child Abuse in Historical Perceptive Abstracts, 1,* 68. (6th International Congress on Child Abuse and Neglect, Sydney, Australia)

Vinson, A. (1992). *An evaluation of the NSW pre-trial diversion of offenders program.* Kensington, Sydney, Australia: Faculty of Professional Studies, University of New South Wales.

Wilson, R. L., & Collingridge, M. (1992). Speaking the same language: An evaluation of child sexual assault protocols in the Wagga Wagga region. Wagga Wagga, Australia: Charles Sturt University, Centre for Rural Social Research.

Wurfel, L. J., & Maxwell, G. M. (1965). The "battered-child" syndrome in South Australia. *Australian Paediatric Journal, 1,* 127-130.

Accommodating Children's Testimony
Legal Reforms in New Zealand

MARGARET-ELLEN PIPE
MARK HENAGHAN

In 1989, New Zealand introduced radical changes to legislation relating to child witnesses. In particular, the Evidence Amendment Act (1989) and the Summary Proceedings Amendment Act (1989) opened the way for a number of different procedures to be used when children give evidence in criminal cases, as well as for expert witnesses to testify on a broader range

AUTHORS' NOTE: We thank the New Zealand Children's and Young Persons Service, the New Zealand Police Sexual Abuse Teams, the judiciary of the District and High Courts, the defense lawyers who participated, and Doctors for Sexual Abuse Care for their assistance and participation. Thanks also to Beverley Bacon, Sue Bidrose, Jan Egerton, and Gina Priestley for assistance with data collection, coding, and analysis; Megan Gollop for assistance with preparation of the chapter; and Sue Bidrose, Jan Egerton, Harlene Hayne, and Larry Owens for helpful comments. Preparation of this chapter was supported, in part, by a grant to the first author from the New Zealand National Children's Health Research Foundation.

of issues than had been possible under existing legislation. In the present chapter, we first provide an overview of the legislative provisions of the two new acts and how they have been interpreted, as reflected in judicial decisions. Second, we report the results of a survey of professionals who have an interest in the legal process when a child is a witness in a criminal case. A number of professionals have now had considerable experience with the functioning of these new legislative provisions. The survey was designed to assess how lawyers, judges, members of the police, social workers, and other child professionals perceive them to be working. Finally, we argue that although the new provisions have by no means solved all of the difficulties child witnesses face when they enter the legal system, in general, those working with children in legal contexts perceive the provisions positively and as working well.

The Law Relating to Child Witnesses in New Zealand

Overview of the Legal System in New Zealand

The legal system in New Zealand is based on common law and, as such, is an adult system created by adults for adults. In New Zealand, the court system is mostly adversarial. It runs on the basis of each side producing its evidence and having it questioned and scrutinized by the other. The main exception is the Family Court, where the judge is given power to call witnesses and, for reports, an inquisitorial role. For reasons of their protection, children are not called as witnesses in the Family Court. The child's perspective is presented by others, such as expert report writers (e.g., psychologists or psychiatrists with specialized training in child development) who comment on the child's needs. In addition, Family Court judges have adopted a procedure whereby they may see a child (normally, age 6 years or older) in their chambers to get a sense of how the issues look from the child's viewpoint.

It is in the criminal courts that children are most commonly called as witnesses. Less serious criminal cases are heard in the District Court, more serious criminal cases (e.g., those involving rape or murder) are heard in the High Court. Appeals from either court can be taken to the Court of Appeal. The criminal courts prefer, and the rules of evidence emphasize, the need for witnesses to give evidence firsthand, and for that evidence to be cross-examined.

Until 1990, children were required to give evidence in the witness box, the same way as adults, and faced the additional hurdle of judges instructing juries that the evidence of children is suspect. The traditional attitude has been that children are untrustworthy witnesses, likely to distort and fantasize. This attitude is best captured in a statement in a 1968 New Zealand Court of Appeal case:

> New Zealand judges almost invariably advise juries to pay particular attention to, or to scrutinize with special care, the evidence of young children and equally invariably explain the tendencies of infants to invention or distortion. We hope that this course will continue to be followed for we think it prudent. (*R. v. Parker,* 1968)

Legislative Changes and the Courts' Reaction

On January 1, 1990, both the Evidence Amendment Act (1989) and the Summary Proceedings Amendment Act (1989) came into force. These legislative changes were made in an attempt to change attitudes toward child witnesses, to make the process of testifying less traumatic, and to better inform juries about children's evidence. The Evidence Amendment Act makes it clear that judges are no longer to instruct juries on the need to scrutinize the evidence of young children with special care, nor to suggest to the jury that young children generally have tendencies to invention or distortion. In 1991, the New Zealand Court of Appeal explained the changes in the following way:

> The interests of justice require that the presentation of the child's evidence be facilitated, both in the manner in which it is done and in making its import accessible to the jury. Recent statutory measures have been designed to achieve both objectives. As aids to the ascertainment of the truth they are important contributions to the course of justice. (*R. v. S.,* 1991a)

Where the offense is one of a sexual nature and the child complainant is under 17 years at the time the proceedings commence, the Evidence Amendment Act (1989) provides for a range of alternative modes of giving evidence by the complainant. Although the legislation is specific as to the nature of crimes and the witnesses with whom the new modes can be used, the New Zealand courts have made it clear that through what they call their "inherent jurisdiction," the modes can be extended to other crimes and to other child witnesses besides the complainant (e.g., *R. v. Accused,* 1989; *R. v. L.,* 1990).

The main alternative means by which children can give evidence in New Zealand are (a) by prerecorded videotape; (b) behind a glass screen or wall partition placed in the courtroom to shield the child from the view of the accused; and (c) via closed-circuit television, with the child in another room within the court precinct but outside the main courtroom. Judges have discretion as to whether they wish to use any of these alternative modes. In exercising that discretion, they are mandatorily required to have regard for the need to minimize stress on the complainant while ensuring a fair trial for the accused. The judge has inquisitorial powers to call for reports from qualified persons advising about the effects on the complainant of giving evidence in person in the ordinary way or of using any of the modes prescribed by the act. A wide variety of persons have been accepted by the courts as qualified to advise on this question, including senior social workers (*R. v. C.,* 1990; *R. v. D.,* 1992), persons with experience in interviewing child complainants at the diagnostic and evidence gathering stage (*R. v. Hauiti,* 1990), a primary school teacher who had been a counselor of sexually abused children (*R. v. N., 1992*), a registered psychologist (*R. v. W.,* 1990a), and even a complainant's mother (*R. v. W.,* 1990a).

There is not, as yet, unanimity of judicial approach as to when the alternative modes of giving evidence should be used. Some judges have started from the position that children should give evidence in the way that adults do unless there is some good, demonstrated possibility of stress for the particular child (*R. v. W.,* 1990a). Other judges have taken the view that the possibility of minimizing stress for children means that one of the new modes should be used in the normal course of events (*R. v. C.,* 1990; *R. v. Lewis,* 1991). The New Zealand Court of Appeal has rejected the argument that the new modes should not be used unless the emotional stress on a child is significantly more than on other witnesses (*R. v. Crime Appeal,* 1988, 163/88). The court was of the view that "a very real possibility" of trauma and stress was enough.

Judges have relied on a variety of factors to determine the possibility of trauma, including the complainant's age, personality, and ability to communicate; the relationship between the accused and the complainant; the possible difficulties of having the accused within sight; the type of charge; and an assessment of the likelihood of intimidation by the court's surroundings and the formality of the process (e.g., *R. v. D.*, 1992; *R. v. Hauiti*, 1990; *R. v. W.*, 1990a). When an alternative mode is used, the judge is mandatorily required to tell the jury not to draw any adverse inference against the accused. This is to protect the accused against the possible inference of guilt or threat and the implication that the child is giving evidence behind a screen or one-way mirror because the accused is a "frightening monster" to the child.

Whichever procedure is used, defense counsel has the right of cross-examination. However, the judge has the power to disallow any questions that, when the complainant's age is taken into consideration, are "intimidating or overbearing." An accused person is entitled to cross-examine the complainant only when the accused is not represented. In such cases, the accused may put questions, either by means of an audio link or, as the judge directs, to a third person who will repeat the questions to the complainant. Where a videotape of the complainant's evidence is to be shown at the trial, the judge determines the manner in which cross-examination or reexamination is to be conducted. When the child complainant gives evidence in chief (i.e., evidence presented by a prosecution witness during the main part of the trial) by means of closed-circuit television or from behind a wall or partition, the judge is required to direct that any questions to be put to the complainant be given through an appropriate audio link to a person, approved by the judge and placed next to the complainant, who will repeat the questions to the complainant.

So far, judges appear to be taking a conservative approach to cross-examination. In one case where the complainant's evidence in chief was given by way of a videotaped interview, the prosecution requested that any further questioning should be via the social worker who had conducted the videotaped interview (*R. v. B.*, 1991). The judge sided with the defense argument for direct questioning, as for any other witness. The judge emphasized the "overall interests of justice and the accused's interests in a fair trial." The most influential point for the judge was a perception that an indirect mode of questioning would lead to a loss of the flavor of questions, such as sternness of voice, thus lessening their possible effect on the complainant (*R. v. B.*, 1991).

The legislative changes concerning modes of giving evidence are wide enough to allow the whole of a child's evidence, both evidence in chief and cross-examination, to be videotaped prior to the trial and shown at the trial. This was recommended by the 1989 UK Pigot Report (*Report of the*

Advisory Group on Video Evidence, 1989). One advantage of completing the child's evidence early in the process is that therapy for the child can proceed with minimum delay. In the case of *R. v. W.* (1990b), for example, counseling was delayed for several months because of concern that such therapy might be perceived as tainting the evidence. The need to retain and recall events over long periods of time is not likely to enhance the recovery process and may have other disadvantages. For example, one New Zealand judge (*R. v. Lewis,* 1991) questioned whether it is meaningful to cross-examine a child with regard to videotaped evidence recorded 8 months previously.

There is some anecdotal comment from judges on the use of videotaped evidence. In a civil case that involved sexual abuse of a sister by her brothers, the judge made the following comments after viewing the video: "The videotape is indeed a remarkable document for it shows A's responses in a way that would have been impossible in court" and "I am satisfied that the video interview is of substantially greater weight than the evidence A could have given if she had been examined in court in the usual way" (*DSW v. H. and H.,* 1987). It is important to emphasize that these comments were made in civil proceedings, in a jurisdiction where the court is able to receive "evidence the court thinks fit" notwithstanding the rules of evidence. Normally, in such a court the child would not give direct evidence and the child's position would be put to the court through other witnesses. Even with these qualifications, it can be seen that judges can be deeply impressed by a videotaped interview.

Legal Constraints on the New Modes of Giving Evidence

Videotaped evidence. Before the videotape of a child's evidence is shown in court, a judge is required to have viewed it to excise any matters that break the rules of evidence (see also Evidence [Videotaping of Child Complainants] Regulations, 1990). The Court of Appeal has indicated that videotaped evidence should be played only once to the court (*R. v. Thomas,* 1992). This is the normal practice with witnesses who give their evidence in person. One High Court judge allowed a jury to have a written transcript of the tape while viewing the tape *(R. v. Anderson,* 1992). The judge said it was a matter of discretion; the length of the interview and the importance of the statements made were material in the decision. Another High Court judge (*R. v. S.,* 1991b), after acknowledging that there were "considerable differences of opinion" on the use of written transcripts of videotapes, allowed the jury to have a transcript while viewing the tape and, furthermore, to take the transcript into the jury room. The judge made the ruling based on the judge's own difficulties in maintaining concentration while viewing the video. However, judges in both the High Court (*R. v. Anderson,* 1992; *R. v. Knowles,* 1992) and the Court of Appeal (*R. v. Thomas,* 1992) have refused to allow the jury access to the written transcript *after* the showing of the videotape. This was seen as giving the prosecution an unfair advantage, the jury effectively being able to revisit evidence that may, as a result, have a disproportionate effect compared with the other evidence.

The competence requirement. The major legal hurdle to the admission of videotaped evidence has been the requirement of the competence examination that the interviewer must carry out at the beginning of the interview. Although young children are not required to take the oath in New Zealand, there is still a legislative concern that they should be competent in terms of knowing the importance of telling the truth and promising to do so. The legal regulations require the interviewer to (a) determine that the complainant understands the necessity to tell the truth and (b) obtain from the complainant a promise to tell the truth, where the complainant is capable of giving, and willing to give, a promise to that effect.

Because the judge is not present when a videotaped interview is recorded, the task of satisfying this provision falls on the interviewer. The Court of Appeal has taken a fairly liberal approach to this requirement (*R. v. Accused,* 1992). The court observed that there is no specification in the law of how the child's understanding of the necessity to tell the truth is to be determined. The court said the purpose behind the requirements is that the child appreciates the full solemnity of the situation. Moreover, it has been argued that there is a distinction between determining the child witness's understanding of the necessity to tell the truth and obtaining a promise to tell the truth (*R. v. Accused,* 1992). The Court of Appeal took the pragmatic position that when a child promises to tell the truth, that shows an understanding of the necessity to tell the truth, and no more is required. Arguments that the child's understanding of the necessity to tell the truth can be established only by the child giving definitions of words like *truth* have failed (e.g., *R. v. Accused,* 1991). The following example of an interviewer establishing competency was acceptable to the courts involved (*R. v. Accused,* C.A. 449/91, 1992).

> **Interviewer**   Okay, before we go on any further, I'd just like to ask you if you know what the difference is between truth and lies. Do you know what the difference is?
>
> **Child**   Um, a bit.
>
> **Interviewer**   "Bit," how would you explain it?
>
> **Child**   That the truth is, you'd tell, you're not, you're telling them the truth, what, um, what really happened.
>
> **Interviewer**   What really happened?
>
> **Child**   Yeah.
>
> **Interviewer**   And will you tell the truth today?
>
> **Child**   Yes.

In another case (*R. v. Neho,* 1992), the court held the child had met the competency requirement by a nodding of the head when questioned by the interviewer as follows: "We need to make an agreement that we only talk about the real stuff, the truth, can we do that?" (Child nods) "Is it OK? That we only talk about the truth?" (Child nods.) In another case, it was held that the competency test was complied with when, in response to the interviewer's statement that "You say I promise to tell the truth today," the child said, "I promise to tell the truth today" (*R. v. Rangi,* 1993).

The wording of the regulations on competency does not say that the interview cannot proceed if the interviewer decides the child is not able to give a promise. Technically, it is sufficient for the interviewer to be satisfied that the child knows it is important to tell the truth. However, this has not prevented some judges from ruling videotaped evidence inadmissible because of failure to obtain a promise to tell the truth. In one case, for example, a videotaped interview was deemed inadmissible because the interviewer failed to determine the child's understanding of a promise and to obtain a promise before carrying out the interview (*R. v. W.,* 1992).

When videotaped evidence is used, children must face two competency tests, one at the time of the video interview, and another at the time the video interview is to be shown and the child is to be available for cross-examination. This is explained by a Court of Appeal judge as follows:

> It is to be remembered that the videotape is simply the means by which the child gives evidence. Therefore, as we have explained, before she gives her evidence the judge must obtain from her the requisite promise to tell the truth. If his questioning demonstrates to him that she is not capable of making that promise and so is not a competent witness, her evidence, including her videotape evidence cannot be received. (*R. v. S.,* 1992)

Many New Zealand judges, to their credit, have not taken a pedantic or technical approach to children's competence. Unless there are clear warning signs, such as the child saying no to a question such as "Will you tell the truth?" (e.g., *R. v. Accused,* C.A. 400, 1992), the courts have largely been satisfied, as long as there is compliance with formality of the regulation.

Issues relating to the interview. A number of decisions have been made with respect to the interviewing conducted for the videotaped interviews. Although it prefers that leading questions be avoided because they may affect credibility, the New Zealand Court of Appeal has been quite liberal if such questions are used to try to focus the issues for young children (*R. v. Lewis,* 1991). In the case of *R. v. Lewis,* the court acknowledged that the questioning on the video was of a "somewhat leading and coaxing character," with a "tendency on the part of the interviewer to seek confirmation of something she had heard from the mothers of the children." The court concluded that the accused's interests had not been overridden, because the jury was capable of evaluating the evidence and because a judge is able to warn the jury about any specific issue that has bearing on the reliability of evidence. In another case, where the evidential interview was interspersed with diagnostic interviews (each child being interviewed 10 times, in total), and the interviewer was also familiar with the background and previous disclosures, the evidential interviews were ruled inadmissible (*R. v. H.,* 1993). The court said that it is essential that the evidential interview be carried out at the earliest stage as a condition for the admission of the videotape in evidence (*R. v. H.,* 1993). In a third case, involving a 4½-year-old child, therapy sessions were commenced between evidential interview sessions (*R. v. Crime Appeal*, 1993). During one of these interviews, the interviewer kept toys from the child "until we get this sorted out." The Court of Appeal believed that this crossed the borderline of impropriety (*R. v. Crime Appeal*, 1993). It also made it clear that the functions of interviewer and therapist should be carried out by different persons.

In a much publicized New Zealand case involving 118 children at a child care center, some significant rulings were made about the interviewing of children (*R. v. Ellis and Others*, 1993). Twenty-eight charges of sexual violation were brought against a male defendant, and one joint charge was brought against three women. The three women were discharged. Defense counsel asked the court to exercise disciplinary control over Social Welfare's Specialist Services Unit for carrying out interviews when the children had been questioned previously by the parents. The court also was asked to discipline the police for prosecuting based on such interviews. The High Court rejected the application. The High Court said that natural and appropriate questioning, even of a leading nature, may be fair and unlikely to lead to false testimony. Defense counsel also objected to the presence of both a parent of the child and a social worker who had worked closely with the child while evidence was given by the child. The High Court judge concluded that a parent had a genuine interest in protecting the child's welfare and a continuing responsibility to ensure the child felt emotionally secure during the court process. Under section 375 A of the Crimes Act (1961), a complainant is able to have some support and comfort during a time of stress. The social worker was allowed to be present for this reason. The Court of Appeal (*R. v. Ellis*, 1994) upheld the High Court rulings. The Court of Appeal said that when dealing with young children, some coaxing and guidance is necessary to aid disclosure on issues that are embarrassing and distasteful to them.

Expert testimony. Experts are able to give opinion evidence in court on matters with which juries are unfamiliar. The Evidence Amendment Act (1989) sets out the specific points on which experts can give evidence in cases of a sexual nature involving children. For the purposes of the legislation, expert is narrowly defined as a child psychiatrist or a child psychologist. The person must have had experience in the professional treatment of sexually abused children. A judge may ask the expert to give opinion evidence on (a) the complainant's intellectual attainment, mental capacity, and emotional maturity; (b) the general developmental level of children of the same sex group; and (c) whether the complainant's behavior (as described in evidence given during the proceedings) is consistent or inconsistent with that of sexually abused children.

Experts may base their opinions on relevant scientific literature or on their professional experience. The expert assessments are to be based on the examination of the child complainant either before the expert's evidence is given or at the time it is given, whether directly or on videotape. The assumption behind the expert being able to comment on the specified matters is that the evidence will provide a context in which the jury can assess the child's credibility. The New Zealand Court of Appeal has commented that the use of the expert "will usually be especially important in assisting the jury to evaluate the truth of the complainant's evidence" (*R. v. Tait*, 1992). It is important to emphasize, however, that the legislative amendments do not allow the expert to express directly an opinion as to the guilt or innocence of an accused or as to the truthfulness of the child complainant.

The New Zealand courts have been strict in confining experts to giving evidence on the specific matters provided for by legislation. The New Zealand Court of Appeal has made it clear that the accused "must be protected against assumptions too readily made and against generalizations too facilely applied to the particular case" (*R. v. S.*, 1991a). The court has also expressed the view that the opinions of experts carry great weight with juries and should be admissible only when the opinion is "solidly based" (*R. v. S.*, 1991a). Case examples show how easy it can be for experts to stray across the boundaries and have evidence excluded or the case appealed. In one case, an expert made the comment that mothers are more likely to take sides with fathers on sexual abuse issues where a child is older (*R. v. S.*, 1991b). The Court of Appeal ruled that this comment was inadmissible, it did not fit within the legislation parameters, and it was a direct attack on the mother's credibility. Another expert, when asked to offer an opinion on the timing of alleged abuse and the change in the child's behavior, said that "it is hard from my point of view to see how the behavior described . . . doesn't tie in with the alleged incident." The Court of Appeal held that this usurped the jury's role and was an opinion on the child's credibility (*R. v. Tait*, 1992). Geddis (1993) suggested the expert should have said "the change in the child's behavior is entirely consistent with the allegation. Such changes can occur for other reasons, but in this case, no evidence has been presented as to their existence" (p. 53). This would be in line with the purpose of the legislative changes to put the child's testimony in a broader context of knowledge and understanding (for further discussion of the Rules of Evidence, see Henaghan, Taylor, & Geddis, 1990).

Perceptions of the Legal Provisions for Child Witnesses: A Survey

The decisions and judgments of the courts reveal the way in which the legislation is interpreted and reflect the views of the judges, but there has been little documentation of how the provisions of the act are seen by other professionals or, indeed, even how frequently the different modes of giving evidence are being used. In part, this situation reflects the relatively recent introduction of the act and consequent logistical problems, with not all procedures, most notably closed-circuit television, being immediately available in all courts.

To obtain some preliminary information as to how the new provisions have been received by different professional groups, we conducted a questionnaire survey. The questionnaire was designed to examine how professionals involved when children are witnesses perceive the legislation to be working. The questionnaire was made up of a series of rating scales and open-ended questions relating to each of the means by which children may give evidence, namely, in court with no special provisions; from behind a one-way glass or screen; on closed-circuit television; or in a prerecorded, videotaped interview. Specific questions related to whether the particular mode of giving evidence had an effect on the trauma of testifying, the quality of the child's testimony, the probability that the child would tell the truth, and the jury's perceptions of the child witness. We also asked whether the procedure was fair or unfair to either the child complainant or to the defendant and whether, overall, the new provisions had had an effect on the number and outcome of trials going to court. Other questions sought an opinion on the expert testimony allowed under the act relating to the abilities, developmental level, and behavior of the child complainant, as well as to the competency requirement. Some of the questions followed those used by Cashmore (1992) in her study for the

Australian Law Reform Commission, whereas others were tailored specifically to the provisions of New Zealand's legislation.

The questionnaire was sent throughout New Zealand to all District court judges with jury jurisdiction ($n = 22$), High Court judges ($n = 46$), crown prosecution lawyers ($n = 52$), police members of police sexual abuse teams ($n = 137$), doctors for sexual abuse care ($n = 116$), social workers, evidential interviewers, and other professionals (e.g., child psychologists) from the Children and Young Persons Service ($n = 120$). In addition, 100 randomly chosen defense lawyers were sent the questionnaire. Response rates ranged from 43% (social workers and interviewers) to 84% (defense lawyers). Not all respondents had dealt with cases of a sexual nature in which children had given evidence in court in the past 3 years. In addition, with the exception of the judges, many respondents from each group had not had experience with all four modes of giving evidence. For these reasons, there were different numbers of respondents answering each of the questions. Doctors, in particular, had seldom had the opportunity to watch children giving evidence, their role most frequently being that of expert witness. Therefore, their responses are not included in this overview. A complete description of the sample, including the number of cases and the age range of children with whom they had had experience, is described in Pipe, Henaghan, Bidrose, and Egerton (1996).

Perception of Alternative Modes for Giving Evidence

The results showed that although there was considerable consensus on some questions relating to the different modes of giving evidence, on others there were marked differences (see Table 9.1). There was consensus that appearing in court without any special provisions was likely to significantly increase the trauma for the child witness whereas, in contrast, the alternative modes were perceived to reduce it. Perhaps not surprisingly, those who work most directly with child complainants (social workers, interviewers, and members of police sexual abuse teams) perceived the most marked differences in the effects of the different modes on the child. Interestingly, however, most groups did not perceive the reduced trauma of testifying using one of the alternative procedures as being at the expense of either the quality or truthfulness of the evidence given. In general, for most professionals, ratings of the quality and likely truthfulness of chil-

TABLE 9.1 Mean Ratings of Each Mode of Giving Evidence for Various Groups

	Group										
	Defense Lawyers		Social Workers		Judges		Prosecutors		Police		Comparison of Modes†
	M	n	M	n	M	n	M	n	M	n	
Does this mode of giving evidence reduce (1) or increase (5) the trauma of testifying for the child witness?											
Direct	3.50[b]	10	4.78[a]	9	3.83[b]	18	3.94[ab]	17	4.42[ab]	26	a
Video	1.87[a]	23	1.60[ab]	30	1.30[a]	27	1.67[ab]	21	1.49[ab]	41	b
Closed-circuit TV	2.00[a]	15	1.45[a]	29	1.69[a]	26	1.77[a]	22	1.68[b]	25	b
Screen/glass	2.15[a]	26	1.69[b]	26	1.89[ab]	27	1.44[b]	25	1.56[b]	48	b
Does this mode of giving evidence have a positive (1) or negative (5) effect on the quality of the child's testimony?											
Direct	2.75[b]		4.34[a]		2.83[b]		2.76[b]		3.50[ab]		ab
Video	2.96[a]		1.85[c]		2.73[ab]		3.37[a]		2.22[bc]		ac
Closed-circuit TV	2.93[ab]		1.89[c]		2.36[abc]		3.14[a]		2.15[bc]		b
Screen/glass	2.50[a]		2.28[a]		2.44[a]		2.36[a]		2.17[a]		c
Does this mode of giving evidence make it more (1) or less (5) likely the child will tell the truth?											
Direct	2.45[b]		3.33[a]		3.00[ab]		3.00[ab]		3.20[a]		a
Video	3.75[a]		2.55[b]		2.95[b]		2.95[b]		2.49[b]		ab
Closed-circuit TV	3.67[a]		2.62[b]		2.67[b]		2.77[b]		2.54[b]		abc
Screen/glass	3.27[a]		2.64[b]		2.71[b]		2.72[b]		2.63[b]		bc
Does this mode of giving evidence have a positive (1) or negative (5) effect on how the jury perceives the child complainant?											
Direct	1.55[b]		3.00[a]		2.44[a]		2.41[a]		2.81[a]		a
Video	2.32[b]		2.36[b]		2.73[b]		3.44[a]		2.83[b]		b
Closed-circuit TV	2.39[a]		2.80[a]		2.92[a]		3.46[a]		2.68[a]		ab
Screen/glass	2.54[a]		2.80[a]		2.81[a]		2.76[a]		2.73[a]		ab
Is this mode of giving evidence fair (1) or unfair (5) to the child complainant?											
Direct	1.91[c]		4.33[a]		3.06[b]		3.41[b]		3.77[ab]		a
Video	2.42[a]		1.76[a]		1.96[a]		1.91[a]		1.76[a]		b
Closed-circuit TV	2.13[a]		1.71[a]		1.96[a]		2.24[a]		1.69[a]		b
Screen/glass	2.04[a]		1.88[a]		2.07[a]		2.12[a]		1.92[a]		b
Is this mode of giving evidence fair (1) or unfair (5) to the defendant (accused)?											
Direct	1.58[a]		2.30[a]		2.44[a]		2.35[a]		2.08[a]		a
Video	4.25[a]		2.44[d]		3.70[b]		3.14[c]		2.42[d]		b
Closed-circuit TV	4.25[a]		2.52[c]		3.24[b]		3.23[b]		2.39[c]		b
Screen/glass	4.00[a]		2.42[c]		3.08[a]		3.04[a]		2.56[c]		b

NOTE: Analyses were univariate analyses of variance, with the significance level set at $p < .01$. Superscript letters refer to post hoc comparisons of different groups for each mode, that is, to comparisons across row means. Means with the same letter do not differ significantly from each other.

†This column summarizes results of pairwise comparisons of the different *modes* of giving evidence, collapsed across groups. The significance level was set at $p < .01$. Modes with same letter do not differ significantly from each other. Numbers contributing to pairwise comparisons of modes differ from the *n*s in the table, depending on numbers of respondents with experience of both modes in the pair being compared.

158

dren's evidence were not significantly different for each of the modes of evidence. Defense lawyers were the exception to this pattern, perceiving children to be more likely to tell the truth when giving evidence directly and, conversely, less likely to tell the truth when any of the other modes of giving evidence was used.

Two questions related to whether the different modes of evidence were fair or unfair to the child complainant and the defendant, respectively. Most respondents viewed giving evidence directly in court as being least fair to the child, with the alternative modes viewed positively by all professional groups except the defense lawyers. Defense lawyers viewed giving evidence directly in court as most fair to the child. With respect to the defendant, evidence in court was seen by all groups as most fair although, in general, the differences in ratings on this question were quite small and not significant. Defense lawyers, again, were an exception to this pattern, as they clearly viewed the alternative means of giving evidence as being very unfair to the defendant.

In addition to general comments, we invited comment as to whether the age of the child giving evidence influenced the respondent's views, concerning each mode of giving evidence. Several respondents from each professional group indicated that giving evidence directly in court is likely to be more useful for older children, whereas closed-circuit television and videotaped evidence were seen as more useful for younger children. Individual comments indicated that if an older child is able to give his or her evidence in court, it will have the most effect on the jury. However, social workers and police members of sexual abuse teams, in particular, commented that facing an abuser may be too difficult, even for older children. Conversely, the main disadvantages noted in relation to closed-circuit television and, to a lesser extent to videotaped interviews, were that they distanced the child from the judge and the jury and lessened the effect of the child's evidence. As one prosecutor commented: "For very young children it [closed-circuit television] is necessary. But it is certainly more difficult to convince juries of the truth of the evidence." Indeed, closed-circuit television was seen by some as clearly being very effective in reducing the stress for the child, so much so that it was this, rather than depersonalization, that might affect the impact of their evidence on the jury.

Interestingly, the same comments seldom came up in relation to screens or one-way glass, which were not seen consistently as either more or less

TABLE 9.2 Mean Ratings for Questions Relating to Outcomes of the New Procedures for Giving Evidence

		Group		
Defense Lawyers *(n = 35)*	*Social Workers* *(n = 39)*	*Judges* *(n = 26)*	*Prosecutors* *(n = 26)*	*Police* *(n = 59)*

Has the provision of the different modes of giving evidence made it *more* (1) or *less* (5) likely that a case involving a child complainant will reach court?

1.89	2.03	1.46	1.59	1.97

Has the provision of the different modes of giving evidence made it *more* (1) or *less* (5) likely that a case involving a child complainant will result in the defendant being found guilty?

2.00	2.31	1.96	2.31	2.39

NOTE: Univariate analyses of variance revealed no significant differences between groups for either question ($p > .01$).

useful for a particular age group. To the contrary, one social worker noted that the "jury often feel sympathy for [the] child when a screen is used as it highlights the powerlessness of [the child]." Comments in relation to screens were related to considerations such as the design of many New Zealand courtrooms and the difficulty of placing the screens in such a way that the child would feel protected yet could still be seen by the jury. The main criticism of screens was, however, raised primarily by defense lawyers and related to the potential implication of guilt or threat when screens are used, despite the warning given by the judge. As one lawyer put it: "I feel that the use of screens is unfair to an accused person because of the negative impact it must have on the jury. In my view it very much goes against the presumption of innocence."

There was general consensus among all of the groups surveyed that the different modes of evidence made it more likely both that a case involving a child complainant would reach court and that the defendant would be found guilty (see Table 9.2). Interestingly, however, defense lawyers did not perceive a greater likelihood of a guilty verdict than did the other professionals, even though the lawyers generally perceived the new procedures as having the most disadvantages.

We cannot verify whether the perceptions of more cases reaching court and of an increased rate of conviction were an accurate reflection of outcome of trials since the introduction of new legislation. There is, at present, no easily accessible record of how frequently these different procedures are being used, or of the outcome of trials in relation to them. It is worth noting, however, that the respondents in our survey were generally much more likely to have had experience with children giving evidence using one or more of the alternative procedures than with children giving evidence in court directly. According to one prosecutor, for example, "Very few cases of a sexual nature, if any proceed without any form of protection." Consistent with this observation, only a small proportion of the respondents from each professional group, apart from the judges, had had experience with children giving evidence directly in court in the past 3 years. This suggests that the new provisions are, indeed, frequently used and that they have become the norm rather than the exception. As one judge commented, cases in which screens and other procedures are not recommended are "now very much the exception."

Several respondents perceived the "fit" between the child and the legal system to be still very poor, in large part a result of the way in which children were interviewed and questioned. For social workers and other child professionals, in particular, a major concern was that children were disadvantaged because of the way they were questioned in court. Although this issue came up in the context of the competency requirement, it frequently was raised also as a more general point, as reflected in comments such as, "In the past, cases have been lost because the children were not asked questions in a way that they could understand." Other respondents expressed concern about the possible effects of the interviewers' knowledge and predisposition on children's accounts.

The Competency Requirement

As described earlier, New Zealand retains a competency requirement; one section of our questionnaire related to this requirement. Responses to these questions are summarized in Table 9.3. Many respondents indicated they believed the competency requirement to be moderately useful. One judge put the case for the competency test in the context of videotaped interview as follows:

> The point to my mind is that the video interview is the "evidence." In court, the solemnity of the occasion, competency, swearing or affirmation and the question-

TABLE 9.3 Mean Ratings for Questions Relating to the Competency Requirement

	Group			
Defense Lawyers (n = 33)	*Social Workers* (n = 39)	*Judges* (n = 27)	*Prosecutors* (n = 26)	*Police* (n = 60)

Do child competency tests serve a *useful* purpose in the trial process (1) or *not* (5)?

3.12^b	3.78^a	2.46^c	2.78^{bc}	2.60^{bc}

Do child competency tests *reduce* (1) or *increase* (5) the trauma of testifying for the child witness?

3.03^{ab}	3.95^c	2.81^a	3.15^{ab}	3.35^b

Do child competency tests have a *positive* (1) or *negative* (5) effect on the quality of the child's testimony?

2.82^a	3.37^b	2.58^a	2.73^a	2.58^a

Do child competency tests make it *more* (1) or *less* (5) likely the child will tell the truth?

2.85^a	2.85^a	2.52^{ab}	2.54^{ab}	2.37^b

Do child competency tests have a *positive* (1) or *negative* (5) effect on how the jury perceives the child?

2.26^b	3.06^a	2.27^b	2.19^b	2.17^b

Are child competency tests *fair* (1) or *unfair* (5) to the child complainant?

2.68^{bc}	4.33^a	2.21^c	2.58^{bc}	2.91^b

Are child competency tests *fair* (1) or *unfair* (5) to the defendant (accused)?

3.7^a	2.46^b	2.57^b	2.33^b	2.20^b

Have child competency tests made it *more* (1) or *less* (5) likely that a case involving a child complainant will reach court?

2.6^a	4.13^c	2.81^{ab}	3.26^b	3.20^b

NOTE: Analyses were univariate analyses of variance, with the significance level set at $p < .01$. Superscript letters refer to post hoc comparisons of different groups for each mode, that is, to comparisons across row means. Means with the same letter do not differ significantly from each other.

ing all take place openly. In the video interview something additional to the deliberately cozy atmosphere is required to bring to the attention of the child, the interviewer, and ultimately counsel and jury precisely what is taking place and the need for sincerity, honesty, and care in protection of all.

Social workers, however, perceived the competency requirement more negatively than did the remaining groups on each question, viewing it as being of little use and unfair to the child, as well as increasing the trauma of testifying and decreasing the probability that a case would proceed through the trial process. One social worker suggested, in addition, that asking children about promises and truth and lies may confuse the child: "It reminds the child about the promises they made to the defendant about not telling anyone about the abuse."

Evidential interviewers are in a unique position with respect to the competency requirement. When the child gives evidence in court, the judge questions him or her and decides whether the competency requirement has been satisfied. In the case of videotaped evidence, the evidential interviewer also must satisfy the requirement that the child demonstrate competence, but unlike the judge, the evidential interviewer does not have the final say in whether the child has met the requirement. This is the role of the judge when the videotaped evidence is presented in court. Given that there is no standardized procedure for assessing competence, and that room exists for considerable variation in interpretation of what satisfies this section of the act (Geddis, 1993), it is not difficult to see how difficulties may arise from the perspective of evidential interviewers.

Expert Testimony

We also asked how useful respondents had found the expert testimony given under the provisions of the act. Ratings in response to these questions are summarized in Table 9.4 and show that, in general, defense lawyers found expert opinion to be least useful (e.g., one described it as "utterly pernicious"), with police, prosecution, and judges evaluating expert testimony either positively or as moderately useful, and social workers evaluating it most positively (e.g., "Expert testimony is vital to inform the jury."). This same pattern was found whether evidence related to (a) the abilities of the child relative to other children, (b) the developmental level of the child, or (c) the consistency of the child's behavior with that of children who have been sexually abused. There was general consensus that the special provisions relating to expert testimony were of most use to the prosecution, a view expressed most strongly by the defense lawyers. Criticisms of expert testimony most frequently related to whether the testimony was impartial, the experts' understanding of their role and

TABLE 9.4 Mean Ratings for Questions Relating to Expert Testimony Given Under Section 23G of the Evidence Amendment Act

		Group		
Defense Lawyers (n = 22)	Social Workers (n = 18)	Judges (n = 19)	Prosecutors (n = 22)	Police (n = 33)

Have you found expert opinion given under section 23G *helpful* (1) or *not helpful* (5) as it relates to the intellectual attainment, mental capacity, and emotional maturity of the complainant?

4.00^a	1.78^c	2.80^b	2.30^{bc}	1.97^c

the general developmental level of children?

3.62^a	1.88^c	2.80^b	2.45^{bc}	1.97^c

whether the complainant's behavior is consistent or inconsistent with the behavior of sexually abused children?

4.09^a	1.50^c	3.00^b	1.95^c	1.82^c

do you think the section 23G expert witness is of most value to the *defense* (1) or the *prosecution* (5)?

4.57^a	3.78^b	3.61^b	3.95^b	3.53^b

their expertise, and the constraints on the kind of testimony that can be given under the act. Evidence relating to questions such as the reliability and suggestibility of children's memory or the effects of long delays on children's accounts are not specifically provided for under the new provisions. This is an area in which research has accumulated very rapidly during the past years (for a review, see Goodman & Bottoms, 1993), and there is now also a considerable body of research within the New Zealand context (e.g., Butler, Gross, & Hayne, 1995; Gee & Pipe, 1995; Pipe, 1993; Pipe & Wilson, 1994; Salmon, Bidrose, & Pipe, 1995). This is one area in which the provisions of the act might be usefully extended.

Conclusion

The middle ground reflected in the responses of a large number of people who completed the survey is best captured by the prosecutor who concluded that "the changes introduced in 1989 have proved beneficial. We need more time to assess the results, both positive and negative, before making further changes." Advantages and disadvantages were perceived with each of the new modes of giving evidence, although there was clear consensus that the new procedures significantly reduced the trauma of testifying for the child witness.

The concerns expressed by defense lawyers that the new provisions favored the child complainant at the expense of the defendant reflect similar concerns raised by defense lawyers in both Britain (e.g., Davies & Westcott, 1992) and Australia (Cashmore, 1992). In contrast, social workers believed that the changes had not gone far enough and that children were still disadvantaged by the way in which they were questioned, by facilities that were not adapted to children, and by the competency requirement. The adoption of standardized, age-appropriate guidelines relating to acceptable questions and responses for establishing that children have satisfied the competency requirement would help to overcome these difficulties (Geddis, 1993). Although there was no consensus across all professional groups that the competency requirement should be removed, the consequences of such changes in other countries will be watched with interest in New Zealand.

In summary, there are issues yet to be addressed if the spirit of the recent legislation, to adapt the legal system to the child witness without compromising the rights of the accused, is not to be undermined. In general, however, the interpretation of the provisions for child witnesses, as reflected in judicial decisions relating to them, has been generally progressive. Moreover, most professionals who work with the new provisions perceive them to be working well.

References

Butler, S. J., Gross, J., & Hayne, H. (1995). The effect of drawing on memory performance in young children. *Developmental Psychology, 31,* 597-608.

Cashmore, J. (1992). *Children's evidence: Research paper 1. The use of closed-circuit television for child witnesses in ACT.* Sydney, Australia: Australian Law Reform Commission.

Crimes Act. (1961). Wellington: New Zealand Government Printer.

Davies, G., & Westcott, H. (1992). Videotechnology and the child witness. In H. Dent & R. Flin (Eds.), *Children as witnesses* (pp. 211-229). Chichester, England: Wiley.

DSW v. H. and H., 4 New Zealand Family Law Reports 397 (1987).

Evidence Amendment Act. (1989). Wellington: New Zealand Government Printer.

Evidence (Videotaping of Child Complainants) Regulations. (1990). Wellington: New Zealand Government Printer.

Geddis, D. (1993). *Children as witnesses. A review of the legislative amendments and some related issues.* Unpublished dissertation, University of Otago, Dunedin, New Zealand.

Gee, S., & Pipe, M.-E. (1995). Helping children to remember: The influence of physical object cues on children's accounts of a real event. *Developmental Psychology, 31,* 746-758.

Goodman, G. S., & Bottoms, B. L. (1993). *Child victims, child witnesses: Understanding and improving testimony.* New York: Guilford.

Henaghan, R. M., Taylor, N. J., & Geddis, D. C. (1990, December). Child sexual abuse: 3. Child witnesses and the rules of evidence. *New Zealand Law Journal,* pp. 425-431.

Pipe, M.-E. (1993). Children's testimony: Current issues and research. In P. R. H. Webb, J. G. Adams, W. R. Atkin, I. D. Johnston, R. M. Henaghan, & J. L. Caldwell (Eds.), *Family law in New Zealand* (pp. 522-533). Wellington, New Zealand: Butterworths.

Pipe, M.-E., Henaghan, M., Bidrose, S., & Egerton, J. (1996, January). Perceptions of the legal provisions for child witnesses in New Zealand. *New Zealand Law Journal,* pp. 18-26.

Pipe, M.-E., & Wilson, C. (1994). Cues and secrets: Influences on children's event reports. *Developmental Psychology, 30,* 515-525.

Report of the Advisory Group on Video Evidence. (1989). London: Home Office, Her Majesty's Stationery Office.

R. v. Accused, 1 New Zealand Law Reports 660 (1989).

R. v. Accused, No. 243/90 (New Zealand Court of Appeal 1991); 2 New Zealand Law Reports 649; 6 Criminal Reports New Zealand 345.

R. v. Accused, No. 449/91 (New Zealand Court of Appeal March 12, 1992).

R. v. Anderson, No. T 151/91 (High Court, Auckland, New Zealand February 12, 1992).

R. v. B., No. T42/91 (High Court, Rotorua, New Zealand August 26, 1991).

R. v. C., 6 Criminal Reports New Zealand 315 (1990).

R. v. Crime Appeal, No. 163/88 (New Zealand Court of Appeal, 1988); 3 Criminal Reports New Zealand 315.

R. v. Crime Appeal, Nos. 400/92 404/92 (New Zealand Court of Appeal March 29, 1993).

R. v. D., No. 33/92 (New Zealand Court of Appeal February 18, 1992).

R. v. Ellis, 12 Criminal Reports New Zealand 172 (1994).

R. v. Ellis and Others, No. T9/93 (High Court, Christchurch, New Zealand October 25, 1993).

R. v. H., No. T34/93 (High Court, Wellington, New Zealand August 27, 1993).

R. v. Hauiti, 6 Criminal Reports New Zealand 599 (1990).

R. v. Knowles, No. T33/91 (High Court, Christchurch, New Zealand August 19, 1992).

R. v. L., 6 Criminal Reports New Zealand 383 (1990).

R. v. Lewis, 1 New Zealand Law Reports 409 (New Zealand Court of Appeal 1991).

R. v. N., No. T59/91 (High Court, Christchurch, New Zealand March 12, 1992).

R. v. Neho, No. 343/92 (New Zealand Court of Appeal November 27, 1992).

R. v. Parker, New Zealand Law Reports 325 (New Zealand Court of Appeal 1968).

R. v. Rangi, No. T 26/92 (High Court, Hamilton, New Zealand May 14, 1993).

R. v. S., No. 244/91 (New Zealand Court of Appeal December 20, 1991a).

R. v. S., 8 Criminal Reports New Zealand 1 (1991b).

R. v. S., No. 105/92 (New Zealand Court of Appeal November 26, 1992).

R. v. Tait, 2 New Zealand Law Review 666 (1992).

R. v. Thomas, No. 130/92 (New Zealand Court of Appeal July 27, 1992).

R. v. W., 6 Criminal Reports New Zealand 157 (1990a).

R. v. W., No. T 87/90 (High Court, Auckland, New Zealand July 26, 1990b).

R. v. W., No. T91/92 (High Court, Wellington, New Zealand December 4, 1992).

Salmon, K., Bidrose, S., & Pipe, M.-E. (1995). Providing props to facilitate children's event reports: A comparison of toys and real items. *Journal of Experimental Child Psychology, 60,* 174-194.

Summary Proceedings Amendment Act (No. 2). (1989). Wellington: New Zealand Government Printer.

10

Listening to Children in South Africa

DAP LOUW
PIERRE OLIVIER

As in most other countries, the legal rights of the child in South Africa received no attention before the 19th century. The first legal steps to rectify the situation were taken in 1856 when an act was passed in the Cape Parliament to ensure that minors received their rightful inheritance (Swanepoel & Wessels, 1992). However, as far as the protection of juvenile complainants and child witnesses is concerned, legal practice in South Africa made no special provision before 1991 when (as will be discussed later) the report of the South African Law Commission was published.

In the past, the evidence of a child was treated with circumspection by South African courts. For example, in *R. v. Manda,* an Appellate Division case in 1951, the judge stated: "The imaginativeness and suggestibility of children are only two of a number of elements that require their evidence to be scrutinized with care, amounting, perhaps, to suspicion," and a similar statement was made by a judge in another Appellate Division case (*Woji v. Santam Insurance Co. Ltd.*) in 1981: "The danger of believing a child where his (*sic*) evidence stands alone must not be understated." In this regard, it should be added that the South African criminal procedure

168

also recognizes so-called cautionary rules. This means that the evidence of certain complainants, including children in sexual abuse cases, should be approached with extreme caution. Because South Africa does not have a jury system, the presiding judge guards over these rules. Corroboration of the evidence of a child is not a strict requirement, but is usually sought. It can be in the form of the evidence of another child or an adult, but in the former case the same rule would apply. The cautionary rule is usually complied with if the evidence of the child witness is found to be credible and supported by the probabilities.

Legal practice in South Africa follows the Anglo-American adversarial system. It thus recognizes the presumption of innocence of an accused and places the burden to prove the guilt of the accused beyond reasonable doubt on the prosecution. It is also a principle of the South African system that trials take place in open court and that the accused is entitled to be present during the trial, to hear all evidence against him or her, and to cross-examine, either personally or through a legal representative, all prosecution witnesses. In the past, this system had a very negative effect on most children because they, for example, were subjected to grueling cross-examination without being allowed any assistance in the witness box. According to the system, the child was obliged to give evidence in the presence of the accused, which was also very traumatic to most children.

There was widespread dissatisfaction with the existing law, especially regarding the suspicion with which the courts approached a child's evidence and that assistance was refused to the child in the witness box. This widespread dissatisfaction was fueled by the results of research projects, which will be discussed next.

South African Research

Two South African research projects that had a significant effect on protecting the rights of the child witness were those of Hammond and Hammond (1987) and Key (1988).

The Hammond and Hammond Study

In a series of experiments that received widespread attention from mental health professionals, Hammond and Hammond (1987) tried to prove their viewpoint that the child is not a less competent witness than an adult.

Immediate Spatial and Delayed Recognition Memory

To compare the immediate and delayed memories of children and adults, the Hammonds made use of the so-called Pelmanism game where picture cards are placed facedown on a table. Each card has a match (one other card with the same picture). The object of the game is to try to turn up matching pairs. You turn over one card, then another. If they match, you remove them and proceed. If they do not match, it is your opponent's turn. Gradually, a spatial memory for the contents of the cards develops and the person whose spatial memory is best is the winner.

Mothers were required to play against their children, achieving at once an adult/child comparison, along with genetic and environmental matching. Twenty pairs of cards were used. (A further six pairs were used in a warm-up session). Eight children and their mothers participated. The children ranged from 5 years 2 months to 7 years 10 months. In a follow-up, a mother/child pair were visited without warning, after 2 days (short interval) or 5 days (long interval) and given a recognition memory test that included previously seen and unseen cards.

In the Pelmanism game, the children of all ages performed better than their mothers. In the recognition memory phase, the children also outdid their mothers, although the difference was not dramatic. Both mothers and children did slightly better after the 5-day delay than the 2-day delay, suggesting that across this time interval, memories had consolidated and not faded. Although the mothers were no more reliable than their children, there was a difference in style. Mothers were more conservative and less likely to guess than their children.

Although this experiment can only be regarded as a pilot study, the results remain interesting because they show that the immediate spatial and the late recognition memory of children in the age 5–7 range is actually superior to that of a matched adult control group.

Recall About a Person

Sixteen mother/child pairs participated in this experiment. Half the children were 4–6 years of age (the young group) and the other half were 7–11 years of age (the older group). They were individually visited by a young woman, who asked them some questions about nutrition. Neither the mothers nor the children were warned that their memory would be tested later. The researcher visited half the sample after a delay of 1 day, and the other half after 7 days. The memories of both mothers and children concerning the young woman were assessed by free recall, a questionnaire, and by asking them to draw the visitors. A composite measure (maximum 100) was derived from these. The results showed that the children were negatively affected by the passage of time. Mothers outdid their children in this experiment, but not by a large margin. There was a general improvement with age, although no quantum changes were evident. The 7- to 11-year-olds performed at 80% of the adult level. The 4- to 6-year-olds were able to perform at 69% of the adult level.

The posing of a leading question was also part of the experiment. The young female visitor had not used a handbag, but the participants were asked whether her bag had a shoulder strap. The results for this leading question were that 50% of the mothers, 56% of the older children, and 64% of the younger children were influenced by the leading question. It thus seems that the children, as well as their mothers, were open to suggestion.

Immediate and Delayed Recognition of Photographs of Faces

In this experiment, the Hammonds assessed the performance of 64 children who varied in age (5- to 12-year-olds), ethnic group (black and white), and gender (boys and girls). There were 8 children in each of these eight (2 × 2 × 2) subgroups. Each child was shown a head-and-shoulder photograph of a black man, and one of a white man (in his early 20s). They saw each photograph for 10 seconds. They were tested after 10 minutes or after 7 days. There were two booklets, one containing 20 photographs of whites and another containing 20 photographs of blacks. In each booklet, one photograph was the target and the other 19 were distracters. The children were told that the faces they had seen previously might occur (a) not at all, (b) once only, or (c) several times in each booklet. Although (b) was the correct one, this procedure was used to be able to compute a "recklessness score" (the number of false positives).

Two analyses were performed. One was on accuracy with a guessing correction applied. The other was conducted on the false positives to assess the mentioned recklessness components. As far as accuracy was concerned, no differences that were attributable to time delay or gender were found. Age, however, was important (older children performed better than younger children). So was ethnic group (white children performed better than black children). The latter may be due to the difference in the background and environmental circumstances of the two groups of children. It should also be added that young children did not fail to recognize the target. They were, however, willing to point out many false positives that with the guessing correction applied, had a negative influence on their accuracy score.

Hammond and Hammond (1987) concluded their pioneering research with the following recommendations:

> In civil and criminal proceedings every child witness should have representation and support. In cases of child abuse specially trained officers should take a statement as soon as the case is reported and videorecord the interview. The minimum of time should elapse before the case is heard in court. Ideally the child should contribute no further to the proceedings. The videorecording should be permitted to speak for him or her. Alternatively a children's courtroom should be used with live video link and a Child Hearing Officer mediating between the court and the child. In sexual abuse cases an assessor can inform the court of the classical symptoms suffered by victims. Corroboration should not be required routinely since children are no less creditable than adults and indeed are very unconvincing liars. More research is needed, but from what we already know it seems that no gulf separates children and adult witnesses as far as their cognitive capabilities are concerned. However, children do have to be treated in an age-appropriate fashion. (pp. 17-18)

In evaluating the Hammond and Hammond study, it is important to note that its major contribution lies more in the fact that it fueled reforms in the South African legal system than in its scientific acceptability. More specifically, methodological flaws (e.g., small samples) led to questionable results. For example, research in other countries indicates that although children's recognition memory is often quite reliable, it is not generally true that children have better recognition memory than adults (Ceci & Bruck, 1993; Spencer & Flin, 1990).

The Key Study

The other study that had a major effect on later legislation was that of Key (1988), a medical doctor from Durban. Key published an article titled "The Child Witness: The Battle for Justice" in the widely read *De Rebus,* official journal and mouthpiece of South African attorneys. She began her article with the following case, which she thought highlighted some of the problems that the child witness has to face:

In August 1985 I was asked to examine two young boys aged 12½ and 2½ years respectively, who gave a history of alleged long-standing sexual abuse by their father. The story was a shocking one and only came to light because the mother became suspicious about her two and half year old's consistent complaints about a painful anus. On gentle questioning he told the story in simple childlike terms. Both children had medical evidence of chronic sexual abuse and the matter was reported to the police and charges were laid. The older boy required admission for six months intensive psychotherapy and will need ongoing psychological counseling for years to come.

Had I known then what I know now, I would have doubted the wisdom of laying charges which would result in this young boy being subjected to the horrendous secondary abuse he received in court.

The younger brother was too young to testify, but the older boy first gave evidence in court at the beginning of April 1986, eight months after the charges were laid. He was subjected to one and a half days of persistent and detailed cross-examination about the appalling sexual abuse to which he had been subjected by his father for as far back as he could remember. Throughout the hearing the boy demonstrated signs of severe anxiety. He held his hands against his face to blinker out the sight of his father. When asked why he was so upset he said that his father had, on numerous occasions, produced a knife and threatened to kill him if he ever told anyone about what his father had done to him. The case was remanded for two months and then remanded again because of a change in defense counsel. Finally, in October 1986, 14 months after the original charge was laid, this unfortunate child once again was required to stand in the witness box for hour upon hour of grueling cross-examination. Within 10 minutes on the first day he was in tears. As before, he held his hand against his face to avoid seeing his father. He was bullied about details he could not remember. He was accused of being a liar and making up the whole story. At this stage he broke down completely and pleaded to know why the defense did not believe him.

Judgement in this case was deferred twice, but finally, on 12 June 1987, nearly two years after the discovery of the abuse, the father was found guilty on two counts of sodomy and two counts of indecent assault. (Key, 1988, pp. 54-55)

As a result of the effect it had, the above-mentioned example can be regarded as a landmark case. Several authors, including Grey (1991) and Zieff (1991) and also the South African Law Commission (1991), have referred to it.

To prove that the above-mentioned case was not a unique one, Key also produced empirical data. The data were based on the outcome of sexual abuse cases seen at the Addington Hospital in Durban during 1985 and 1987 that were referred to the police for investigation.

Key found that 62% of 42 cases involving children under the age of 6 years were withdrawn because the child was too young to testify or refused to testify. In a further 26%, the child's testimony, with or without support-ing medical evidence, was considered insufficient without corroboration, and the accused was acquitted. Five children in this group testified. In two cases, the accused were found not guilty. Key's experience led her to believe that except in the unlikely event of an adult witness being able to testify to having seen the child being abused, it was almost impossible to secure a conviction in cases of abuse involving a child who was younger than 6 years.

Key found a similar pattern in the age 6-12 group. Twelve percent of 49 cases refused to testify, and the accused were acquitted. In 55% of the cases, the evidence was considered insufficient in the absence of corroboration.

Far more children in the group between the ages of 12 and 16 testified (58% of 19 cases). The number of convictions was also significantly higher than in either of the two other groups (73%). The only child who refused to testify was slightly mentally retarded.

When all 110 cases referred for police investigation are combined, it seems that 19% of child witnesses were considered too young to testify. Eleven percent refused to testify, and in 48% of the cases the evidence was considered insufficient. Twenty-nine percent testified, and in just over half of the cases the accused were found guilty.

Key made the following suggestions for reform:

- A social worker should be appointed to represent the child and the child's interests as soon as possible.
- The prosecution authority should do everything in its power to obtain an early date for the trial. There is no shortage of lawyers and if counsel of the accused's choice is not available, the accused should be obliged to brief some other lawyer who is available.
- The (young) child witness should give evidence in a playroom environment. The demeanor of the child can be observed by the judicial officer, by the accused, and by the other parties in the proceedings through one-way glass.
- A clinical psychologist should question the child, and the psychologist should be entitled to express an opinion on the reliability of the child's evidence. The questions put by the psychologist should be subjected to consultation with the accused, the prosecution, and the judicial officer.

- Videotapes of the discussions between the child and the social worker during the investigation should be admissible evidence and should be made available to the accused before the hearing.

The Report of the South African Law Commission

Research, especially that conducted by the Hammonds and Key, had such an effect on expert and public opinion that then Minister of Justice, Mr. H. J. Coetzee, instructed the South African Law Commission on November 8, 1988 to investigate new means of protecting the child witness. Mr. Justice P. J. J. Olivier was appointed as project leader. (The South African Law Commission is a permanent commission with full-time researchers whose task it is to enquire into the improvement and reform of South African law.)

After a thorough investigation, during which numerous experts were consulted and a working paper was announced in the government *Gazette* and in the press to stimulate comment, the final report (*Report on the Protection of Child Witnesses*) was published in February 1991.

The main recommendations of the report are summarized as follows:

National child support program. The commission recommended a national child support program consisting of a multidisciplinary team to assist abused children prior to, and subsequent to, court cases.

Special courtrooms and "translated" cross-examination. Probably the most practical, beneficial recommendation of the commission was that children under the age of 18 years should give evidence somewhere other than in court, for example, via electronic equipment such as closed-circuit television in a room adjacent to the courtroom (see Figure 10.1). This will enable children to testify without coming into contact with the accused, their legal representatives, or prosecutors. The manipulation and intimidation of the witness are thus eliminated. This procedure also has the advantage that it does not expose the child to the unfamiliar and often threatening court atmosphere.

Another result of the commission's recommendation is that new courts will have to be designed to provide for one-way mirrors to view young

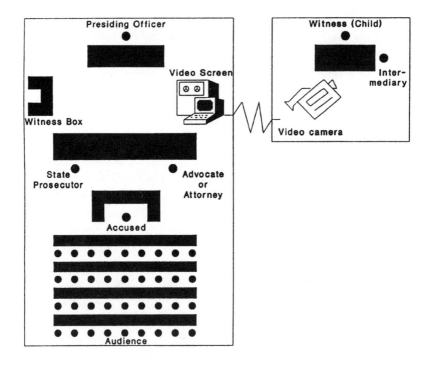

Figure 10.1. Room to Protect Child Witnesses

witnesses from courts. This system will be used as an alternative for the mentioned electronic equipment.

The commission also recommended that an intermediary be present in the adjoining room with the child to "translate" questions into the "child's language." More specifically, the judicial officer/prosecutor will pose the questions to the intermediary through a set of earphones. The intermediary will, in turn, relay the questions to the child in simple, understandable terms. Everyone present in the courtroom will be able to hear and see what is said or demonstrated in the adjoining room. This adjoining room will be tastefully decorated to set the child at ease.

An intermediary can be appointed from the following categories:

- Pediatrician
- Psychiatrist
- Family counselor who is also registered as a social worker, teacher, or psychologist

- Child care worker with at least 4 years' experience in child care
- Social worker with at least 2 years' experience in social work
- Teacher with at least 4 years' experience in teaching
- Psychologist registered as a clinical, educational, or counseling psychologist

The commission also recommended that the giving of evidence in the case of a witness who is hearing impaired should also include sign language, and in the case of a witness under the age of 18 years, demonstrations, gestures, and any other form of nonverbal expression.

Legal assistance for child witnesses. The commission was of the opinion that in view of the recommendations just discussed and especially the role of the intermediary, the need for a legal representative for the child diminishes.

Initial statement taking. The commission regarded the sympathetic and careful taking of the child's initial statement by the police as very important. It is obvious that the legal importance lies in the fact that full and correct statements should be taken because they are used by the prosecution during preparation for the trial as well as in leading the child's evidence. A poor, unsympathetic, or incomplete statement taken during the initial interview could have seriously negative implications for the prosecution and for the child, because it opens the door to devastating cross-examination.

Videorecordings of the initial statement of the child as admissible evidence. The commission stated that "the recording of the child's initial statement on video may be of much practical use to both the police and prosecutor, but that according to current rules of law such a recording does not carry any weight" (South African Law Commission, 1991, p. 62). The vast majority of jurists who commented on this matter were in complete agreement with the commission's conclusion in this regard. The commission quotes the Bar Council of the Cape, which correctly stated:

> It cuts across the fabric of our law, to the extent that the accused is not permitted to confront his (*sic*) accuser. It does make it easier for the child complainant who has been indoctrinated, or who is fabricating, to give false testimony without having to look at the accused face to face. (p. 64)

A similar objection cannot be raised against the viva voce evidence of a child witness in court behind one-way mirrored glass, because in such a case the child can be observed by the court and counsel and can be cross-examined. The same holds true for viva voce evidence given by medium of closed-circuit television.

Expert evidence concerning the credibility of child witnesses. On the proposal that experts should give evidence concerning the credibility of a specific child witness, the commission clearly pointed out that the use of compurgators to testify on the credibility of other witnesses has long been extinct and impermissible in South African and most other legal systems.

Delay avoidance. The commission strongly advised that everything possible should be done to avoid unnecessary delays during the trial and remands. However, the commission did not believe that this problem can be regulated by statute. The commission rightly points out that this is a practical matter where too many genuine factors may cause inevitable delays. The matter therefore lies in the discretion of the court (p. 68). It is, however, of paramount importance that all concerned, that is, the investigating officer, the prosecutor, the legal representative, and others, should collaborate to restrict delays to the bare minimum and that the court should, as far as possible, control matters with a view to disposing of cases of this nature with the least possible delay.

Identification. Concerning the important aspect of identification, the commission recommended the following:
First, if a child is requested by the investigating police officer to identify a suspect, whether in the course of a private confrontation or of a formal identification parade (line-up), the child should not be asked to identify the suspect by physically touching him or her. The commission made an appeal to the police to implement this undertaking immediately by way of an internal standing order or some other suitable instruction. The commission felt so strongly about this that they went further and made an appeal to prosecutors, legal practitioners, presiding officers, and all other parties to bring noncompliance with such an instruction to the notice of the Commissioner of the South African Police.
Second, regardless of criticism that their recommendation could affect the accused's fundamental rights, the commission recommended that a

one-way mirror facility may be used at identification parades. This will enable the child witness to identify without being identified.

Preparation by the prosecutor. The commission found, at the time of their research, an unequal contest between prosecutor and defense. The main reason for this was the inexperience on the part of prosecutors regarding child witnesses and a lack of time for preparation and consultation with witnesses. The commission therefore proposed that specially trained prosecutors should, as far as possible, be employed in cases where children have to testify about sexual acts. The commission also pointed out that many other professional groups like social workers and psychologists are more than willing to share their knowledge and experience with prosecutors.

Legislative Implementation of the South African Law Commission's Report

The report of the South African Law Commission had a dramatic effect in South Africa. Administrative measures were taken to offer specialized training courses to prosecutors to enable them to deal more effectively with child witnesses. The most far-reaching result, however, was achieved when Parliament adopted the commission's main recommendation, dealing with the treatment of child witnesses in court so as to protect them from the ravages of destructive cross-examination. In 1991, the following enactment (§ 170 A of the Criminal Procedure Act, 51 of 1977, as amended) was placed on the statute book:

Evidence through intermediaries. (1) Whenever criminal proceedings are pending before any court and it appears to such court that it would expose any witness under the age of 18 years to undue mental stress or suffering if he testifies at such proceedings, the court may, subject to subsection (4), appoint a competent person as an intermediary in order to enable such witness to give his evidence through that intermediary.

(2)(a) No examination, cross-examination or re-examination of any witness in respect of whom a court has appointed an intermediary under subsection (1), except examination by the court, shall take place in any manner other than through that intermediary.

(b) The said intermediary may, unless the court directs otherwise, convey the general purport of any question to the relevant witness.

(3) If a court appoints an intermediary under subsection (1), the court may direct that the relevant witness shall give his evidence at any place—

(a) which is informally arranged to set that witness at ease;

(b) which is so situated that any person whose presence may upset that witness, is outside the sight and hearing of that witness; and

(c) which enables the court and any person whose presence is necessary at the relevant proceedings to see and hear, either directly or through the medium of any electronic or other devices, that intermediary as well as that witness during his testimony.

(4)(a) The Minister may by notice in the Gazette determine the persons or the category or class of persons who are competent to be appointed as intermediaries.

(b) An intermediary who is not in the full-time employment of the State shall be paid such travelling and subsistence and other allowances in respect of the services rendered by him as the Minister, with the concurrence of the Minister of Finance, may determine.

Conclusion

The legal enactment just cited took effect on July 30, 1993. According to informal reports so far received from prosecutors, magistrates, and police officers, the new system is being implemented with marked success.

However, it is hoped that the new system is only the beginning of a tradition to protect the legal rights of the child in South Africa. To firmly establish such a tradition, there are especially two prerequirements. First, it is important to have a daily monitoring system to ensure that the present system is used to the fullest. Second, an ongoing research program to determine the weaknesses and strengths of the system should be introduced. Such steps could only contribute to keeping South Africa in the forefront of legal systems that are concerned about the protection of child witnesses. After all, South Africa, with its tragic history of violation of human rights, owes it to the world.

References

Ceci, S. J., & Bruck, M. (1993). Suggestibility of the child witness: A historical review and synthesis. *Psychological Bulletin, 113,* 403-439.

Hammond, J. C., & Hammond, E. J. (1987). Justice and the child witness. *South African Journal of Criminal Law and Criminology, 11,* 3-20.

Key, J. J. A. (1988, January). The child witness: The battle for justice. *De Rebus,* pp. 54-58.

Grey, E. (1991). Die gemolesteerde kind as getuie [The molested child as witness]. *Koers, 56,* 77-91.

R. v. Manda, 3 SA 158 AD (1951).

South African Law Commission. (1991, February). *Report on the protection of child witnesses.* Pretoria, South Africa: Government Printer.

Spencer, J. R., & Flin, R. C. (1990). *The evidence of children: The law and psychology.* London: Blackstone.

Swanepoel, H. M., & Wessels, P. J. (1992). *'n Praktiese benadering tot die Wet op Kindersorg* [A practical to the law of child care]. Pretoria, South Africa: Digma.

Woji v. Santam Insurance Co. Ltd., 1 SA 1020 AD (1981).

Zieff, P. (1991). The child victim as witness in sexual abuse cases—A comparative analysis of the law of evidence and procedure. *South African Journal of Criminal Justice, 4,* 21-43.

11

Children's Evidence
Mandating Change in the Legal System of Hong Kong

TING-PONG HO

The public's attention is often turned toward the plight of abused children, and child care workers often respond to promote children's rights and protection. Hong Kong is no exception.

Before the enactment of the Protection of Women and Juveniles Ordinance in 1951, protection of children from abuse in Hong Kong was primarily focused on the sexual exploitation of girls (Wingfield, 1987). On October 5, 1978, a 10-year-old girl weighing 40 pounds, with multiple bruises, cigarette burns, fractured ribs, and tufts of hair ripped out, stum-

AUTHOR'S NOTE: This chapter would not have been possible without the expert advice and information provided by Grenville Cross from the Attorney General's Chamber, Yuk-Shan Lee from the Child Protective Services Unit, Priscillia Lui from Against Child Abuse, Roger Booth and Eddie Li from the Royal Hong Kong Police, Janice Brabyn and James Garrity from the Law Faculty of the University of Hong Kong, Maggie Leung from the Social Welfare Department, and Deborah Wong from the Child Custody Services Unit. I am grateful to the librarian of the Supreme Court Library for permission to access the library facilities. Although every effort has been made to ensure that the chapter is factually correct, any errors are mine.

bled into a police station. When the injuries were discovered to be the result of repeated battering at home, outcries raged in the community. Two months later, a voluntary agency, Against Child Abuse, was created. Public education programs, counseling, and hotline services were set up. In 1980, the first interdisciplinary working group on child abuse met. One year later, the Social Welfare Department issued guidelines to handle child abuse cases. In June 1983, the Child Protective Services Unit (CPSU) was established to provide intensive casework for children whose safety is endangered. In 1986, the central registry for child abuse and neglect was opened. In 1993, the increase in child sexual abuse allegations in the territory and legislation changes in other parts of the world led to the establishment of an interdisciplinary committee to review the system regulating the giving of evidence by children in criminal proceedings in Hong Kong.

This chapter aims to review legal practices regarding child witnesses in cases of child abuse in Hong Kong. The official statistics of child abuse allegations and prosecutions will be described. This is followed by a review of the procedures for handling child abuse allegations, relevant legislation, and existing practices with regard to child witnesses in the territory. Recommendations from the Committee on the Evidence of Children in Criminal Proceedings (1994) in Hong Kong will be summarized and discussed.

Child Abuse Allegations and Prosecutions

There are no local epidemiological data on child abuse, but a glimpse of the extent of the problem is possible through the official statistics. In 1990, my colleagues and I conducted a study examining the characteristics of sexual abuse cases referred to child care workers in Hong Kong. A total of 134 sexual abuse cases was recorded from 1986 to 1989 (Ho & Lieh-Mak, 1992). Out of these 134 cases, 84 were known to police and only 17 were brought to the court. It was noteworthy that out of these 17 court cases, 6 had physical findings of sexual abuse.

In 1993, the CPSU managed a total of 326 child abuse cases in which physical abuse constituted the majority ($n = 239$), followed by sexual abuse ($n = 36$). The number of sexual abuse allegations and prosecutions known to the police and CPSU from 1991 to 1993 is listed in Table 11.1

TABLE 11.1 Number of Reported and Prosecuted Child Sexual Abuse Cases in Hong Kong, 1991–1993

Types of Cases	1991 Reported	1991 Prosecuted	1992 Reported	1992 Prosecuted	1993 Reported	1993 Prosecuted	1991–1993 Reported	1991–1993 Prosecuted
Police:								
Rape	57	35	40	21	35	15	132	71
Indecent assault	333	129	385	113	320	110	1,038	352
Unlawful sexual intercourse	335	193	356	210	333	204	1,024	607
Indecent conduct toward a child	10	1	9	4	11	2	30	7
Incest	3	2	10	7	6	4	19	13
Total	738	360	800	355	705	335	2,243	1,050
Child Protective Services Unit:								
Sexual abuse	7	2	21	8	36	12	64	22

(Royal Hong Kong Police & CPSU, personal communication, 1994). Overall, less than half the alleged cases were prosecuted. From these official figures, it is impossible to know how many alleged cases are substantiated after police investigation but not prosecuted. The difficulties of prosecution were explored through a review of CPSU case notes for 1991-1993. Out of the 42 nonprosecuted cases, 12 involved victims who were either mentally retarded ($n = 2$) or too young (below age of 7, $n = 10$) to give evidence in court, 8 cases had no corroborative evidence, and in the remaining cases children gave inconsistent statements or the allegations were "unfounded." Among the 22 prosecuted cases, only 3 required the child victim to give evidence in court. Successful prosecution usually relied on confessions of the aggressors or positive physical findings.

Two points merit elaborations from these official figures. First, even if all alleged sexual abuse cases are genuine, the absolute number is small relative to the 1.2 million population under age of 15 (Census and Statistics Department, 1992). The extent of unreported cases remains largely unknown. The legal implications and administrative difficulties of mandatory reporting of child abuse had been considered by a working group under the Secretary of Health and Welfare in 1983, but mandatory reporting remains unenforced in the territory. In the United States, reporting behaviors have been linked to perceived seriousness, fear of inducing harm by reporting, training background, and countertransference (Attias & Goodwin, 1985; Pollack & Levy, 1989; Zellman, 1990). Although these factors probably affect Hong Kong child care workers as well, research indicates that a lack of experience and ignorance regarding the identification of child abuse are primary obstacles to reporting in Hong Kong. Specifically, preliminary results of a survey of 478 child care workers in Hong Kong reveal that reporting is often problematic because workers (a) are unsure how to identify actual child abuse (58%), (b) fear disrupting the family-worker relationship (28%), (c) are confused about whom to report abuse to (20%), (d) feel that reporting is ineffective (13%), and (e) feel that reporting is a breach of confidentiality (10%) (Against Child Abuse, personal communication, 1994). To address the issue of identifying child abuse, the Working Group on Child Abuse (1992) published the *Guide to the Identification of Child Abuse*. This booklet described situations, behaviors, and signs that are conducive to, or possibly indications of, child abuse.

Second, prosecution of sexual abuse aggressors is not common. There are no fixed guidelines for the decision to prosecute in Hong Kong. Although it is often considered in the interest of the public to proceed on a case of child sexual abuse, lack of evidence and practical difficulties in producing children at court could be major obstacles (Hood, 1988). The above figures seemed to suggest that a large number of sexual abuse cases were not prosecuted because of the anticipated difficulties under present legal requirements and court procedures.

Handling of Child Abuse Allegations

The Social Welfare Department of Hong Kong issued standard procedural guidelines to handle child abuse allegations (Social Welfare Department, 1993a). In short, when notified of a suspected abuse case, an initial investigation will be taken either by the CPSU or other social agencies that happen to know the child or the family. A regionalized child abuse assessment team had been suggested in the past but the idea has not materialized. Where circumstances require, police will be informed and the suspected victim will be brought to a hospital for medical examination.

If the parents/guardians are uncooperative and the child appears to be in need of care and protection, the right of entry into premises, child assessment, detention in hospital, and place of refuge are provided in the Protection of Women and Juveniles Ordinance (1993, Amendment No. 25). The application of such orders can be made by police or social workers. In the ordinance, a child in need of care and protection refers to one

(a) who has been or is being assaulted, ill-treated, neglected or sexually abused; or (b) whose health, development or welfare has been or is being neglected or avoidably impaired; or (c) whose health, development or welfare appears likely to be neglected or avoidably impaired; or (d) who is beyond control, to the extent that harm may be caused to him or to others and who requires care or protection.

A multidisciplinary conference is usually called within 10 days to decide the nature of the case and the welfare plan of the child. Membership of the case conference consists of those with relevant knowledge of the child and the family. They usually include social workers, police officers, psychiatrists, pediatricians, and other child care workers. Because there is no designated team that conducts investigations, membership of the case conference changes for every case, even in the same hospital. It is not uncommon to find inexperienced staff attending the case conference. As a partial remedy, the Social Welfare Department published the *Guide to the Participants of the Multidisciplinary Case Conferences on Child Abuse* (Social Welfare Department, 1993b).

For established abuse or at-risk cases, the particulars of the child victim will be registered in the Child Protection Registry operated under the Social Welfare Department. Prosecution of the suspected perpetrator is often discussed in the conference but the decision rests primarily in the hands of police. Police are not compelled to launch a prosecution, although the decision to not prosecute is subjected to the possibility of judicial review. In the case of incest, a consent from the attorney general must be obtained before prosecution is instituted (Crimes Ordinance, 1993, sec. 51).

Overall, Hong Kong adopts the English legal system. If the prosecution is initiated and the accused is under age 18, the case will be transferred to juvenile court unless otherwise indicated. If the accused is over age 18, the case will be dealt with by the magistrate, district court, or High Court depending on the nature of offense. It usually takes 9 to 12 months for the case to be heard.

Existing Legislation Governing Children's Testimony

The relevant legislation that governs the evidential status of children in Hong Kong is found in sections 3 and 4 of the Evidence Ordinance (1992). Section 3 of the Evidence Ordinance provides: "The following persons only shall be incompetent to give evidence in any proceedings: (a) children under 7 years of age, unless they appear capable of receiving just impressions of the facts respecting which they are examined and of relating them truly."

Section 4 of the Evidence Ordinance (1992) provides:

> Where, in any proceeding against any person for an offense, any child of tender years who is tendered as a witness does not in the opinion of the court understand

the nature of an oath, the evidence of that child may be received, though not given upon oath, if, in the opinion of the court, the child is possessed of sufficient intelligence to justify the reception of the evidence, and understands the duty of speaking the truth; and the provisions of section 70[1] shall extend to the evidence of the child, though not given on oath, but otherwise taken and reduced into writing in accordance with the provisions of section 81[2] of the Magistrates Ordinance (Cap. [chap.] 227): Provided that—

(a) no person shall be liable to be convicted of the offense unless the testimony admitted by virtue of this section and given on behalf of the prosecution is corroborated by some other material evidence in support thereof implicating the accused; and

(b) any child, whose evidence is received as aforesaid and who willfully gives false evidence under such circumstances that, if the evidence had been given on oath, he would have been guilty of perjury, shall, subject to the provisions of the Juvenile Offenders Ordinance (Cap. 226), be liable on summary conviction to such punishment as might have been awarded had he been charged with the perjury and the case been dealt with summarily under section 8 of that Ordinance.

In 1991, the Bill of Rights Ordinance was enacted in Hong Kong. Although many of the rights guaranteed in the bill are derived from the International Covenant on Civil and Political Rights and may be found explicitly or implicitly in English common law, Hong Kong courts, from then on, had to deal with explicit and enforceable statutory rights (Bruce & McCoy, 1991). The rights of confrontation and cross-examination are embodied in Articles 11(2)(d) and 11(2)(e) of the bill. Article 10 of the bill guaranteed the rights of the accused to a fair and public hearing except "where the interest of juvenile persons otherwise requires or the proceedings concern matrimonial disputes or the guardianship of children." Provisions in other ordinances also empower the court to exclude the public if the interests of justice, public order, or security so require (Criminal Procedure Ordinance, 1993, sec. 122). In addition, section 11 of the Magistrates Ordinance (1993) provides that the magistrate may, where the evidence is of an indecent character, exclude the public provided that he or she delivers the determination in open and public court. Moreover, in any proceedings in any court, except insofar as the court otherwise permits, no person shall publish, broadcast the name, address, or school, or any particulars calculated to lead to the identification of a child witness (Juvenile Offenders Ordinance, 1991, sec. 20A).

In short, the circumstances where a child can be allowed to give evidence, the protection of child witnesses, and the rights of the accused are provided in the existing legislation. However, few provisions specifically address the difficulties child witnesses may face, especially in abuse cases.

Existing Practices Regarding Child Witnesses

Issue of Competency

There is no statutory definition of the expression "child of tender years" in section 4 of the Evidence Ordinance (1992). Indeed, the laws of Hong Kong have different definitions for the word *child*. For example, under the Reformatory Schools Ordinance (1991) and Juvenile Offenders Ordinance (1991), child means a person under the age of 14 years. Under the Employment Ordinance (1992) and Education Ordinance (1992), it is 15.

Whether a person is regarded as a child of tender years is a matter left to the discretion of the court. In *Chan Chi v. R.* (1968), a 14-year-old boy was a prosecution witness. The judge did not think the boy looked of tender years and said, "The Courts have never so far as I know decided exactly where to draw the line as regards [to] tender years and it well may be it need not be drawn as it is only necessary to know on which side of it a proposed witness falls. This could depend on other matters than years since birth." The appeal court added, "It may not be necessary or desirable to attempt to do so [to define child of tender years] and preferable merely to decide each case ad hoc as it arises."

In *Tam Hoi-hon v. R.* (1963), a 12-year-old prostitute had been sworn and evidence taken without some previous enquiry by the judge as to her capacity to understand an oath. The appeal court held that the child had attained a maturity considerably beyond that normally associated with a child of 12 years, and it was not incumbent on the judge to hold any formal or other enquiry before allowing her to be sworn. More recently, a case of murder (*R. v. Fung Kam-keung,* 1991) was appealed on the ground that the trial judge had erred in failing to inquire as to whether a 13-year-old witness was old enough or mature enough to understand the taking of an oath. The appeal court commented,

It is always at the discretion of the trial judge as to whether a child of tender years should be sworn. There is no absolute rule that a child in Hong Kong under 14

> must be the subject of an enquiry in the presence of the jury, before the judge can
> properly form an opinion whether to receive the child's unsworn evidence.

However, when the appeal was brought to the United Kingdom, the quoted judgment was not recommended to be followed: "Their Lordships consider that an enquiry should have been made and would not want to give countenance to children under the age of fourteen not being submitted to an enquiry and the judge not saying what the result of that enquiry was."

It appears that some form of competency assessment of child witnesses is recommended, and it has to be performed by the judge. In *R. v. Wong Yat-tan* (1990), the prosecutor questioned a 15-year-old witness as to her understanding of the truth. The practice was regarded as serious irregularity in the appeal court:

> The magistrate should not have permitted the prosecution (nor the defense had
> they applied) to ask her (the child witness) any questions on this subject. The duty
> to determine whether a witness is competent is solely that of the judge or
> magistrate.

The actual assessment performed may best be understood by examining the court recordings. In *Chung Kwong v. R.* (1959), the presiding judge asked a 9-year-old witness whether he understood the nature of an oath and the child answered, "I do not know what is an oath." Although it was unrecorded, the judge asked the child if he understood the duty of speaking the truth to which the child replied yes. The judge then decided that his evidence should be taken unsworn. In the appeal court, it was held that

> the section [sec. 4 of the Evidence Ordinance, 1992] does not itself lay down any
> particular procedure to be followed by the Court in order that it may form the
> opinion in question. . . . It is clearly desirable that the Judge should in fact record
> his conclusion on such a point and show how he has reached it.

However, the judgment does not imply that the assessment will not be challenged. In *R. v. Wong Yat-tan* (1990), the appeal court was not satisfied concerning whether the magistrate came to any conclusive view on the competency of the child witness, and it was not clear whether the witness was treated as affirmed or not affirmed. The enquiry was recorded as follows:

Q (magistrate)   Been in court before?

A (child)   No.

Q   Do you understand the importance of telling the truth?

A   What?

Q   (Repeat)

A   I don't know what to do.

Q   You have given oath?

A   I did not hear it.

Q   What just done?

A   I don't understand.

(Takes oath again)

Q   Understand that?

A   No.

Q   What am I required to do?

A   To tell the truth.

Q   Do you understand you are in the court and you have taken oaths to tell the truth?

A   But I don't know what truth is.

Q   Do you know what truth is?

A   No.

Thus, the controversies about child witnesses' competency focus on the age at which children should be assessed and how assessment should be performed.

Issue of Corroboration

Section 4 of the Evidence Ordinance (1992) states the unsworn evidence of a child is admissible if the child is sufficiently intelligent and understands the duty of speaking the truth. The trial judge has to direct the jury that unsworn evidence must be corroborated. The omission of this direction from the trial judge lead the appeal court to quash conviction in *Yeung Ming v. R.* (1966). Even so, sworn evidence from a child does not require corroboration as a matter of law, although the jury will be warned that it is dangerous to act on the uncorroborated testimony of a child (Bruce & McCoy, 1991).

Child Witnesses in Court

Although open court is the prevailing practice in Hong Kong, there are provisions and precedents to protect child witnesses from extreme embarrassment. In *Fan Siu-Man v. R.* (1986), a 15-year-old girl appeared very uneasy about giving evidence on a charge of indecent assault. The magistrate made an order to exclude the public from the trial. It was contended that the magistrate had no jurisdiction to close the court because "evidence which consists of a description of indecent acts is not itself of an indecent character." The appeal court ruled that oral evidence of indecency is just as much evidence of an indecent character as a written description, film, or three-dimensional representation of such indecency.

Although videorecordings can be admissible evidence in the courts of Hong Kong (*Li Shu-Ling v. R.,* 1986, in which video records concerned the confession of the accused; *Tam Wing-kwai v. R.,* 1976), video record of a child interview has never been submitted as court evidence. In a retrial of a case of indecent assault on a 10-year-old girl (*R. v. Lin Chun-wing,* 1991), the girl said some 38 times "I can't remember" when she was cross-examined about whether she had said something on a different occasion. It seemed that the quality of evidence was far from satisfactory, yet little was available to assist the child. Instead, the magistrate resorted to examining the notes of the previous trial. The appeal court considered it as a material irregularity and the conviction was quashed.

There is no family court in Hong Kong, and civil proceedings such as child custodial disputes are dealt with in the Supreme Court or district courts. The hearing is usually conducted in a formal manner, and the child is rarely called to give evidence.

Expert Witnesses

As in many other countries, evidence of opinion is inadmissible in the courts of Hong Kong. Expert evidence, in both criminal and civil proceedings, is one of the exceptions. In the case of civil proceedings, section 58(1) of the Evidence Ordinance (1992) provides that "where a person is called as a witness in any civil proceedings his opinion on any relevant matter on which he is qualified to give expert evidence shall be admissible in evidence."

There is a general reluctance to allow experts to give opinions as to matters that are for the courts to decide. For example, to determine whether a photograph is or is not indecent, obscene, revolting, or offensive, the magistrate must exercise the community's conscience and treat himself or herself as representing the community's feelings in the matter (*Yeung Kam-tsuen v. R.,* 1962). In *Pang Bing-yee v. R.* (1984), the appellant was charged with the murder of a 2-year-old child in her care. The defense sought to call psychiatrists to say that the appellant did not form the requisite intent to kill the baby at the time she inflicted the injury. The trial judge refused to admit the psychiatrists' reports as evidence. The appeal court held that the judgment of intent in this case did not fall outside the experience and knowledge of a judge and jury.

Although psychiatrists are often consulted in suspected child abuse cases, they are rarely called to give expert evidence in court. Psychiatric opinions will be incorporated in the minutes of the multidisciplinary conference. Whether these minutes will be submitted to the court is a decision made by the police. Clinical psychologists in the police force have developed a set of questioning techniques recommended for emotionally traumatized victims, children, and individuals with mental impairments (Tam, 1988). The essence of the questioning techniques consists of (a) assessment and preparation of the witness, (b) helping the individual to give a free-narrative account, and (c) examining statement authenticity. Over 70% of the cases in which these are applied are sex-related offenses (Li, 1990a). The decision to request help from the clinical psychologist is at the discretion of the police officers. Similar to that of psychiatrists, clinical psychologists are rarely summoned by the courts for expert testimony in child abuse cases. Nonetheless, the courts appear to be more receptive to the expert opinions of social workers in civil proceedings such as child custodial disputes.

The courts of Hong Kong do not rely on experts to testify on the truthfulness of a child's evidence. Many clinical techniques used to establish sexual abuse, like the use of anatomically correct dolls, remain largely uncontested in the courts of Hong Kong.

Proposed Changes and Their Implications

Realizing the various insufficiencies and difficulties of existing laws and practices governing child witnesses, especially in abuse cases, the Committee on the Evidence of Children in Criminal Proceedings was formed in 1993 in Hong Kong. The specific recommendations made by the committee (1994) are summarized and discussed in the following sections.

Age of Competence

The committee recommended that sections 3(a) and 4 of the Evidence Ordinance (1992) should be repealed. The presumption of a child's incompetence to testify should cease. Accordingly, the power of a court to determine that a particular person is not competent to give evidence shall apply to children as it applies to any other persons. All children should give their evidence unsworn. A child, here, refers to a person under the age of 14 years. This recommendation in no way affects the inherent power of the court to decide on the competency of any witness at any stage of his or her evidence, be that witness a child or an adult.

The recommendation, if put into practice, facilitates children, especially young children, to give unsworn evidence. Existing legislation basically does not allow children under age 7 to testify unless the trial judge determines otherwise. A "child of tender years" may give unsworn evidence but the clause is ambiguous and subject to dispute. The age of 14 is recommended as a cutoff in the report. It is compatible with the idea that from 14 onward, a juvenile is capable of having criminal intent (Juvenile Offenders Ordinance, 1991).

It seems the burden of proof with regard to the competency of children has shifted from that of presumed incompetence in existing legislation to that of assumed competence as recommended in the report. This lenient attitude, more comparable to that in the United States and the United Kingdom, does not completely eliminate the need for competency assessment. On the contrary, the court has to decide how much reliance to place on the child's evidence, and this has to rely, in part, on the competency of the child (Perry & Wrightsman, 1991). The decision can be a more complicated consideration than ruling on the admissibility of evidence.

The court retains broad discretion in reaching its competency decisions, but there is no guidance as to what it is expected to assess. As far as court records tell, the assessment varies from one judge to another. It can be anticipated that jurors, without legal training, may have a more varied attitude regarding the competency of a child witness and consequently different reliance on evidence coming from children.

Corroboration Requirement

The committee recommended that the requirement of corroborating evidence in unsworn testimony of a child should be abolished. The courts are obliged to give direction as to the dangers inherent in convicting the accused on the uncorroborated evidence of a child. The unsworn evidence of a child should be capable of corroborating the evidence, sworn or unsworn, given by any other person. The courts retain a general discretion in appropriate cases to issue a warning of the dangers of relying solely on the evidence of a child.

The obligatory corroboration requirement in unsworn evidence of children in present legislation has, in effect, made prosecution very difficult in sexual abuse cases involving young children and no physical evidence. Although child welfare rather than prosecution is the overriding concern in abuse cases, dropped prosecutions have been used as "evidence" of innocence by some abusers. This created serious difficulties in securing the welfare of the child victim, especially in intrafamilial abuse cases. On the other hand, the suggested cancellation of the corroboration rule is likely to lead the courts and jurors to weigh the child's evidence more carefully. The credibility of the child's evidence will become a greater concern and will be subjected to intense scrutiny in the courts. Rival experts may be called to attack or defend the evidence of the child. Experience in the West has shown that the practice can be costly, time-consuming, and run the risk of turning the experts into "hired guns" (King & Trowell, 1992). It remains to be tested if the courts of Hong Kong will admit these expert opinions, especially those in regard to the truthfulness of a child's evidence, in the future. Case precedents quoted above seem to suggest that the court would believe truthfulness of evidence is within the province of the judge or jurors, but there is no test case in the context of sexual abuse. There is still a lot of judicial disagreement over the issue in both the United Kingdom (Spencer & Flin, 1990) and the United States (Myers, 1992).

Television Video Link in Court

The committee recommended that child witnesses should be able to give evidence through a live television link at a trial if the offenses involve (a) sexual abuse, (b) physical abuse, or (c) cruelty to a child. In relation to offenses of sexual abuse, a child should be defined as a person under the age of 17 years. The use of television link is not to be treated as automatic in any case falling within the three categories and ought only to occur with the leave of the court. Practical procedures were recommended to reduce the stress to child witnesses. First, the child should only see the person speaking on the screen, and this will usually mean the head and shoulders of the judge or counsel. Second, there are guidelines for the identification of the accused. In case the accused is a member of the child's family, the identification should, if possible, be undertaken by another family member or familiar adult. The child should be able to identify the accused by way of closed-circuit television. In case the use of television link is considered to be inappropriate for identification of the accused, the child witness should be in the presence of the accused solely for the purpose of identification and only after the child's evidence is complete. However, the accused must be allowed to ask questions of the accuser, although the stress may be diminished by the use of television link.

Currently, the courts of Hong Kong have few specific provisions to accommodate child witnesses. The author recently saw an adolescent boy who attempted suicide because of the intense fear of facing the abuser in court, shame of reporting the abuse incidents in front of the public, and mounting training pressures from parents to ensure he spoke the right thing in court. How far the recommended television link can protect the child witness from undue stress in court proceedings remains to be seen. Experience in other countries has shown that the television link is not a complete solution and that it may even be one that leads to more vigorous cross-examination (Spencer & Flin, 1990). To the extent that the Bill of Rights Ordinance (1991) in Hong Kong guarantees that the accused has a statutory right of confrontation, test cases are likely to appear soon after the recommendation is put into practice. Furthermore, this provision is limited to the three defined categories of abuse. Child witnesses in other criminal proceedings are not given such "privileges," and they can be equally distressed.

It has to be noted that the recommendations still allow the accused to question the child if the defendant chooses not to be represented. This is slightly different from the practice in the United Kingdom in which the accused is not allowed to cross-examine the child witness. In the report, the committee clearly expressed their reluctance to compel anybody against his or her wishes to accept legal representation.

Videorecorded Evidence

To reduce the stress from repeated questioning, the committee recommended that a videorecorded interview of a child witness may be allowed if the alleged offense falls within one of the three categories of abuse. The court retains discretion as to whether to allow videorecorded evidence to be introduced. The child should be asked formally to adopt it at trial and must be available for cross-examination. If any matter has not been dealt with adequately, it should be opened to the party calling the witness to ask further questions. To ensure the quality of the videorecorded evidence, the recording should be conducted by trained personnel of the Royal Hong Kong Police and the Social Welfare Department, and a comprehensive guide for videorecording of interviews with children has to be adopted. Moreover, rules on the regulation and admissibility of videorecorded evidence has to be adopted locally.

The acceptance of videorecorded interviews as evidence in court could have implications regarding the staffing and training for and handling procedures of child abuse cases in Hong Kong. Trained personnel from the police and Social Welfare Department will be required to conduct videorecorded interviews that are supposed to replace examination by an advocate in open court. Most workers in Hong Kong do not have the experience necessary for this. The police force in Hong Kong ran structured training programs for selected officers to improve their skills and knowledge in handling victims of sexual assault and child abuse (Li, 1990b), but the program is not exactly designed for this purpose. The current practice of conducting investigation by those who happen to know the case is unlikely to meet the highly demanding jobs. It is hoped that expert assessment teams will be established if the recommendations are adopted.

Similar to the proposed television link, the child must be available for cross-examination even if videorecorded interviews are accepted as evidence. Thus, the proposed protection is not complete or absolute, but represents an attempt to balance the rights of the child and the accused.

Timing of Court Hearing

The committee recommended that once the prosecution notifies the magistrate of its intention to prosecute, the case should be committed for trial quickly. This procedure should apply to offenses falling within the three categories and involving child witnesses as defined. As a safeguard against any possible injustice, the accused must have the right to apply to a judge, before arraignment, to dismiss a charge if there is not sufficient evidence to justify a trial. This privilege is limited to child abuse cases only. It is hoped that reducing the waiting time to trial may improve the quality of children's evidence in courts.

Conclusion

In Hong Kong, systematic efforts to deal with child abuse began only in the late 1970s. Based on official statistics, the prevalence of child abuse, especially sexual abuse, is much lower than that reported in the West. Although there are guidelines to handle suspected abuse cases, a low awareness and a lack of experience in identification remain major obstacles to reporting. Only a fraction of alleged cases go to court, and very often, successful convictions are based on confessions of the aggressors or positive physical findings. The current court process is failing children who are victims of abuse and subjecting them to avoidable trauma. An interdisciplinary committee in Hong Kong proposed that the system regulating the evidential status of children requires restructuring. Their recommendations included changing the competence and corroboration requirements of children's evidence, introduction of television link in court, acceptance of videorecorded evidence, and reducing waiting time to court hearing. These recommendations represent a major step to facilitate children testifying. At the time of this writing, it remains unknown if all or part of the recommendations will be accepted, if these recommendations will be truly effective, or if concerned parties will take necessary steps to ensure a smooth transition.

Notes

1. Section 70 refers to the admissibility in evidence in criminal proceedings of the deposition of a dead person.

2. Section 81 of the Magistrates Ordinance refers to the taking of evidence at preliminary inquiry at magistrate.

References

Attias, R., & Goodwin, J. (1985). Knowledge and management strategies in incest cases: A survey of physicians, psychologists and family counselors. *Child Abuse & Neglect, 9,* 527-533.

Bruce, A., & McCoy, G. (1991). *Criminal evidence in Hong Kong* (2nd ed.). Hong Kong: Butterworths.

Bill of Rights Ordinance, Laws of Hong Kong. (1991).

Census and Statistics Department. (1992). *Annual digest of statistics, 1992.* Hong Kong: Hong Kong Government.

Chan Chi v. R., 61 HKLR (1968).

Chung Kwong v. R., 261 HKLR (1959).

Committee on the Evidence of Children in Criminal Proceedings. (1994). *The report of the committee on the evidence of children in criminal proceedings.* Unpublished report.

Crimes Ordinance, 200 Laws of Hong Kong. (1993).

Criminal Procedure Ordinance, 221 Laws of Hong Kong. (1993).

Education Ordinance, 279 Laws of Hong Kong. (1992).

Employment Ordinance, 8 Laws of Hong Kong. (1992).

Evidence Ordinance, 8 Laws of Hong Kong. (1992).

Fan Siu-Man v. R., 1001 Mag App (1986).

Ho, T.-P., & Lieh-Mak, F. (1992). Sexual abuse in Chinese children in Hong Kong: A review of 134 cases. *Australian and New Zealand Journal of Psychiatry, 26,* 639-643.

Hood, P. M. (1988). The prosecution file—Aspects of proof. In Zonta Club of Hong Kong (Ed.), *Proceedings of symposium on the sexual abuse of the mentally handicapped in Hong Kong* (pp. 50-54). Hong Kong: Zonta Club of Hong Kong.

Juvenile Offenders Ordinance, 226 Laws of Hong Kong. (1991).

King, M., & Trowell, J. (1992). *Children's welfare and the law: The limits of legal intervention.* London: Sage.

Li, E. K. W. (1990a). A profile of sexual assault victim referred to Force clinical psychologist. In F. Cheung, R. G. Andy, & R. C. Tam (Eds.), *Research on rape and sexual crimes in Hong Kong* (pp. 19-27). Hong Kong: Chinese University of Hong Kong, Institute of Social Studies.

Li, E. K. W. (1990b). Teaching police officers to handle victims of sexual assault and child abuse. In M. L. Ng & L. S. Lam (Eds.), *Sexuality in Asia* (pp. 161-172). Hong Kong: Hong Kong College of Psychiatrists.

Li Shu-Ling v. R., 1165 HKLR (1986).

Magistrates Ordinance, 227 Laws of Hong Kong. (1993).

Myers, J. E. B. (1992). *Legal issues in child abuse and neglect.* Newbury Park, CA: Sage.

Pang Bing-yee v. R., 298 HKLR (1984).

Perry, N. W., & Wrightsman, L. S. (1991). *The child witness: Legal issues and dilemmas.* Newbury Park, CA: Sage.

Pollack, J., & Levy, S. (1989). Countertransference and failure to report. *Child Abuse & Neglect, 13,* 515-522.

Protection of Women and Juveniles Ordinance, Amendment No. 25, 213 Laws of Hong Kong. (1993).

R. v. Fung Kam-keung, 377 HKLR (1991).

R. v. Lin Chun-wing, 589 Mag App (1991).

R. v. Wong Yat-tan, 1395 Mag App (1990).

Reformatory Schools Ordinance, 225 Laws of Hong Kong. (1991).

Social Welfare Department. (1993a). *Procedure for handling child abuse cases.* Unpublished manual.

Social Welfare Department. (1993b). *Guide to the participants of the multidisciplinary case conferences on child abuse.* Unpublished manual.

Spencer, J. R., & Flin, R. (1990). *The evidence of children: The law and the psychology.* London: Blackstone.

Tam, K. O. (1988). Psychological questioning techniques for obtaining testimony from the mentally handicapped. In Zonta Club of Hong Kong (Ed.), *Proceedings of symposium on the sexual abuse of the mentally handicapped in Hong Kong* (pp. 45-46). Hong Kong: Zonta Club of Hong Kong.

Tam Hoi-hon v. R., 20, HKLR (1963).

Tam Wing-kwai v. R., 401 HKLR (1976).

Wingfield, I. (1987). The role of the courts in the protection of children. In Organizing Committee of the MD Conference on Child Abuse (Ed.), *Combating child abuse—A multi-disciplinary responsibility* (pp. 119-124). Hong Kong: Organizing Committee of the MD Conference on Child Abuse.

Working Group on Child Abuse. (1992). *Guide to the identification of child abuse.* Hong Kong: Hong Kong Government Printer.

Yeung Kam-tsuen v. R., 663 HKLR (1962).

Yeung Ming v. R., 591 HKLR (1966).

Zellman, G. L. (1990). Report decision-making patterns among mandated child abuse reports. *Child Abuse & Neglect, 14,* 325-336.

12

Children on the Witness Stand

The Use of Expert Testimony and Other Procedural Innovations in U.S. Child Sexual Abuse Trials

MARGARET BULL KOVERA
EUGENE BORGIDA

As in all criminal litigation, perceptions of witness credibility play a significant role in cases involving adult sexual assault and child sexual abuse. To date, psycholegal researchers have focused on various individual and contextual variables that influence perceptions of credibility in cases involving allegations of child sexual abuse. Insofar as perceptions of credibility are linked to trial outcomes in these cases, it is not surprising that prosecutors and victim witness programs throughout North America have introduced procedural innovations aimed at enhancing the credibility

AUTHORS' NOTE: The research reported in this chapter was supported in part by a subcontract from the National Council of Jewish Women's Center for the Child and the National Center on Child Abuse and Neglect, Grant 90-CA-1273 and a University of Minnesota Graduate School Grant-in-Aid of Research. We are extremely grateful for the substantial contributions of our collaborators, April W. Gresham and Janet K. Swim, to this research. We also thank Bradley D. McAuliff for his thoughtful comments on an earlier version of this chapter.

of child witnesses or minimizing the stressfulness of a child's court appearance. These innovations have their critics. Indeed, a major obstacle to such innovations has been concerns about both the defendant's Sixth Amendment right to confrontation and the defendant's Fourteenth Amendment right to due process (*Coy v. Iowa,* 1988; *Maryland v. Craig,* 1990). The tension between protecting child witnesses from harm and preserving the constitutional rights of defendants is a significant feature of child sexual abuse trials in America today.

In our own research, we have examined the decision-making processes associated with several procedural innovations that have been designed to alleviate the stress experienced by child witnesses or to enhance the credibility of child sexual abuse victims. To understand the effects of procedural innovation, however, one must understand how jurors perceive child witnesses and render verdicts in cases in which these young witnesses play crucial roles. To this end, we first review studies that have examined perceptions of child witnesses in cases that do and do not involve child sexual abuse. It is important to review both sets of studies because the type of case (e.g., vehicular homicide, drug possession, child sexual abuse) has emerged as a potentially powerful contextual variable that influences mock jurors' perceptions of child witnesses.

Survey Research on Perceptions of Child Witnesses

The first researchers to examine the beliefs that individuals hold about the capabilities of child witnesses used survey methodology. Generally, respondents to these surveys indicated that they questioned the credibility of child witnesses. For example, Yarmey and Jones (1983) surveyed potential jurors, law students, psycholegal researchers, and legal professionals to examine their beliefs in the capabilities of a hypothetical 8-year-old witness. In general, respondents believed that the child was an unreliable, inaccurate witness who could be easily manipulated by any investigator. Psycholegal researchers were more likely to endorse these beliefs than were laypersons. However, one must keep in mind that these responses reflect perceptions of a hypothetical, average 8-year-old child and that in the context of a trial, jurors' perceptions of a child witness who has been prepared for the courtroom experience might be very different.

Similarly, respondents to a survey conducted by Leippe and Romanczyk (1989) held unfavorable beliefs about the capabilities of child witnesses.

Respondents were presented with descriptions of the conditions of the Marin, Holmes, Guth, and Kovac (1979) study in which children and adults attempted to identify the perpetrator of a staged theft. Subsequently, Leippe and Romanczyk's participants estimated the number of accurate eyewitness identifications made by participants in the Marin et al. study. Leippe and Romanczyk found that their participants consistently underestimated the accuracy of the participants in the Marin et al. study. Taken together with the research by Yarmey and Jones (1983), this study suggests that jurors believe children are less accurate and more suggestible than are older witnesses.

However, young children who testify in child sexual abuse cases may appear to be more credible than their older counterparts. Corder and Whiteside (1988) surveyed jurors in North Carolina to determine whether beliefs about children's abilities and about issues related to child sexual abuse differed as a function of witness age. These respondents believed that most children 3 years of age or older are capable of providing accurate testimony about sexual abuse. Their respondents viewed older children as more capable of lying about being sexually abused than children under 5, although 55% of the respondents thought that children as young as 3 were capable of fabricating sexual abuse allegations. Ninety-eight percent of jurors believed that a mental health professional can determine whether children's allegations of sexual abuse are false. Although these self-report data suggest that jurors may be unduly biased by the testimony of an expert psychologist, people are often unaware of the factors that influence their decisions (Nisbett & Wilson, 1979). Therefore, it is possible that jurors may not rely on an expert's testimony when rendering a verdict at trial.

Experimental Studies

Although these survey results are informative, it is unclear whether jurors would respond similarly to child witnesses when presented with the live testimony of a child in a trial context. Several researchers have conducted experimental studies that begin to address this issue. For example, Goodman and her colleagues (Goodman, Golding, Helgeson, Haith, & Michelli, 1987) conducted the first experiments to examine jurors' reactions to a child's testimony. Participants viewed a videotape of a vehicular homicide or murder trial in which the eyewitness was either 6, 10, or 30 years old. Participants rated the 6-year-old witness to be less perceptive, less accurate, and more easily manipulated than the adult. However, participants who heard the child's testimony, in conjunction with other evidence, were as likely to render guilty verdicts as were participants who heard testimony from an adult eyewitness. Therefore, Goodman et al. concluded that participants did not disregard the child's testimony, they merely gave a child's testimony less weight when determining their verdict. An identical pattern of results was found for college undergraduates and a more representative sample of potential jurors from the community. Results also converged whether the crime was vehicular homicide or murder (Goodman et al., 1987).

Leippe and Romanczyk (1989) also conducted a series of four experiments in which they demonstrated that jurors believe children make unreliable witnesses. In one study, these researchers manipulated eyewitness age (6, 10, or 30 years old) and the strength of the prosecution's case (weak, ambiguous, or strong) in a description of a robbery-murder case. The findings from this study replicated Goodman et al.'s (1987) findings that children are perceived to be less credible than adults. Unlike Goodman et al., however, Leippe and Romanczyk (Study 2, 1989) found that the age of the eyewitness did affect the number of guilty verdicts that participants rendered, particularly when the other evidence in the case was strong. Specifically, when the case for the prosecution was strong, participants were more likely to convict if an adult eyewitness testified than if either a 6- or a 10-year-old testified. The age of the eyewitness did not influence participants' verdicts when the strength of the prosecution's case was moderate or weak.

In their next experiment, Leippe and Romanczyk (Study 3, 1989) presented participants with a description of a mugging-murder case in which they varied eyewitness age (6, 10, or 30 years old) as well as the consistency of the eyewitness testimony provided. These researchers found that witness inconsistency negatively affected participants' credibility ratings of the 6-year-old witness but had no effect on their ratings of the 10- or 30-year-old witness's credibility. Consistent with Goodman et al. (1987), Leippe and Romanczyk found that eyewitness age did not influence the frequency of guilty verdicts. In a similar experiment, Leippe and Romanczyk (Study 4, 1989) manipulated the eyewitness age (6 or 30 years old) and the consistency of the eyewitness's testimony; however, in this study, the researchers attempted to make the eyewitness's speech style consistent with their age (e.g., the 6-year-old's testimony contained childlike phrases). In contrast with earlier studies, jurors perceived a 6-year-old child to be more credible than an adult witness. Leippe and Romanczyk suggest that these contradictory results were obtained because jurors underestimate the abilities of child witnesses and therefore were impressed with the coherence and quality of the child's testimony relative to their stereotypes about a typical child's performance.

Ross, Dunning, Toglia, and Ceci (1990) presented participants with a brief videotaped simulation (Study 1) or a written transcript (Study 2) of a drug possession trial in which the key prosecution witness was either 8, 21, or 74 years old. Participants judged the child witness to be more credible than either the 21- or the 74-year-old witness, irrespective of the trial medium. Participants also judged the elderly witness to be more credible than the young adult witness. Participants indicated that they believed the child witness and the elderly witness were somewhat less likely to give accurate testimony than was the young adult witness, but were likely to be more honest and trustworthy than was the young adult witness. Ross et al. suggest that although the participants could have viewed the young adult witness as a potential accomplice to the alleged drug transaction, it is less likely that the participants viewed the 8- or the 74-year-old witnesses as potential accomplices. Other researchers have also demonstrated that under certain conditions, jurors judge children to be more credible than adults (Leippe & Romanczyk, Study 3, 1989).

Several authors (Bottoms & Goodman, 1994; Leippe & Romanczyk, 1987, 1989; Ross et al., 1990) have argued that a persuasion framework is useful for understanding the inconsistent findings in the child witness literature. Specifically, these authors have argued that the trial context influences jurors' appraisals of child witnesses by influencing their judgments of children's memorial capabilities and trustworthiness. Indeed, social psychologists have generally conceived of credibility as a multidimensional construct consisting of expertise and trustworthiness dimensions (McGuire, 1985). Thus, in the absence of indicators such as the consistency of the child's testimony (e.g., Leippe, Manion, & Romanczyk, 1992; Leippe & Romanczyk, 1989) or the powerfulness of the child's speech (e.g., Nigro, Buckley, Hill, & Nelson, 1989), jurors may judge a child's credibility to be a function of the child's age because the child's age provides information about the likely memorial capabilities (i.e., expertise) of the child. However, some trial factors (e.g., type of case) may direct jurors' attention to the trustworthiness of the witnesses; this possibility seems especially likely when the witness is the alleged victim of the crime at issue.

Juror Perceptions of Child Victims

If jurors judge the credibility of a child witness by assessing the probable accuracy of the testimony and the probable honesty of the child, child witnesses in sexual abuse cases may be scrutinized with regard to a different set of criteria than are young eyewitnesses in other types of trials. For example, an average child's knowledge of sexual details at a particular age may play an important role in jurors' evaluations of whether the child has the ability to fabricate the allegation and thereby could affect jurors' ratings of the child's trustworthiness and credibility. Or jurors may question the child's ability to differentiate between fantasy and reality—an ability that is rarely at issue with older witnesses—and therefore devote particular attention to indications of the accuracy of the child's testimony. Given the competing possibilities suggested by this persuasion framework, it is necessary to examine jurors' perceptions of child witnesses within the context of child sexual abuse cases to determine the factors that might affect a child's credibility in that particular type of case. Witness credibility is especially important in child sexual abuse trials. Due to the nature of child sexual abuse, material evidence is seldom found. Because it is a secretive crime, there are often only two witnesses: the child and the alleged perpetrator. Thus, the child witness's credibility becomes a key aspect of the prosecution's case (McCord, 1986). Jurors' standards for the child witness's demeanor and their expectations about how a child witness should talk and act on the stand should strongly influence assessments of the credibility of a child witness.

Several researchers have begun to examine factors that affect the perception of a child witness's credibility in child sexual abuse cases. For example, Duggan et al. (1989) presented potential jurors with a videotaped simulation of a child sexual abuse trial. In the trial simulation, Duggan et al. manipulated both the age of the victim/witness and the strength of an adult's versus a child's corroborative testimony. Jurors who viewed the 9-year-old victim were more likely to convict the defendant than jurors who viewed the 5- or 13-year-old victim. The jurors who viewed the 13-year-old victim were the least likely to render a guilty verdict. Jurors' ratings of the credibility of the victim/witness followed the same pattern found in their verdicts. Although Duggan et al. did not report data on either the perceived trustworthiness or accuracy of the child witness, it is possible that participants believed both that the 5-year-old was less capable of providing veridical testimony (e.g., Leippe, Brigham, Cousins, & Romanczyk, 1989) and that the 13-year-old was more likely to fabricate (i.e., less trustworthy) than the 9-year-old witness. Indeed, subsequent research confirms that participants attribute more responsibility for the sexual abuse to older victims than they do to younger victims (Isquith, Levine, & Scheiner, 1993).

Bottoms and Goodman (1994) demonstrated that in child sexual abuse cases, a witness's credibility is likely to be an inverse function of witness age. In one study, Bottoms and Goodman (Study 1, 1994) had participants read a one-page description of an alleged sexual assault case in which the victim's age was varied (i.e., the witness was either 6, 14, or 22 years old). The victim alleged that her teacher called her into his classroom after school on the pretense of discussing class grades but instead forced her to perform an act of oral copulation. Participants judged the 6-year-old victim to be significantly more credible than the 22-year-old victim. Participants' ratings of the 14-year-old's credibility did not differ from their credibility ratings of the other two witnesses. In a different and necessarily less well-controlled study, participants who watched actual depositions from two alleged sexual abuse victims judged the younger child to be a more credible witness than the older child (Bottoms & Goodman, Study 3, 1994). Although these effects of witness age on perceptions of child victim credibility are not always reliable (e.g., Bottoms & Goodman, Study 2, 1994), trial factors that heighten the salience of witness trustworthiness (e.g., child sexual abuse allegations) may result in an inverse relationship between witness age and witness credibility.

Procedural Innovations That Influence Mock Juror Judgments in Child Sexual Abuse Cases

Because medical evidence of sexual abuse is often not available (Herbert, 1987; Mian, Wehrspann, Klajner-Diamond, LeBaron, & Winder, 1986), an allegation of sexual abuse may be based primarily on a child's claims. In these cases, jurors' perceptions of a child witness's credibility play a role in jurors' determinations of the defendant's guilt (Goodman,

Bottoms, Herscovici, & Shaver, 1989). With assumptions about the importance of child credibility in mind, child advocates have used various procedural innovations that might enhance the perceived credibility of a child (e.g., expert psychological testimony). Moreover, some advocates have sought to protect child sexual abuse victims from the psychological trauma that might result from a court appearance and the diminished credibility that might accompany an in-court demonstration of distress. It is thought, for example, that children might be protected by the videotaping of their testimony for later viewing at trial or by presenting their testimony via closed-circuit television. Our research team has examined the nature of the psychological processes associated with three legal tools that may indeed affect jurors' perceptions of a child witness: expert psychological testimony, witness preparation, and videotaped testimony. The results of these investigations are discussed in the next few sections.

Expert Testimony

Psychological researchers have begun to examine the possible effects of different types of expert testimony that are offered in child sexual abuse cases (e.g., McCord, 1986; Sagatun, 1991). For example, expert testimony about child sexual abuse accommodation syndrome (Summit, 1983) has been used to explain a child's counterintuitive reactions to child sexual abuse (e.g., delays in reporting, recanting allegations). An assumption of this type of syndromal testimony is that children who have been victimized exhibit prototypical responses such as delays in reporting the abuse, a fear of men, and nightmares with assaultive content; if a child exhibits these prototypical behaviors, a psychologist may infer that abuse has occurred. In a few cases, expert psychologists have testified about a child witness's credibility (e.g., State v. Kim, 1982). In this type of testimony, an expert directly addresses the alleged victim's credibility as a witness without addressing the ultimate issue of the trial (i.e., whether the defendant is guilty). The assumption underlying credibility testimony is that clinical experience with child sexual abuse victims provides a sound foundation for making judgments of credibility. In State v. Batangan (1990), however, the Supreme Court of Hawaii overturned the Kim decision. According to this ruling, expert psychological testimony can be introduced to rehabilitate the complainant's credibility, but not to establish directly that the complainant is truthful. In addition, experts sometimes testify about the details of clinical interviews with children during which anatomically detailed (AD) dolls are used as an investigative tool (Sagatun, 1991). Some investigators assume that because children generally do not have detailed sexual knowledge, only children who have been sexually abused will demonstrate sexual acts with AD dolls; other investigators have argued that AD dolls should be viewed only as a communicative tool and not as a diagnostic one (for a discussion of this controversy, see Everson & Boat, 1994).

These kinds of expert testimony differ in their reliance on probabilistic evidence (i.e., evidence on general characteristics of abuse victims). Syndromal testimony is based on group probability data; this type of testimony—in its standard form—does not seem to have an effect on juror judgments in adult sexual assault cases (Brekke & Borgida, 1988). However, credibility and AD doll testimony are based on often vivid case histories (i.e., specific information about a particular child victim), and research suggests that under certain circumstances, vivid as opposed to pallid information can be influential and persuasive (e.g., Frey & Eagly, 1993). In contrast, Imwinkelreid (1981) has argued that the effect of expert testimony depends on whether that testimony is based on a technique that relies on a visual display of information or on the judgment of an expert. If his hypothesis is correct, then AD doll testimony should have a greater effect on juror judgments of witness credibility than would syndromal or credibility testimony.

To examine whether different types of expert psychological testimony result in different perceptions of child witnesses or cause other trial judgments to differ, Kovera, Levy, Borgida, and Penrod (1994) presented jurors with a videotaped simulation of a child sexual abuse trial in which the type of expert testimony proffered (e.g., none, syndromal, witness credibility, and AD doll) was varied. Participants then made a variety of judgments regarding the trial and the trial participants. A key finding of this research was that expert evidence influenced participants' judgments: Those participants who heard expert testimony—irrespective of type— were more likely to convict the defendant than were participants who did not hear expert testimony. That expert testimony influences decision making in the child sexual abuse domain is consistent with research findings demonstrating the influence of expert testimony on juror decision making in other domains, including eyewitness identification (Cutler, Dexter, & Penrod, 1989; Cutler, Penrod, & Dexter, 1989) and sexual assault (Brekke & Borgida, 1988).

The probabilistic content of the expert's testimony in the Kovera et al. (1994) study *did* appear to moderate the effect of the expert on participants' judgments, as had been hypothesized. Participants' ratings of the expert and her testimony were less positive when the expert presented syndromal evidence (i.e., probabilistic information) than when she presented credibility or AD doll evidence (i.e., case history information). In particular, participants judged the syndromal expert evidence to be less important and less helpful than both the credibility and AD doll expert evidence. Moreover, participants actually recalled less of the evidence presented by the syndromal expert. Given the pattern of results, it seems that participants were less influenced by syndromal testimony because it is based on how well an alleged victim's behavioral responses match characteristics of abuse victims more generally, as opposed to more anecdotal evidence offered by an expert psychologist about the alleged victim's credibility or the truthfulness of her report of abuse. It is important to note that although expert evidence type influenced some participant judgments, it did not affect either participants' verdicts in the case or participants' ratings of the alleged victim. It is possible that the high conviction rates in all expert testimony conditions constrained the detection of the differential influence of expert evidence types. However, the Kovera et al. study suggests that expert testimony involving AD dolls and witness credibility does seem to influence decision making in a direction that is favorable to the child witness (i.e., a pro-prosecution shift in judgments) by influencing participants' perceptions of the expert and her testimony.

Child Witness Age and Expert Testimony

Research suggests that jurors judge adolescents to be less credible than younger children in a sexual assault case (Duggan et al., 1989; Bottoms & Goodman, 1994). However, few researchers have examined evidentiary variables that may enhance or diminish the influence of age on decision making. For example, little is known about how jurors' perceptions of children who differ in age might be affected by the presentation of expert testimony about typical reactions to child sexual abuse. Jurors may be more trusting of older children, who are typically perceived as less trustworthy when testifying about child sexual abuse (Bottoms & Goodman, 1994; Duggan et al., 1989), if an expert testifies that the child's behavior indicated that she had been sexually abused. Although two studies have varied both witness age and the presence of expert testimony in a single trial scenario (Crowley, O'Callaghan, & Ball, 1994; Gabora, Spanos, & Joab, 1993), the ages of the children in these scenarios present problems for a persuasion analysis of their findings. The witnesses in Crowley et al. (1994) were 12 years old or younger, and the witnesses in Gabora et al. (1993) were 13 and 17 years old. Because participants believe children are unlikely to have detailed sexual knowledge until they are over the age of 12 (Isquith et al., 1993; Scheiner, 1988), neither study allows for a comparison between jurors' perceptions of children who presumably are able to fabricate allegations of abuse and their perceptions of children who presumably would be unable to fabricate. If one expects that expert testimony will enhance the perceived trustworthiness of a child witness, it is crucial to compare jurors' perceptions of child witnesses who vary in their perceived trustworthiness (e.g., children who are younger and older than 12).

A social psychological model of persuasion like the heuristic systematic model (HSM) of persuasion (Chaiken, Liberman, & Eagly, 1989) suggests that jurors may rely on their heuristic beliefs about children and as a result differentially perceive child witnesses in the absence of expert testimony. However, this general model of persuasion also suggests that expert testimony may enhance jurors' ability to evaluate systematically the evidence presented at trial, thereby reducing the effect of the child's age on juror judgments (see Brekke, Enko, Clavet, & Seelau, 1991). Therefore, we designed a study to investigate whether expert testimony serves as a persuasion cue for systematic processing of the evidence and thereby lessens the influence of jurors' heuristic beliefs about children's capabilities on juror judgments (Kovera & Borgida, 1992).

In this study, participants watched a 3½-hour videotape simulation of a child sexual abuse trial. The child witness was played by either an 8-year-old or 14-year-old actress. The type of expert psychological testimony was varied orthogonally with the age of the child witness. In the standard testimony, the expert described the typical set of victim reactions to child sexual abuse, including behaviors such as nightmares and delays in reporting the allegation (i.e., standard syndromal testimony). In the hypothetical condition, after the expert presented the standard summary of the psychological research, the prosecuting attorney described a hypothetical abuse scenario that closely paralleled the case fact pattern. The expert was then asked to discuss the implications of the psychological research for this hypothetical scenario.

In the absence of expert testimony, jurors were more likely to convict the defendant when the child witness was 14 than when the child was 8. Moreover, jurors who did not view expert testimony were more likely to find the evidence to be consistent with the alleged victim's story when the child was 14 than when she was 8. Finally, in the absence of expert testimony, the age of the victim was less important to jurors who viewed a 14-year-old witness than to jurors who viewed an 8-year-old witness. However, jurors who viewed the 8-year-old witness judged her to be more likable than did jurors who viewed the 14-year-old witness. The child witness's age did not influence any juror judgments when jurors were presented with expert psychological testimony of either type (i.e., standard or hypothetical).

As suggested by the HSM, jurors' beliefs about children's witnessing capabilities affect juror judgments. In particular, jurors' ratings of the evidence, the child witness, and the trial outcome differed as a function of the child witness's age in the absence of expert testimony. Our findings indicate that for some judgments, a 14-year-old witness is judged more favorably; for other judgments, an 8-year-old witness is judged more favorably. Further analyses suggested that these differences may be explained by the heuristics that mediate specific judgments, specifically, whether the beliefs are about the memorial capabilities of children or about children's ability to differentiate between fantasy and reality. Moreover, the effects of the child witness's age on juror judgments appear to be attenuated by the introduction of either standard or hypothetical expert testimony. To the extent that jurors' beliefs about children's capabilities are sometimes inaccurate, it appears that expert testimony provides jurors with information about children and their behavior that counteracts their previous beliefs about children's witnessing abilities.

Although informative, these studies of the influence of expert testimony in child sexual abuse cases did not address a central scientific question in the debate surrounding expert testimony (Saks, 1992): Does expert testimony educate the jury (i.e., provide jurors with critical information needed to make an informed decision) or does such testimony prejudicially influence the jury (i.e., bolster a witness's testimony, irrespective of whether the trial evidence is congruent with the expert's testimony)? We chose to address this question by investigating the effect of expert testimony in cases in which the preparation of the child witness for the courtroom experience seemed to differ.

Witness Preparation

Although some prosecutors believe that jurors rely on a victim's emotions to make determinations about credibility (Limber & Etheredge, 1989), one prosecutorial strategy for increasing witness credibility involves spending time with child witnesses to better prepare them for the courtroom experience and to ensure that they maintain their composure when testifying and provide consistent responses to questions (Kovera, Gresham, Borgida, Gray, & Regan, 1995; Saywitz & Snyder, 1993). A child who has been prepared for the courtroom experience and has become comfortable in that environment might appear more confident, composed, and credible. Not only might he or she demonstrate behaviors indicative of greater poise, but he or she might also provide coherent testimony relatively free from hesitancies and nonfluencies.

In the absence of expert testimony, jurors may evaluate the child's credibility by determining how well the child's testimony matches expectations about the events involved in an instance of sexual abuse (Leippe & Romanczyk, 1987). For example, jurors, relying on their preconceived beliefs and expectations, may infer that a child who nervously fidgets while testifying about abuse is lying, because people tend to believe that nervousness and fidgeting are behavioral indicants of deception (e.g., Zuckerman, DePaulo, & Rosenthal, 1981). If jurors have heard an expert testify that sexually abused children often appear nervous and uncertain when describing their experience, they may be more likely to believe a child who nervously fidgets on the stand (e.g., an unprepared child) because her behavior is congruent with the typical behavior of abuse victims. Indeed, a child who is confident and poised (i.e., prepared) during his or her testimony may be judged a liar by jurors who have heard expert evidence suggesting that this is atypical behavior for an abuse victim.

Therefore, we had participants watch a simulated trial in which the actress portraying the child witness acted either more prepared (e.g., the child made eye contact, sat still, and responded confidently) or less prepared (e.g., the child looked down, fidgeted, and responded hesitantly) for her testimony (Kovera et al., 1995). The trial contained no expert testimony, standard syndromal expert testimony, or testimony that explicitly linked the psychological research with the trial evidence (hypothetical expert testimony). In both expert testimony conditions, the expert explained that the combination of a child's fear, guilt, and lack of sexual knowledge often results in a child appearing confused and hesitant when describing sexual abuse. Therefore, the less prepared child's behavior was congruent with the expert's description of typical victim behavior, whereas the more prepared child's behavior was incongruent with the expert's description.

As expected, jurors who heard hypothetical expert testimony were more likely to make pro-prosecution judgments when a child witness's behavior was congruent with the expert's testimony (i.e., less prepared) than when her behavior was incongruent with that testimony (i.e., more prepared). Specifically, those jurors who viewed hypothetical expert testimony judged the child's mother to be more credible, judged the defendant to be less credible, and were more likely to convict when the child witness was less prepared than when the child was more prepared. Conversely, jurors who heard standard testimony were more likely to make pro-prosecution judgments when the child's behavior was incongruent with the expert's testimony (e.g., more prepared) than when it was congruent. That is, jurors who heard standard expert testimony rated the prosecution witness (e.g., the mother) more favorably, rated the defendant less favorably, and were more likely to convict when the child was less prepared.

Therefore, standard expert testimony had the greatest influence on juror judgments when the child witness's demeanor was incongruent with the description provided by the expert (i.e., when the child was more prepared). It appears that when standard expert testimony was presented, jurors used this corroborative testimony to bolster the testimony of the more prepared child witness—a witness who may already be seen as more credible than the less prepared child witness. These findings suggest that the explicit link between the psychological research and the alleged victim's behavior that is provided exclusively in the hypothetical expert testimony is indeed an important key to understanding the process by which expert testimony influences decision making. It appears that the concrete link provided in the hypothetical testimony enables jurors not just to use the information provided by the expert but to use the information when it is appropriate to do so (i.e., where juror misconceptions about human behavior shape their perceptions of witness credibility).

We also conducted analyses to determine whether jurors' attention to certain topics in their deliberations mediated the interactive effect of expert testimony and witness preparation on juror judgments. According to these mediational analyses, the child witness's perceived motivations constitute the single most important variable that mediates the effect of expert testimony on juror judgments. That is, expert testimony specifically focuses jurors' attention on the child witness's behavior and her motivations for alleging sexual abuse occurred—issues that were specifically addressed by the expert when she testified. It is the discussion of these specific topics that influences jurors' ultimate decisions about the alleged victim, the defendant, and the verdict. In sum, these data suggest that hypothetical expert testimony enables jurors to think more systematically about the evidence presented at trial.

Videotaped Testimony

Many have expressed concern about the stress created for a child by requiring that child to testify in the physical presence of the defendant (Goodman, Levine, Melton, & Ogden, 1991). Videotaped depositions and closed-circuit camera coverage have been proposed as alternative methods of presenting a child's testimony that could alleviate the stress experienced by a child on the witness stand (Hill & Hill, 1987). However, if jurors suspect that videotaped depositions are being used so that the child does not have to speak in front of the defendant, maybe to prevent the defendant from scaring the child, then jurors may be more likely to conclude that the defendant is guilty. Alternatively, a persuasion analysis of the likely effects of videotaped depositions suggests that videotaped testimony may actually harm the prosecution's case. For example, if a child testifies on videotape, jurors may believe that the child cannot withstand the scrutiny of a trial process; therefore, the videotaped deposition may increase the salience of the child's trustworthiness (or lack thereof).

Only a few studies have examined these issues. Swim, Borgida, and McCoy (1993), for example, presented jurors with a videotape of a child sexual abuse case in which the child's testimony was given in court or via a videotaped deposition. This experimental manipulation of the medium of presentation had little effect on juror judgments. The one significant effect of presentation medium indicated that jurors were more likely to render guilty verdicts when the child testified in court than when her testimony was presented via videotape. These findings suggest that the credibility of child witnesses may be undermined by such a "mediated" form of presentation. Other research has demonstrated a similar influence of mediated presentations of child witness testimony on verdicts (Ross et al., 1994; Tobey, Goodman, Batterman-Faunce, Orcutt, & Sachsenmaier, 1995).

Conclusions

We have argued—as have others (e.g., Bottoms & Goodman, 1994; Leippe & Romanczyk, 1987, 1989; Ross et al., 1990)—that a persuasion framework is useful for understanding the seemingly inconsistent findings about how jurors make decisions about child witnesses. As in other areas of impression formation and decision making, jurors seem to assess the credibility of a child witness by assessing both the accuracy of the child's testimony and the trustworthiness of the child. Therefore, the trial context can influence jurors' appraisals of child witness credibility by making salient either children's memorial capabilities or their trustworthiness.

However, this depiction of juror decision making casts jurors in a rather passive role; that is, to assume that jurors' decisions are always affected by their beliefs about children's capabilities implies that jurors do not systematically process the evidence that is presented at trial. Clearly, theory and research in social psychology suggest that individuals are not passive recipients of information; rather, individuals actively engage in processing new information when they are motivated and able to do so (Chaiken et al., 1989; Petty & Cacioppo, 1986). Therefore, it is our opinion that to gain a deeper understanding of juror perceptions of child witness credibility, psycholegal researchers must begin to incorporate into their research variables that increase or decrease jurors' motivation or ability to process the evidence presented at trial.

Our research (Kovera & Borgida, 1992; Kovera et al., 1995) suggests that the application of persuasion theories to studying child witness credibility is warranted, especially when evaluating the potential effects of procedural innovations. For example, if we assume that expert testimony enhances jurors' ability to evaluate the trial evidence deliberately and carefully, then we should predict that trial variables such as witness age (Kovera & Borgida, 1992) or witness confidence (Kovera et al., 1995) would have a diminished effect on juror judgments. Indeed, our research findings support this interpretation. Other research has demonstrated that gender differences in perceptions of child victims (e.g., women find child sexual abuse victims to be more credible than do men) are in part due to women's greater empathy for these victims (Bottoms, 1993); perhaps these differences in empathy lead to different processing goals (e.g., women may be more motivated to process than are men), which in turn result in different perceptions of the child victim.

However, to determine whether persuasion models can offer useful predictions about juror perceptions of child witnesses, researchers will need to include measures of decision-making process, not just outcome measures (e.g., ratings of child credibility). Process measures directly address routinely expressed legal concerns about the potentially prejudicial effects of procedural innovations on juror decision making. Expert evidence, although scientifically reliable and valid, may still be ruled inadmissible if it prejudicially alters the trial *process* (McCord, 1986). Similarly, measures to protect children from the trauma of testifying in court (e.g., screens, closed-circuit television, videotaped depositions) may be ruled inadmissible if they prejudice the defendant's case (Swim et al., 1993). In this regard, contributing to an understanding of the processes by which procedural innovations influence decision making is crucial to the quality of justice dispensed to both victims and defendants.

References

Bottoms, B. L. (1993). Individual differences in perceptions of child sexual assault victims. In G. S. Goodman & B. L. Bottoms (Eds.), *Child victims, child witnesses: Understanding and improving testimony* (pp. 229-261). New York: Guilford.

Bottoms, B. L., & Goodman, G. S. (1994). Perceptions of children's credibility in sexual assault cases. *Journal of Applied Social Psychology, 24,* 702-732.

Brekke, N., & Borgida, E. (1988). Expert psychological testimony in rape trials: A social-cognitive analysis. *Journal of Personality and Social Psychology, 55,* 372-386.

Brekke, N. J., Enko, P. J., Clavet, G., & Seelau, E. (1991). Of juries and court-appointed experts: The impact of nonadversarial versus adversarial expert testimony. *Law and Human Behavior, 15,* 451-475.

Chaiken, S., Liberman, A., & Eagly, A. (1989). Heuristic and systematic information processing within and beyond the persuasion context. In J. S. Uleman & J. A. Bargh (Eds.), *Unintended thought* (pp. 212-251). New York: Guilford.

Corder, B. F., & Whiteside, R. (1988). A survey of jurors' perceptions of issues related to child sexual abuse. *American Journal of Forensic Psychology, 6,* 37-43.

Coy v. Iowa, 487 U.S. 1012 (1988).

Crowley, M. J., O'Callaghan, M. G., & Ball, P. G. (1994). The juridical impact of psychological expert testimony in a simulated child sexual abuse trial. *Law and Human Behavior, 18,* 89-105.

Cutler, B. L., Dexter, H. R., & Penrod, S. D. (1989). Expert testimony and jury decision making: An empirical analysis. *Behavioral Sciences and the Law, 7,* 215-225.

Cutler, B. L., Penrod, S. D., & Dexter, H. R. (1989). The eyewitness, the expert psychologist, and the jury. *Law and Human Behavior, 13,* 311-322.

Duggan, L. M., Aubrey, M., Doherty, E., Isquith, P., Levine, M., & Scheiner, J. (1989). The credibility of children as witnesses in a simulated child sexual abuse trial. In S. J. Ceci, D. F. Ross, & M. P. Toglia (Eds.), *Perspectives on children's testimony* (pp. 71-99). New York: Springer-Verlag.

Everson, M. D., & Boat, B. W. (1994). Putting the anatomical doll controversy in perspective: An examination of the major uses and criticisms of the dolls in child sexual abuse evaluations. *Child Abuse & Neglect, 18,* 113-129.

Frey, K. P., & Eagly, A. H. (1993). Vividness can undermine the persuasiveness of messages. *Journal of Personality and Social Psychology, 65,* 32-44.

Gabora, N. J., Spanos, N. P., & Joab, A. (1993). The effects of complainant age and expert psychological testimony in a simulated child sexual abuse trial. *Law and Human Behavior, 17,* 103-119.

Goodman, G. S., Bottoms, B. L., Herscovici, B. B., & Shaver, P. (1989). Determinants of the child victim's perceived credibility. In S. J. Ceci, D. F. Ross, & M. P. Toglia (Eds.), *Perspectives on children's testimony* (pp. 1-22). New York: Springer-Verlag.

Goodman, G. S., Golding, J. M., Helgeson, V., Haith, M., & Michelli, J. (1987). When a child takes the stand: Jurors' perceptions of children's eyewitness testimony. *Law and Human Behavior, 11,* 27-40.

Goodman, G. S., Levine, M., Melton, G. B., & Ogden, D. W. (1991). Child witnesses and the confrontation clause: The American Psychological Association brief in *Maryland v. Craig. Law and Human Behavior, 15,* 13-30.

Herbert, C. P. (1987). Expert medical assessment in determining probability of alleged child sexual abuse. *Child Abuse & Neglect, 11,* 213-221.

Hill, P. E., & Hill, S. M. (1987). Videotaping children's testimony. *Michigan Law Review, 85,* 809-833.

Imwinkelried, E. J. (1981). A new era in the evolution of scientific evidence—A primer on evaluating the weight of scientific evidence. *William and Mary Law Review, 23,* 261-290.

Isquith, P. K., Levine, M., & Scheiner, J. (1993). Blaming the child: Attribution of responsibility to victims of child sexual abuse. In G. S. Goodman & B. L. Bottoms (Eds.), *Child victims, child witnesses: Understanding and improving testimony* (pp. 203-228). New York: Guilford.

Kovera, M. B., & Borgida, E. (1992, August). *Children on the witness stand: A persuasion analysis of jurors' perceptions.* Paper presented at the meeting of the American Psychological Association, Washington, DC.

Kovera, M. B., Gresham, A. W., Borgida, E., Gray, E., & Regan, P. C. (1995). *Does expert testimony inform or influence jury decision-making? A social cognitive analysis.* Unpublished manuscript, Florida International University.

Kovera, M. B., Levy, R. J., Borgida, E., & Penrod, S. D. (1994). Expert testimony in child sexual abuse cases: Effects of expert evidence type and cross-examination. *Law and Human Behavior, 18,* 653-674.

Leippe, M. R., Brigham, J. C., Cousins, C., & Romanczyk, A. (1989). The opinions and practices of criminal attorneys regarding child eyewitnesses: A survey. In S. J. Ceci, D. F. Ross, & M. P. Toglia (Eds.), *Perspectives on children's testimony* (pp. 100-130). New York: Springer-Verlag.

Leippe, M. R., Manion, A. P., & Romanczyk, A. (1992). Eyewitness persuasion: How and how well do fact finders judge the accuracy of adults' and children's memory reports. *Journal of Personality and Social Psychology, 63,* 181-197.

Leippe, M. R., & Romanczyk, A. (1987). Children on the witness stand: A communication/ persuasion analysis of jurors' reactions to child witnesses. In S. J. Ceci, M. P. Toglia, & D. F. Ross (Eds.), *Children's eyewitness memory* (pp. 155-177). New York: Springer-Verlag.

Leippe, M. R., & Romanczyk, A. (1989). Reactions to child (versus adult) eyewitnesses: The influence of jurors' preconceptions and witness behavior. *Law and Human Behavior, 13,* 103-132.

Limber, S., & Etheredge, S. (1989, August). Prosecutors' perceptions of sexually abused children as witnesses. In G. S. Goodman (Chair), *Child sexual abuse victims in court.* Symposium presented at the meeting of the American Psychological Association, New Orleans, LA.

Marin, B. V., Holmes, D. L., Guth, M., & Kovac, P. (1979). The potential of children as eyewitnesses: A comparison of children and adults on eyewitness tasks. *Law and Human Behavior, 3,* 295-305.

Maryland v. Craig, 497 U.S. 836 (1990).

McCord, D. (1986). Expert psychological testimony about child complainants in sexual abuse prosecutions: A foray into the admissibility of novel psychological evidence. *Journal of Criminal Law and Criminology, 77,* 1-68.

McGuire, W. J. (1985). Attitudes and attitude change. In G. Lindzey & E. Aronson (Eds.), *The handbook of social psychology* (Vol. 2, pp. 233-346). New York: Random House.

Mian, M., Wehrspann, W., Klajner-Diamond, H., LeBaron, D., & Winder, C. (1986). Review of 125 children 6 years of age and under who were sexually abused. *Child Abuse & Neglect, 10,* 223-229.

Nigro, G. N., Buckley, M. A., Hill, D. E., & Nelson, J. (1989). When juries "hear" children testify: The effects of eyewitness age and speech style on jurors' perceptions of testimony. In S. J. Ceci, D. F. Ross, & M. P. Toglia (Eds.), *Perspectives on children's testimony* (pp. 57-70). New York: Springer-Verlag.

Nisbett, R. E., & Wilson, T. D. (1979). Telling more than we can know: Verbal reports on mental processes. *Psychological Review, 90,* 339-363.

Petty, R. E., & Cacioppo, J. T. (1986). The elaboration likelihood model of persuasion. In L. Berkowitz (Ed.), *Advances in experimental social psychology* (Vol. 19, pp. 123-203). New York: Academic Press.

Ross, D. F., Dunning, D., Toglia, M. P., & Ceci, S. J. (1990). The child in the eyes of the jury: Assessing mock jurors' perceptions of the child witness. *Law and Human Behavior, 14,* 5-23.

Ross, D. F., Hopkins, S., Hanson, E., Lindsay, R. C. L., Hazen, K., & Eslinger, T. (1994). The impact of protective shields and videotape testimony on conviction rates in a simulated trial of child sexual abuse. *Law and Human Behavior, 18,* 553-566.

Sagatun, I. J. (1991). Expert witnesses in child abuse cases. *Behavioral Sciences and the Law, 9,* 201-215.

Saks, M. J. (1992). Normative and empirical issues about the role of expert witnesses. In D. K. Kagehiro & W. S. Laufer (Eds.), *Handbook of psychology and law* (pp. 185-203). New York: Springer-Verlag.

Saywitz, K. J., & Snyder, L. (1993). Improving children's testimony with preparation. In G. S. Goodman & B. L. Bottoms (Eds.), *Child victims, child witnesses: Understanding and improving testimony* (pp. 117-146). New York: Guilford.

Scheiner, J. (1988, April). The use of the minimalist vignette as a method for assessing the generalizability of videotape trial simulation results. In M. Levine (Chair), *Simulated jury research on the child as a witness.* Symposium conducted at the meeting of the Eastern Psychological Association, Buffalo, NY.

State v. Batangan, 71 Haw. 552, 799 P.2d 48 (1990).

State v. Kim, 64 Haw. 598, 645 P.2d 1330 (1982).

Summit, R. C. (1983). The child sexual abuse accommodation syndrome. *Child Abuse & Neglect, 7,* 177-193.

Swim, J. K., Borgida, E., & McCoy, K. (1993). Videotaped versus in-court witness testimony: Does protecting the child witness jeopardize due process? *Journal of Applied Social Psychology, 23,* 603-631.

Tobey, A. E., Goodman, G. S., Batterman-Faunce, J. M., Orcutt, H., & Sachsenmaier, T. (1995). Balancing the rights of children and defendants: Effects of closed-circuit television on children's accuracy and jurors' perceptions. In M. S. Zaragoza, J. R. Graham, G. C. N. Hall, R. Hirschman, & Y. S. Ben-Porath (Eds.), *Memory and testimony in the child witness* (pp. 214-239). Thousand Oaks, CA: Sage.

Yarmey, A. D., & Jones, H. P. T. (1983). Is the psychology of eyewitness identification a matter of common sense? In S. M. A. Lloyd-Bostock & B. R. Clifford (Eds.), *Evaluating witness evidence: Recent psychological research and new perspectives* (pp. 13-40). Chichester, England: Wiley.

Zuckerman, M., DePaulo, B. M., & Rosenthal, R. (1981). Verbal and nonverbal communication of deception. In L. Berkowitz (Ed.), *Advances in experimental social psychology* (Vol. 14, pp. 1-59). San Diego, CA: Academic Press.

13

A Decade of International Reform to Accommodate Child Witnesses
Steps Toward a Child Witness Code

JOHN E. B. MYERS

Children are no strangers to the courtroom, although courtrooms must certainly be strange to them. Not only are the courtroom trappings formal and intimidating, some of the "grown-ups aren't nice." For most children, interaction with adults is positive. Teachers, doctors, coaches, and others are supportive and concerned. In court, by contrast, at least one adult—the defense attorney—is likely to be incredulous of everything the child says and may portray the child as incompetent, coached, or confused.

Beginning in the early 1980s, the number of young witnesses escalated as prosecutors focused increased attention on child sexual abuse (*Regina v. D.O.L.*, 1993). As more and more children took the long walk to the witness stand, legislators and judges altered time-honored procedures to accommodate them, and today we find a patchwork of reforms. Few efforts

This chapter is reprinted with permission from *Criminal Justice and Behavior,* Vol. 23 No. 2, June 1996 402-222. © 1996 American Association for Correctional Psychology.

have been made, however, to distill these reforms into a comprehensive set of laws comprising a child witness code. This chapter marks a step toward such a code. The chapter begins by describing an important distinction between the common law and the civil law systems—a distinction that makes reform more important yet more difficult in countries that adhere to the common law. Following discussion of the common law and civil law systems, the chapter describes 14 categories of legal reform intended to accommodate children. Finally, as an appendix, the chapter sets forth a child witness code that legislators and policymakers may consider as they contemplate reform.

The Difficulty of Reform in Countries
That Follow the Common Law Tradition

A chapter discussing legal reforms to accommodate young witnesses must point out an important difference between the two legal systems that dominate the Western world: the common law and the civil law. The difference between these systems helps explain why reform is more difficult in the former than the latter.

Most European countries are traditionally classified as following the civil law system, with France and Germany as examples. By contrast, "common law is, essentially, the law of England and the law of those countries in which the law of England has been received or implanted" ("Evolution of Modern," 1991, p. 917). Countries following the common law include Australia, Canada, New Zealand, the Republic of Ireland, Scotland, South Africa, and the United States. Quebec, Canada and Louisiana in the Unites States—with their French roots—are a blend of common law and civil law traditions.

When it comes to accommodating children in court, the most important difference between the civil and common law systems concerns trial procedure rather than substantive law. Although the procedural distinction between civil and common law countries is far from pure, it is a distinction with a difference. Common law countries generally follow the adversarial or, as it is sometimes called, accusatorial system of justice. Civil law countries, on the other hand, employ an inquisitorial trial procedure. Spencer and Flin (1993) describe the difference:

It is generally accepted that there are two main systems of trial in the civilized world: the accusatorial (alias adversarial) and the inquisitorial. In an accusatorial system each side presents a case before a court the function of which is limited to deciding who has won. The judges have nothing to do with the preliminary investigations, give no help to either side in presenting its case, and take no active steps to discover the truth, which emerges—or so the theory goes—from the clash of conflicting accounts. . . . In an inquisitorial system, on the other hand, the court is viewed as a public agency appointed to get to the bottom of the disputed matter. The court takes the initiative in gathering information as soon as it has notice of the dispute, builds up a file on the matter by questioning all those it thinks may have useful information to offer—including, in a criminal case, the defendant— and then applies its reasoning powers to the material it has collected in order to determine where the truth lies. (p. 75)

In the adversary system, the attorneys for the parties question the witnesses, and tremendous significance is placed on cross-examination and face-to-face confrontation between witnesses and the accused. In the inquisitorial system, by contrast, less significance is attributed to face-to-face confrontation. Moreover, the judge rather than the lawyers often takes the lead in interrogating witnesses. By its very nature, the inquisitorial system is less hostile to children than the adversary system and less in need of reform.

Reforms to accommodate children are difficult in common law countries, which are deeply wedded to adversarial cross-examination and face-to-face confrontation. Indeed, in the United States, cross-examination and confrontation are guaranteed by the U.S. Constitution, and the constitutional stature of these rights makes reform particularly difficult. It is not surprising that most contributions in this volume describe common law countries, where reform is urgently needed and strenuously opposed.

The Reform Movement to
Accommodate Child Witnesses

This section describes legal reforms to accommodate children. During the past 10 years, reforms occurred primarily in three arenas: (a) investigative interviewing, (b) preparing children for court, and (c) courtroom accommodations.

Investigative Interviews

The way children are interviewed has a direct bearing on their credibility (Home Office, 1992; Lamers-Winkelman & Buffing; Sternberg, Lamb, & Hershkowitz; Warren & McGough, this volume). Defense attorneys increasingly argue that child witnesses should not be believed because they were interviewed improperly (*Idaho v. Wright,* 1990). Although there is no gainsaying the existence of defective investigative interviewing, there is no evidence such interviewing is the norm. Moreover, serious efforts are under way to improve the skills of the police officers, social workers, and others who interview children (California Attorney General, 1994; Myers, 1994). Concerted efforts to train interviewers are among the most laudable reforms of the child protection system. Several American states have laws on interviewing. Alabama and West Virginia, for example, authorize judges to limit the number of interviews (Alabama Code, 1994, § 15-1-2(a); West Virginia Code, 1994, § 61-8-13(a)). New York encourages use of multidisciplinary teams to investigate and prosecute cases (N.Y. Executive Law, 1995, § 642-a 1.).

Preparing Children to Testify

Testifying is difficult for young witnesses, and professionals owe it to children to prepare them for the experience (Flin, 1995). Saywitz and Snyder (1993) remind us that "preparation of children for painful medical procedures has proven successful in lowering children's perceptions of pain and raising their level of cooperation" (Jay, 1984). "Children facing similarly stressful forensic procedures deserve no less" (p. 119). Groundbreaking research by Sas and her colleagues demonstrates the utility of preparation (Sas, Wolfe, & Gowdey, 1996 in this volume). Sas, Hurley, Austin, and Wolfe (1991) write:

> The court preparation offered by the Child Witness Project [in London, Ontario, Canada] benefitted the child witnesses in four distinct ways:
>
> 1. By educating them about court procedures
> 2. By helping them deal with their stress and anxieties related to the abuse and to testifying
> 3. By helping them tell their story competently on the stand in court
> 4. By providing an advocacy role on their behalf with the other mandated agencies in the criminal justice system. (pp. 195-196)

Innovative court preparation programs operate in a number of communities, including Huntsville, Alabama (Keeney, Amacher, & Kastanakis, 1992); San Diego, California (C. Tammariello, Project Coordinator, Kids in Court Program, Center for Child Protection, Children's Hospital, personal communication, July 20, 1995); and Seattle, Washington (D. Belin, Executive Director, King County Kid's Court Program, personal communication, August 9, 1995). Empirical research suggests that preparation can increase children's memory, reduce suggestibility, and lower stress (Saywitz & Snyder, 1993).

Courtroom Testimony

Considerable legislative and judicial effort has focused on reforming the criminal justice system to accommodate child witnesses (McGough, 1994; Murray, 1995; Spencer & Flin, 1993). Less energy has been devoted to reforming noncriminal proceedings such as family and juvenile court. The paucity of reform in noncriminal forums is likely due to two factors. First, judges feel greater flexibility to accommodate children in noncriminal proceedings, thus the need for reform is less compelling. Second, although noncriminal proceedings are extremely important for children, disproportionate attention focuses on the more highly visible and contentious criminal justice system.

For purposes of discussion, it is convenient to place courtroom reforms into 12 categories, with the 12th serving as a catchall for reforms that do not fit conveniently elsewhere. The categories are the following:

1. Admissibility of children's hearsay statements.
2. Competence to testify as a witness; the oath.
3. Altering the courtroom to accommodate child witnesses.
4. Judicial control of the proceedings and questioning.
5. Support persons for child witnesses.
6. Sequestration or exclusion of witnesses during the child's testimony.
7. Closing the courtroom to the public and the press.
8. Video link technology and other modifications that effect the accused's right to confront the child.
9. Counsel or guardian ad litem for the child.
10. The corroboration requirement.
11. Jury instructions regarding child witnesses.
12. The residual category.

These reforms are discussed briefly below.

Children's Hearsay Statements

Children disclose sexual abuse to parents, teachers, medical and mental health professionals, friends, and others. In many cases, children's disclosure statements are powerful evidence of abuse. Yet such out-of-court statements are hearsay, and hearsay is disallowed in Anglo-American legal proceedings unless the hearsay meets the requirements of an exception to the rule against hearsay. In countries following the civil law, hearsay is generally admissible.

Children's hearsay statements are important for three reasons. First, the child's hearsay statements are often the most compelling evidence of abuse. As one court put it, "The child's out-of-court statements often make or break an entire case" (*Zinger v. State*, 1995, p. 429). Second, in many cases the need for the child's hearsay is magnified by the paucity of medical and corroborating evidence. As the U.S. Supreme Court observed, "Child abuse is one of the most difficult crimes to detect and prosecute, in large part because there often are no witnesses except for the victim" (*Pennsylvania v. Ritchie*, 1987, p. 60). Finally, although most children possess the capacity to testify in court, some children are ineffective witnesses, and others cannot take the witness stand at all. For a child who cannot testify, hearsay statements made prior to trial are the child's only way to communicate with the judge or jury. For a child who testifies but performs poorly, earlier hearsay statements may bolster the child's credibility.

Although numerous exceptions to the rule against hearsay exist, only a handful play a major role in child abuse litigation. The "excited utterance" exception allows hearsay statements made shortly following startling events. All U.S. jurisdictions, England, Scotland, and other countries recognize the excited utterance exception (Scottish Law Commission, 1988; Spencer & Flin, 1993). Another important exception is the so-called medical diagnosis or treatment exception that allows certain hearsay statements made to medical personnel. Most U.S. jurisdictions have a version of the medical exception. A slim majority of U.S. states also have a residual or catchall exception that allows admission of reliable hearsay that does not meet the requirements of one of the more traditional exceptions, such as excited utterance. The residual exceptions play an important role in child abuse litigation by allowing reliable hearsay that would otherwise be excluded.

Until 1982, hearsay exceptions did not, for the most part, draw lines based on age. Beginning in Washington State in 1982, however, an increasing number of U.S. states adopted hearsay exceptions for children's statements describing sexual abuse, and today, a small majority of states have "child hearsay exceptions."

In the United States, the rule against hearsay applies in noncriminal as well as criminal proceedings. Some American states have special exceptions that allow hearsay in noncriminal proceedings designed to protect children (*In re Carmen O.,* 1994). In England, "any civil [i.e., noncriminal] court that is concerned with the welfare of a child may now receive and act on hearsay evidence" (Spencer & Flin, 1993, p. 146). In Scotland, the Civil Evidence Act of 1988 abolished the hearsay rule in relation to civil cases (Flin, Kearney, & Murray, 1996 in this volume).

Competence to Testify and the Oath

To testify as a witness, a person must possess the cognitive and moral capacities that comprise testimonial competence. In addition, the person must take a religious oath or a secular affirmation. Although it is common to speak in one breath of competence and the oath—as though they were a single requirement—they are separate and distinct.

Testimonial competence. A prospective witness—child or adult—must be testimonially competent. The individual must have sufficient memory to recall events (Melton, 1981), must be able to communicate intelligibly (Weinstein & Berger, 1995), must apprehend the difference between truth and lies (*Ricketts v. State,* 1985), and must comprehend the duty to testify truthfully (*Swanigan v. Board of Education,* 1988).

In the United States, there are three approaches to children's testimonial competence. First, in a diminishing number of states children below a specified age—typically 10 or 12—are presumed to lack testimonial competence. Before a "presumptively incompetent" child may testify, the judge conducts a competency examination to assess the child's memory, comprehension of the difference between truth and lies, and appreciation of the duty to testify truthfully.

The second approach to evaluating testimonial competence abandons arbitrary age limits and holds that "every person is competent to be a witness" (Federal Rules of Evidence, 1975, Rule 601). Under this approach, which predominates in the United States, many children are permitted to testify without a preliminary competency examination. Despite the apparently all-inclusive—"every person is competent"—language of modern law, judges continue holding competency examinations when legitimate questions arise about individual children (*State v. Eldredge,* 1989).

The third approach to the issue of testimonial competence exists in several American states that have laws guaranteeing that child abuse victims testify without preliminary examination (see Myers, 1992a, § 2.9). Alabama, for example, has a statute stating: "Notwithstanding any other provision of law or rule of evidence, a child victim of a physical offense, sexual offense, or sexual exploitation, shall be considered a competent witness and shall be allowed to testify without prior qualification in any judicial proceeding" (Alabama Code, 1994, § 15-25-3(c)).

The oath or affirmation. In addition to possessing the cognitive and moral capacity to testify, a witness must take an oath or affirmation. The oath is religious, and the witness must appreciate the divine penalty awaiting perjurers. As an alternative to a religious oath, a witness may make an affirmation, which is a secular declaration that the witness will testify truthfully.

In Canada, England, Scotland, and civil law countries, children may testify unsworn (*Halsbury's Statutes of England and Wales,* 1992, p. 515 [Children Act 1989, § 96]; Spencer & Flin, 1993).

Altering the Courtroom to Accommodate Child Witnesses

The courtroom is a forbidding place to children. Is it permissible to tinker with the solemn halls of justice to accommodate young children? If doing so improves the quality of their testimony, the answer is yes. The law does not preordain that courtrooms be configured in a particular way (Myers, 1992b), and, as long as the defendant's right to a fair trial is protected, minor alternations to accommodate children are proper (*Hicks-Bey v. United States,* 1994).

Judges have inherent authority to accommodate children (*State v. Ford,* 1993). The Alaska Supreme Court observed that "the rules of evidence were not developed to handle the problems presented by the child witness. Therefore our courts must be free to adapt these rules, where appropriate, to accommodate these unique cases" (*In re T. P.,* 1992). The Massachusetts Supreme Judicial Court approved a trial judge's decision to allow children to testify from a child-sized table and chair placed in front of the jury (*Commonwealth v. Amirault,* 1989). The Massachusetts court wrote that "a judge is afforded wide discretion in fashioning procedures and modifying standard trial practices to accommodate the special needs of child witnesses" (p. 207).

Judges have approved a variety of accommodations for children. For example, the witness chair may be turned slightly away from the defendant, provided the defendant can observe the child testify (*United States v. Thompson,* 1990; *United States v. Williams,* 1993). In *United States v. Romey* (1991), a child witness was allowed to whisper her answers to her mother, who repeated them aloud. In another case, "the prosecutor positioned herself in the courtroom so that one of the young victim witnesses, Tammy G., did not have to look at [defendant] while testifying about his acts of sexual molestation. . . . [T]he prosecutor sat or stood next to the witness stand so Tammy could look away from the defense table while she was testifying" (*People v. Sharp,* 1994, pp. 120, 122). The defendant complained that this procedure violated his right under the confrontation clause of the U.S. Constitution to confront the child, but the California Court of Appeals disagreed, writing:

> The mere fact that the prosecutor facilitated Tammy's decision to look away from [defendant] does not transform this innocuous act into a violation of the confrontation clause.
>
> A contrary holding would border on the absurd. Surely, [defendant] cannot be claiming a constitutional right to stare down or otherwise subtly intimidate a young child who would dare to testify against him. Nor can he claim a right to a particular seating arrangement in the courtroom. (*People v. Sharp,* 1994, p. 123)

Legislators have been active regarding child witnesses. For example, Connecticut has a statute that authorizes the judge to prohibit people from entering or leaving the courtroom during a child's testimony (Conn. Gen. Stat., 1994, § 54-86g(b)(1)). Another Connecticut law provides that the judge may require attorneys to remain seated during questioning, and may instruct attorneys to make objections "in a manner which is not intimidating to the child" (Conn. Gen. Stat., 1994, § 54-86g(b)(4)). A California law states that "the taking of the child's testimony may be limited to the hours during which the child is normally in school" (Cal. Penal Code, 1995, § 868.8(d)). Another California statute provides that a child "may be allowed reasonable periods of relief from examination and cross-examination during which he or she may retire from the courtroom" (Cal. Penal Code, 1995, § 868.8(a)). A third California law states that "in the court's discretion the judge, parties, witnesses, support person, and court personnel may be relocated within the courtroom to facilitate a more comfortable and personal environment for the child witness" (Cal. Penal Code, 1995, § 868.8(c)). West Virginia law states that "the court may permit a child who is eleven years old or less to use anatomically correct dolls, mannequins or drawings to assist such child in testifying" (W. Va. Code, 1994, § 61-8-13(b)). An Alabama statute provides that "the court may allow leading questions at trial by the prosecution or defense of any victim or witness in a case who is under the age of 10" (Ala. Code, 1994, § 15-25-1). Although a judge would have inherent authority to implement all the accommodations listed above, a legislative pronouncement gives judges guidance and confidence to approve accommodations.

There are limits, of course, to accommodating children, particularly in criminal cases. In *Duffitt v. State* (1988), for example, the Indiana Supreme Court disapproved a trial judge's decision to put posters on the courtroom walls, writing that "the practice of decorating in deference to [a] certain witness is altogether inappropriate" (p. 608). In *State v. Michaels* (1993), the trial judge went too far when he allowed young children to sit on his knee while they testified. And in *State v. R. W.* (1986), the trial judge told the child witness she would receive ice cream if she told what was "real." At the conclusion of her direct examination, the youngster refused to be cross-examined until she received the promised treat. The ice cream was provided in the presence of the jury, and the New Jersey Supreme Court stated "without hesitation that the trial judge abused his discretion by promising the child ice cream and in subsequently giving it to her, thereby suggesting to the jury, albeit inadvertently, that the infant had indeed testified truthfully" (*State v. R. W.*, 1986, p. 1289).

Although limits are necessary on accommodations for children, some courts seem remarkably insensitive to children's needs. In *State v. Palabay* (1992), for example, the Hawaii Court of Appeals ruled that a 12-year-old should not have been permitted to hold a teddy bear while testifying unless the state first demonstrated a compelling justification for this simple accommodation.

Judicial Control of the Proceedings and Questioning

The judge has authority to control the proceedings and interrogation of witnesses. In the United States, Rule 611(a) of the Federal Rules of Evidence is typical of laws on this subject, and states,

> The court shall exercise reasonable control over the mode and order of interrogating witnesses and presenting evidence so as to (1) make the interrogation and presentation effective for the ascertainment of the truth, (2) avoid needless consumption of time, and (3) protect witnesses from harassment or undue embarrassment.

Several states have laws specifically addressing the judge's authority to protect child witnesses. A New York statute provides that "the judge presiding should be sensitive to the psychological and emotional stress a child witness may undergo when testifying" (N.Y. Executive Law, 1995, § 642-a 4). A California law states that in sexual offense cases "the court shall consider the needs of the child victim and shall do whatever is necessary, within existing budgetary resources, and constitutionally permissible to prevent psychological harm to the child victim" (Cal. Penal Code, 1995, § 288(d)). California law specifically allows judges to "forbid the asking of a question which is in a form that is not reasonably likely to be understood by a person of the age of the witness" (Cal. Evidence Code, 1995, § 765(b)). This statute is important in light of attorneys' inexhaustible appetite for incomprehensible queries. Two questions from actual trials illustrate the point:

Q   On the evening of January third, you did, didn't you, visit your grandmother's sisters' house and didn't you see the defendant leave the house at 7:30, after which you stayed the night? (Saywitz & Snyder, 1993, p. 117)

Q   Well, I have jumped ahead a bit, so you will have to go back to what you were telling us about before that first incident. You told us of what you did and what he did to you. On the next occasion you went there,

> what kind of thing happened between you? (Kranat & Westcott, 1994,
> p. 21)

It is any wonder children get confused? Judges have ample authority to
stop such nonsense. A judge also has authority to forbid unduly embarrassing questions. In the context of child sexual abuse, however, the crime
often makes embarrassing questions necessary. The judge may disallow
cross-examination on irrelevant issues and may forbid confusing, misleading, ambiguous, and unintelligible questions. Finally, the judge has authority to curtail questions designed merely to harass or badger a witness.

Although judges have authority to control cross-examination, judges in
the adversary system are reluctant to interfere with attorneys' questioning.
Within broad parameters, attorneys have the right to question witnesses as
they see fit. Judges are particularly deferential to defense counsel's right
to cross-examine prosecution witnesses, including children. The U.S.
Supreme Court ruled that the right of defense counsel to cross-examine is
protected by the Constitution. "The cross-examiner is not only permitted
to delve into the witness' story to test the witness' perceptions and memory,
but the cross-examiner has traditionally been allowed to impeach, i.e.,
discredit, the witness" (*Davis v. Alaska,* 1974, p. 316).

Attorneys place extraordinary confidence in cross-examination to un-
cover the truth and unmask the liar. Spencer and Flin (1993) observed that
"among English-speaking lawyers no belief is more deeply held than the
value of cross-examination. It has been the subject of fervent professions
of faith in so many speeches and writings that a collection of them would
fill a sizeable book" (p. 270). American legal scholar John H. Wigmore
(1974) opined that cross-examination "is beyond any doubt the greatest
legal engine ever invented for the discovery of truth" (§ 1367).

Not everyone genuflects before the alter of cross-examination. Some
European lawyers and judges are less enthusiastic. Spencer and Flin
(1993) write,

> If we really want to know what foreign lawyers think of cross-examination we
> should read what a distinguished French judge and legal writer, François Grophe,
> had to say about it:
> "The Anglo-American system has grave faults which cry out for it to be
> abolished. In the first place, it over-uses the right of questioning, to which it
> attributes an exaggerated efficiency in the case of suspect witnesses, whilst paying
> insufficient respect to witnesses who are sincere. Even more deplorably, it takes

absolutely no precautions against the witness being influenced, or even badgered, and it takes no account of the distorting effect of suggestive questions, which get worse as the case is more bitterly contested." (Grophe, 1927, p. 90, quoted in Spencer & Flin, 1993, p. 271).

From the perspective of the adversary system, Judge Grophe's criticism of cross-examination is interesting but beside the point. Cross-examination is so thoroughly ensconced in the Anglo-American legal system that the only hope for more humane treatment of children is to pare away clear abuses. The statutes cited earlier in this section are steps in the right direction.

Support Persons for Child Witnesses

Imagine 5-year-old Susie, about to enter the hospital for the first time in her life. Susie is scheduled to undergo an unfamiliar and painful medical procedure. Mother drives Susie to the hospital, opens the car door, and says, "Okay honey, run along into the hospital and find the doctor. I'll be back in a couple of hours to pick you up. Bye." Mother drives off, leaving little Susie all alone outside the hospital. Preposterous you say? Mother won't do that. She'll walk Susie into the hospital and remain by her side to provide comfort, reassurance, and support. Moreover, the nurses and doctors understand the importance of emotional support for young patients, and unless there is some overriding medical reason to exclude mother during the procedure, she is welcome.

Now change the scene from the hospital to the courthouse. Susie is about to enter a courtroom for the first time, where she is to testify in the trial of the man accused of molesting her. Just as Susie's mother did not abandon her at the hospital, mother accompanies Susie to court. Mother holds Susie's hand as they approach the courtroom. At the door, however, Susie's mother is told she cannot go in. All by herself, Susie steps into the huge room. She can feel the stare of unfamiliar grown-ups. Most of all, though, she feels the piercing gaze of the one adult she knows too well, the defendant. The bailiff points to the witness stand and says, "Take a seat up there." Susie inches her way to the witness box and sits down. She can barely see over the rail around the box, and her feet dangle far above the floor. For a moment she lifts her eyes, but quickly drops them when she sees the defendant sitting a few feet away.

At the hospital, emotional support is an integral part of treatment, and parents are partners in therapy. At the courthouse, however, things are different. The tradition in court is that the child must go it alone. Fortunately, this tradition is giving way to a more enlightened approach. An increasing number of states have laws that allow support for children testifying in court (see, e.g., Conn. Gen. Stat., 1994, title 54, § 54-86g(b)(2); Delaware Code, 1994, title 11, § 5134(b); Idaho Code, 1995, § 19-3023; N.Y. Exec. Law, 1995, § 642-a 6; U.S. Code, 1995, title 18, § 3509(i)).

Emotional support is not only humane, it is effective. Goodman and her colleagues (Goodman et al., 1992) conducted research on children testifying in American criminal proceedings. The research disclosed that the presence of a supportive adult increased some children's capacity to testify. Goodman et al. write that "presence of a parent/loved one was associated with children answering more questions during direct examination" (p. 92).

In the present author's opinion, no courtroom reform is more important than allowing child witnesses to be accompanied by a supportive and trusted adult. During the past decade, the most hotly debated, legislated, and litigated reform was live-link video testimony. Yet, in the final analysis, video testimony pales in importance to simple propinquity. It is ironic that so much energy focuses on "high tech" solutions like video testimony when more may be accomplished with the decidedly "low tech" solution of a familiar face.

Excluding Witnesses While They Are Not Testifying

Witnesses may be excluded from the courtroom while they are not testifying. The purpose of exclusion is to prevent witnesses from shaping their testimony in light of what others say. The practice goes back to the Old Testament, where Susanna was convicted and sentenced to die based on testimony from two of the elders. Before Susanna could be executed, however, Daniel rose to her defense. Daniel said, "Are ye such fools, ye sons of Israel, that without examination or knowledge of the truth ye have condemned a daughter of Israel? Return again to the place of judgment: for they have borne false witness against her." As Daniel prepared to cross-examine the accusing elders he said, "Put these two aside one far from another, and I will examine them." Once the elders were separated they told inconsistent stories and their perjury was revealed. The practice of excluding witnesses from the courtroom has changed little since Biblical times.

In child abuse litigation, the exclusion rule becomes important when a child witness needs the supportive presence of an adult who is also a witness, and who normally would be excluded from the courtroom during the child's testimony (*Government of Virgin Islands v. Edinborough,* 1980). In some cases, the prosecutor can arrange for a support person who is not a witness. If the only adult who can provide emotional support is also a witness, however, the adult can testify before the child, and in that case, the adult may remain in the courtroom during the child's testimony.

Closing the Courtroom to the Public and the Press

One way to reduce the stress of testifying is to close the courtroom to the public and the press. Under the U.S. Constitution, however, the defendant in a criminal case has a right to a public trial (*Waller v. Georgia,* 1984). The right is not absolute, and competing interests may be balanced against the defendant's right to an open proceeding. Closure is particularly appropriate where a child must describe degrading and embarrassing acts (*Press-Enterprise Co. v. Superior Court,* 1986). Nevertheless, in the United States open trials are the norm, and closure the exception.

In addition to the defendant's right to a public trial, the American public and press have a constitutional right to attend criminal trials. Here too the right is not absolute, and in selected cases, the public and press may be excluded. The U.S. Supreme Court's decision in *Globe Newspaper Co. v. Superior Court* (1982) is the leading American authority on closing the courtroom when children testify. In *Globe Newspaper,* the Court declared unconstitutional a Massachusetts law that required exclusion of the press and public *whenever* young sexual offense victims testified. The Supreme Court wrote that "the circumstances under which the press and public can be barred from a criminal trial are limited; the State's justification in denying access must be a weighty one" (p. 606). The Court went on to state that protecting the physical and psychological well-being of a child is a sufficiently compelling governmental interest to override the public and press right of access in some cases. In deciding when to close the courtroom, the judge considers the child's "age, psychological maturity and understanding, the nature of the crime, the desires of the victim, and the interests of parents and relatives" (p. 609).

A number of American states and the federal government have laws regarding closure of the courtroom (e.g., Louisiana Statutes, 1995, § 15:469.1; New Hampshire Code, 1994, title 57, § 632-A:8; U.S. Code, 1995, title 18, § 3509(e)).

Video Testimony

No reform has generated more legislation and debate than allowing children to give evidence outside the physical presence of the defendant. Although several methods are available to accomplish this goal, the technique that garners the most attention is closed-circuit television or, as it is called in Scotland and England, live television link. Unfortunately, the goal of sparing children the ordeal of a face-to-face encounter with the accused collides head-on with the defendant's right to confront accusatory witnesses. Spencer and Flin (1993) capture the importance in the adversary system of face-to-face confrontation when they write that "it is a widely held belief among lawyers in the English-speaking world that confronting the accuser with the person he accuses ensures he tells the truth" (p. 277). The U.S. Supreme Court wrote,

> The perception that confrontation is essential to fairness has persisted over the centuries because there is much truth to it. A witness "may feel quite differently when he has to repeat his story looking at the man whom he will harm greatly by distorting or mistaking the facts. He can now understand what sort of human being that man is." . . . It is always more difficult to tell a lie about a person "to his face" than "behind his back." In the former context, even if the lie is told, it will often be told less convincingly. . . . [F]ace-to-face presence may, unfortunately, upset the truthful rape victim or abused child; but by the same token it may confound and undo the false accuser, or reveal the child coached by a malevolent adult. (*Coy v. Iowa*, 1988, pp. 1019-1020)

Thus, face-to-face confrontation between witness and defendant is a cornerstone of adversarial criminal trials. In the United States, confrontation takes on added significance because the right is enshrined in the confrontation clause of the U.S. Constitution, which provides that "in all criminal prosecutions, the accused shall . . . be confronted with the witnesses against him" (U.S. Constitution, Amendment VI, 1787, 1791). In the early and mid-1980s, numerous states in the United States passed video testimony laws designed to spare children face-to-face confrontation. Like the governor on an engine, however, the confrontation clause regulates how fast and how far these laws may travel on the road to reform.

Video testimony laws are of three types: (a) videotaped investigative interviews, (b) videotaped testimony taken prior to trial, and (c) trial testimony through live-link television.

Videotaped investigative interviews. England leads the way regarding use at trial of videotaped investigative interviews (Bull & Davies, 1996 [this volume]). The Criminal Justice Act of 1991 "permits, for the first time, the admission of videotaped interviews with a child, conducted by a police officer or social worker as a substitute for the child's evidence-in-chief at trial" (Davies, Wilson, Mitchell, & Milsom, 1995). The judge has limited authority to exclude the tape "in the interests of justice," and the child must appear at trial to be cross-examined by defense counsel (*Halsbury's Statutes of England and Wales,* 1993, p. 253 [Criminal Justice Act, 1988, § 32A]).

Canadian law "contains a provision for the admissibility of videotaped interviews of child complainants of sexual abuse as long as the child adopts the contents of the tape on the witness stand, and the tape has been made within a reasonable length of time after the offense" (Sas et al., 1996, in this volume, p. 346). In *Regina v. D.O.L.* (1993), the Supreme Court of Canada ruled that allowing videotaped interviews to be considered in court "neither offends the principles of fundamental justice nor violates the right to a fair trial as guaranteed by . . . the Canadian Charter of Rights and Freedoms." During the 1980s, a number of American states enacted laws authorizing videotaped investigative interviews to be used in lieu of the child's testimony at trial (e.g., Kan. Stat. Ann., 1988, § 22-3433; Ky. Rev. Stat., 1995, § 421.350). Several of these laws compromised the defendant's constitutional right to confront and cross-examine child witnesses, and at least three of the laws were ruled unconstitutional (*Burke v. State,* 1991; *Lowery v. Collins,* 1993; *State v. Pilkey,* 1989).

Videotaped testimony taken prior to trial. A substantial number of states have laws allowing pretrial videotaping of children's testimony. The taping occurs in the courtroom or at some other location. By and large, the laws require that the defendant be present at the videotaping (e.g., Tenn. Code, 1994, § 24-7-116). A number of statutes allow the judge to exclude the defendant if face-to-face confrontation would traumatize the child (e.g., Iowa Rules Crim. Pro. 12. 2. b., 1994); U.S. Code, 1995, title 18, § 3509(b)(2)(B)(iv)).

Trial testimony through live television link. In the United States, the most controversial courtroom reform is live television link, which allows selected children to testify outside the physical presence of the defendant via closed-circuit television. The live television link often entails a complete abrogation of the defendant's constitutional right to face-to-face confrontation, and it is on constitutional grounds that the American battle over live link has been waged.

In 1990, the U.S. Supreme Court resolved the constitutional issue with its decision in *Maryland v. Craig* (1990). The Court reiterated the importance of confrontation but concluded that a face-to-face encounter at trial is not required in every case. The Court wrote that "a State's interest in the physical and psychological well-being of child abuse victims may be sufficiently important to outweigh, at least in some cases, a defendant's right to face his or her accusers in court" (p. 853). Before confrontation may be curtailed, however, a judge must determine that the defendant's presence will cause emotional distress that "is more than de minimis, i.e., more than 'mere nervousness or excitement or some reluctance to testify' " (p. 856). Moreover, the child's distress must emanate from the defendant, not from fear of the courtroom, spectators, or other factors. Although the Court declined to say how much emotional distress is required, the Court stated that " 'serious emotional distress such that the child cannot reasonably communicate,' clearly suffices to meet constitutional standards" (p. 856).

The Supreme Court made clear that states may not enact laws that authorize all children to testify via live television link. Before a defendant's right to confrontation may be impaired, the judge must determine that the particular child would be traumatized by face-to-face confrontation.

Countries that do not have a constitutional confrontation right do not ignore the importance of confrontation (Spencer & Flin, 1993). Nevertheless, such countries have greater flexibility to employ video testimony. Canada, England, and New Zealand authorized live television link in 1988 and 1989 (Bull & Davies, 1996; Davies & Noon, 1991; Pipe & Henaghan,

1996; Sas et al., 1996, in this volume). In Scotland, "statutory authority for the use of live television link by child witnesses" went into effect in 1991 (Murray, 1995, p. i; see also Flin et al., 1996, in this volume). By the early 1990s, most Australian states enacted "legislation allowing the use of closed-circuit television for child witnesses" (Shrimpton, Oates, & Hayes, 1996 in this volume).

Counsel, Guardian Ad Litem, or Advocate for the Child

One way to help children cope with the adversary legal system is to assign an advocate to protect their interests. The advocate may be an attorney or a trained lay person. In the United States, the advocate's role varies with the type of litigation. In noncriminal cases, a child's advocate takes an active role in investigating the case, making recommendations to the court, and, if the advocate is an attorney, examining and cross-examining witnesses at trial (Haralambie, 1993). In criminal trials, however, a child's advocate plays a more limited role. For example, in North Dakota a child's advocate—called a guardian ad litem—"may not separately introduce evidence or directly examine or cross-examine witnesses" (N.D. Century Code, 1993, § 12.1-20-16). Outside the courtroom itself, however, a child's advocate may take an active part in assisting the child and family through the labyrinth of the legal system (Fla. Stat., 1994, § 914.17; Whitcomb, 1988).

Children, like other crime victims, sometimes get "lost in the shuffle." Children need a voice—an adult who understands the legal system and who has authority to speak for them. Research indicates that judges seldom implement accommodations that are available under existing law (Goodman et al., 1992; Murray, 1995; but see Pipe & Henaghan, 1996, in this volume). An important reason for infrequent accommodation is probably the child's voicelessness in the process. An effective antidote to this unsatisfactory state of affairs is to ensure that every child witness involved in the criminal justice system has an advocate to protect his or her interests.

The Corroboration Requirement

Throughout most of the 20th century, children's testimony in sexual offense cases was viewed with such skepticism that a conviction could not be predicated on the uncorroborated testimony of the victim. During the 1970s and 1980s, however, courts moved away from the corroboration requirement, and nearly all of the United States have diluted or eliminated the corroboration requirement (Myers, 1992a, § 5.17).

Jury Instructions Regarding Child Witnesses

It was once common in the United States to instruct jurors to consider children's testimony with care (Myers, 1992a, § 8.14). The modern trend is away from such cautionary instructions, however (e.g., *Guam v. McGravey,* 1994).

Residual Category

The accommodations outlined above by no means cover the waterfront. Judges make on-the-spot decisions to meet the exigencies of particular cases, and legislatures refine existing laws and generate new ideas.

Conclusion

The past decade witnessed unprecedented change to improve the skills of professionals who interview children and to accommodate children in court. Foment for change came primarily from judges and lawyers, on the one hand, and mental health and medical professionals, on the other. On the American legal front, pioneering writing by prosecutor Mary Avery (1983), law professor David Liabi (1969), and judge Charles Schudson (Dziech & Schudson, 1989), among others, propelled the reform agenda. In England, the reports by Lord Clyde and Judge Thomas Pigot on interviewing and video evidence were highly influential (Clyde, 1992; Home Office, 1989), as was the excellent book by law professor John Spencer and psychologist Rhona Flin (1993). In other countries, including Canada, Hong Kong, Ireland, Israel, Scotland, and South Africa, government commissions on child witnesses were influential (in this volume see, e.g., Ho, 1996; Ireland Law Reform Commission, 1989; Louw & Olivier, 1996; Sas et al., 1996; Scottish Law Commission, 1988; Sternberg et al., 1996).

Psychological research contributed to the reform movement, and this volume provides an excellent overview of the research and its effect on reform. Louw and Olivier (1996) describe how reform in South Africa was fueled by psychological research on children's competence and by the evocative writing of a physician who was shocked by the treatment accorded children in South African courts. Flin et al. (1996) describe the role of psychological research in changing Scottish law (see also Murray, 1995), and Bull and Davies (1996) bespeak the English experience and that of other countries when they observe that psychological research demonstrates that "children *are* usually able to provide a worthwhile oral account of what has happened to them" and that psychological research has had a positive effect on legislative change (see also Davies et al., 1995). In Australia, research on court delays, developmentally inappropriate questioning by attorneys, and "children's perceptions of the court process" influenced important legal reforms (Shrimpton et al., 1996). Although Canada is on the cutting edge of many areas of reform, Canada's most lasting contribution to date is innovative research on pretrial preparation of child witnesses (Sas et al., 1996).

Reforming the legal system is no mean feat. Many judges and lawyers are reluctant to tinker with traditional courtroom practices. Birks (1972) observed that "there is no doubt that lawyers have always clung to the relics of by-gone days, be they antiquated laws, outmoded dress or ancient ceremonial" (p. 1). Despite the pull of tradition, impressive gains have been made to accommodate children in court. Reform came in fits and starts and was opposed at every turn. Moreover, reform is far from complete. Some reforms trammeled the rights of defendants and appropriately fell by the wayside. Nevertheless, the tide of reform appears irreversible and, in the end, beneficial to children and the search for truth.

References

Alabama Code.

Avery, M. (1983). The child abuse witness: Potential for secondary victimization. *Criminal Justice Journal, 7,* 1-48.

Birks, M. (1972). Court architecture. In G. R. Winters (Ed.), *Selected readings: Courthouses and courtrooms* (pp. 1-3). Chicago: American Judicature Society.

Bull, R., & Davies, G. (1996). The effect of child witness research on legislation in Great Britain. In B. L. Bottoms & G. S. Goodman (Eds.), *International perspectives on child abuse and children's testimony: Psychological research and law* (pp. 96-113). Thousand Oaks, CA: Sage.

Burke v. State, 820 P.2d 1344 (Okla. Crim. App. 1991).

California Attorney General. (1994). *Child victim witness investigative pilot projects: Research and evaluation* (Final report). Sacramento: Author.

California Evidence Code. (1995).

California Penal Code. (1995).

Clyde, Lord. (1992). *The report of the inquiry into the removal of children from Orkney in February 1991* (HC 195). Edinburgh, Scotland: Her Majesty's Stationery Office.

Commonwealth v. Amirault, 535 N.E.2d 193 (Mass. 1989).

Connecticut General Statutes. (1994).

Coy v. Iowa, 487 U.S. 1012 (1988).

Davies, G. M., & Noon, E. (1991). *An evaluation of the live link for child witnesses* (Grant report). London: Home Office.

Davies, G., Wilson, C., Mitchell, R., & Milsom, J. (1995). *Videotaping children's evidence: An evaluation.* London: Home Office.

Davis v. Alaska, 415 U.S. 308 (1974).

Davies, G. & Noon, E. (1991). *An evaluation of the live link of child witnesses.* London: Home Office.

Delaware Code. (1994).

Duffitt v. State, 525 N.E.2d 607 (Ind. 1988).

Dziech, B. W., & Schudson, C. B. (1989). *On trial: America's courts and their treatment of sexually abused children.* Boston: Beacon.

Evolution of modern Western legal systems. (1991). In *Encyclopedia Britannica* (15th ed., Vol. 22, pp. 917-947). Chicago: Encyclopedia Britannica.

Federal Rules of Evidence. (1975).

Flin, R. (1995). Children's testimony: Psychology on trial. In M. S. Zaragoza, J. R. Graham, G. C. N. Hall, R. Hirschman, & Y. S. Ben-Porath (Eds.), *Memory and testimony in the child witness* (pp. 240-254). Thousand Oaks, CA: Sage.

Flin, R., Kearney, B., & Murray, K. (1996). Children's evidence: Scottish research and law. In B. L. Bottoms & G. S. Goodman (Eds.), *International perspectives on child abuse and children's testimony: Psychological research and law* (pp. 114-131). Thousand Oaks, CA: Sage.

Florida Statutes. (1994).

Globe Newspaper Co. v. Superior Court, 457 U.S. 596 (1982).

Goodman, G. S., Taub, E. P., Jones, D. P. H., England, P., Port, L. K., Rudy, L., & Prado, L. (1992). Testifying in criminal court. *Monographs of the Society for Research in Child Development, 57* (5, Serial No. 229).

Grophe, F. (1927). *La critique du Temoignage* (2nd ed.). Paris: Dalloz.

Government of Virgin Islands v. Edinborough, 625 F.2d 472 (3rd Cir. 1980).

Guam v. McGravey, 14 F.3d 1344 (9th Cir. 1994).

Halsbury's statutes of England and Wales (Vols. 6, 17). (1993). London: Butterworths.

Haralambie, A. M. (1993). *The child's attorney.* Chicago: American Bar Association.

Hicks-Bey v. United States, 649 A.2d 569 (D.C. App. 1994).

Ho, T.-P. (1996). Children's evidence: Mandating change in the legal system of Hong Kong. In B. L. Bottoms & G. S. Goodman (Eds.), *International perspectives on child abuse and children's testimony: Psychological research and law* (pp. 182-200). Thousand Oaks, CA: Sage.

Home Office. (1989). *Report of the advisory group on video evidence* (Chairman Judge Thomas Pigot QC). London: Author.

Idaho Code. (1995).

Idaho v. Wright, 497 U.S. 805 (1990).

In re Carmen O., 33 Cal. Rptr.2d 848 (Ct. App. 1994).

In re T. P., 838 P.2d 1236 (Alaska 1992).

Iowa Rules of Criminal Procedure. (1994).

Ireland Law Reform Commission. (1989). *A law reform commission consultation paper on child sexual abuse.*

Jay, S. M. (1984). Pain in children: An overview of psychological assessment and intervention. In A. Zener, D. Bendell, & C. E. Walker (Eds.), *Health psychology treatment and research issues* (pp. 167-196). New York: Plenum.

Kansas Statutes Annotated. (1988).

Keeney, K. S., Amacher, E., & Kastanakis, J. A. (1992). The court prep group: A vital part of the court process. In H. Dent & R. Flin (Eds.), *Children as witnesses* (pp. 201-209). Chichester, England: Wiley.

Kentucky Revised Statutes. (1995).

Kranat, V. K., & Westcott, H. L. (1994). Under fire: Lawyers questioning children in criminal courts. *Expert Evidence, 3,* 16-24.

Lamers-Winkelman, F., & Buffing, F. (1996). Children's testimony in the Netherlands: A study of statement validity analysis. In B. L. Bottoms & G. S. Goodman (Eds.), *International perspectives on child abuse and children's testimony: Psychological research and law* (pp. 45-61). Thousand Oaks, CA: Sage.

Liabi, D. (1969). The protection of the child victim of a sexual offense in the criminal justice system. *Wayne State Law Review, 15,* 977-1032.

Louisiana Statutes. (1995).

Louw, D. A., & Olivier, P. J. J. (1996). Listening to children in South Africa. In B. L. Bottoms & G. S. Goodman (Eds.), *International perspectives on child abuse and children's testimony: Psychological research and law* (pp. 168-181). Thousand Oaks, CA: Sage.

Lowery v. Collins, 988 F.2d 1364 (5th Cir. 1993).

Maryland v. Craig, 497 U.S. 836 (1990).

McGough, L. S. (1994). *Child witnesses: Fragile voices in the American legal system.* New Haven, CT: Yale University Press.

Melton, G. B. (1981). Children's competence to testify. *Law & Human Behavior, 5,* 73-85.

Murray, K. (1995). *Live television link: An evaluation of its use by child witnesses in Scottish criminal trials.* Glasgow, Scotland: Scottish Office, Central Research Unit.

Myers, J. E. B. (1992a). *Evidence in child abuse and neglect cases.* New York: John Wiley.

Myers, J. E. B. (1992b). Steps toward forensically relevant research. In G. S. Goodman, E. P. Taub, D. P. H. Jones, P. England, L. K. Port, L. Rudy, & L. Prado, Testifying in criminal court. *Monographs of the Society for Research in Child Development, 57* (5, Serial No. 229), 143-152.

Myers, J. E. B. (1994). Taint hearings for child witnesses? A step in the wrong direction. *Baylor Law Review, 46,* 873-946.

New Hampshire Code. (1994).

New York Executive Law.

North Dakota Century Code. (1993).

Pennsylvania v. Ritchie, 480 U.S. 39 (1987).

People v. Sharp, 36 Cal. Rptr.2d 117 (Ct. App. 1994).

Pipe, M.-E., & Henaghan, M. (1996). Accommodating children's testimony: Legal reforms in New Zealand. In B. L. Bottoms & G. S. Goodman (Eds.), *International perspectives on child abuse and children's testimony: Psychological research and law* (pp. 145-167). Thousand Oaks, CA: Sage.

Press-Enterprise Co. v. Superior Court, 478 U.S. 1 (1986).

Regina v. D.O.L., 85 C.C.C. 3d 289 (Canada Supreme Court 1993).

Ricketts v. State, 488 A.2d 856 (Del. 1985).

Sas, L., Hurley, P., Austin, G., & Wolfe, D. (1991). *Reducing the system-induced trauma for child sexual abuse victims through court preparation, assessment and follow-up.* London, Canada: London Family Court Clinic.

Sas, L. D., Wolfe, D. A., & Gowdey, K. (1996). Children and the courts in Canada. In B. L. Bottoms & G. S. Goodman (Eds.), *International perspectives on child abuse and children's testimony: Psychological research and law* (pp. 77-95).Thousand Oaks, CA: Sage.

Saywitz, K. J., & Snyder, L. (1993). Improving children's testimony with preparation. In G. S. Goodman & B. L. Bottoms (Eds.), *Child victims, child witnesses: Understanding and improving testimony* (pp. 117-146). New York: Guilford.

Scottish Law Commission. (1988). *The evidence of children and other potentially vulnerable witnesses* (Discussion Paper No. 75). Edinburgh, Scotland: Author.

Shrimpton, S., Oates, K., & Hayes, S. (1996). The child witness and legal reforms in Australia. In B. L. Bottoms & G. S. Goodman (Eds.), *International perspectives on child abuse and children's testimony: Psychological research and law* (pp. 132-144). Thousand Oaks, CA: Sage.

Spencer, J. R., & Flin, R. (1993). *The evidence of children: The law and the psychology* (2nd ed.). London: Blackstone.

State v. Eldredge, 773 P.2d 29 (Utah 1989).

State v. Ford, 626 So.2d 1338 (Fla. 1993).

State v. Michaels, 625 A.2d 489 (N.J. Super Ct. App. Div. 1993).

State v. Palabay, 844 P.2d 1 (Hawaii Ct. App. 1992).

State v. Pilkey, 776 S.W.2d 943 (Tenn. 1989).

State v. R. W., 514 A.2d 1287 (N.J. 1986).

Sternberg, K. J., Lamb, M. E., & Hershkowitz, I. (1996). Child sexual abuse investigations in Israel: Evaluating innovative practices. In B. L. Bottoms & G. S. Goodman (Eds.), *International perspectives on child abuse and children's testimony: Psychological research and law* (pp. 62-76).Thousand Oaks, CA: Sage.

Swanigan v. Board of Education, 527 N.E.2d 1030 (Ill. Ct. App. 1988).

Tennessee Code. (1994).

U.S. Code.

United States v. Romey, 32 M.J. 180 (C.M.A. 1991).

United States v. Thompson, 31 M.J. 168 (C.M.A. 1990).

United States v. Williams, 37 M.J. 289 (C.M.A. 1993).

Waller v. Georgia, 467 U.S. 39 (1984).

Warren, A. R., & McGough, L. S. (1996). Research on children's suggestibility: Implications for the investigative interview. In B. L. Bottoms & G. S. Goodman (Eds.), *International perspectives on child abuse and children's testimony: Psychological research and law* (pp. 12-44). Thousand Oaks, CA: Sage.

Weinstein, J., & Berger, M. (1995). *Weinstein's evidence.* New York: Matthew Bender.

West Virginia Code. (1994).

Whitcomb, D. (1988). *Guardians ad litem in the criminal courts.* Washington, DC: U.S. Department of Justice, National Institute of Justice.

Wigmore, J. H. (1974). *Evidence in trials at common law.* Boston: Little, Brown.

Zinger v. State, 899 S.W.2d 423 (Tex. Ct. App. 1995).

APPENDIX

Child Witness Code

The Child Witness Code that follows pertains to criminal cases. The code draws heavily on existing law in the United States and several other countries. Several sections of the code—particularly sections dealing with live television link— are perhaps unique to the United States, with its constitutional guarantee of face-to-face confrontation at trial.

§ 1 Legislative Intent

The legislature hereby finds and declares as follows:

(a) This state has a compelling interest in protecting children from abuse. The law plays an important role in protecting children and punishing persons who abuse them.

(b) Testimony from children is often essential to prove that abuse occurred, to identify the perpetrator of abuse, and to prove other crimes. Thus, children often must testify in legal proceedings.

(c) The courtrooms of this state and other states are not designed with children in mind, and the formal nature of the courtroom and the proceedings that occur there cause fear and anxiety that interferes with some children's ability to provide full and accurate testimony. In addition to fear and anxiety that interferes with full and accurate testimony, testifying in the traditional fashion is emotionally harmful for some children. Because testifying is very stressful for many children, and because testifying traumatizes some children and can interfere with full and accurate testimony, this state has a compelling interest in accommodating child witnesses to reduce unnecessary stress, anxiety, fear, and trauma, and to increase the accuracy and completeness of testimony.

(d) Accommodations for child witnesses can be made without compromising the right to a fair trial and without unnecessarily undermining the right to confront and cross-examine witnesses.

(e) The judges of this state have a responsibility to protect vulnerable witnesses, including children, from unnecessary stress and trauma. Judges can accommodate child witnesses without compromising judicial neutrality and without undermining the rights of persons accused of crime. Research discloses that judges seldom implement accommodations that are available to them under existing law. It is the intent of the legislature that the judges of this state make liberal use of the provisions set forth in this code to ensure maximum accommodation for child witnesses and to protect children from unnecessary trauma and stress. Judges should take an active role in accommodating child witnesses to reduce trauma and increase the accuracy and completeness of testimony.

(f) The cooperation of children and their families is essential to the successful prosecution of child abuse and other crimes. Release of information identifying child victims and witnesses and their families may subject the child and the child's family to unwanted contacts by the media, public scrutiny, severe embarrassment and humiliation, and psychological harm and may place the child and the child's family at risk from some perpetrators. Release of information regarding a child victim or witness or the child's family to the press and the public harms the child and the child's family and has a chilling effect on the willingness of children and their families to report child abuse and other crimes and to cooperate with the investigation and prosecution of crime. Public dissemination of the child's name, address, phone number, school, and other identifying information about the child and the child's family is not necessary for the accurate release of information to the public concerning the operation of the criminal justice system. Therefore, the legislature intends to assure child victims and witnesses and their families that the identities and locations of child victims and witnesses and their families will remain confidential.

§ 2 Title of Code

This code shall be known as the Child Witness Code.

§ 3 Purpose

The purposes of this code are to ascertain the truth, reduce trauma to children, create conditions that will allow children to provide reliable and complete evidence, increase the number of children who are able to testify in legal proceedings, and protect the rights of persons accused of crime.

§ 4 Applicability of Child Witness Code

(a) This code applies in all criminal proceedings, including pretrial and posttrial proceedings, conducted in this state. The term criminal proceeding includes juvenile delinquency proceedings conducted in the juvenile court.

(b) This code applies to children who are victims of crime and children who witness crime but are not victims thereof. Certain sections of this code apply only to children who are victims of crime.

(c) To the extent provisions of this code provide guidance in civil litigation, a judge may rely on provisions of this code to accommodate children in civil cases.

§ 5 Code to Be Liberally Construed to Accommodate Children

This code shall be liberally construed to ensure maximum accommodation of child witnesses. The rule of the common law, that statutes in derogation thereof are to be strictly construed, has no application to this code.

§ 6 Inherent Judicial Authority

Judges of this state have inherent judicial authority to accommodate children in addition to the specific accommodations authorized by this code.

§ 7 Definitions

(a) "Child" means a person under the age of 18 years.

(b) "Child abuse" means physical abuse, sexual abuse, and criminal neglect as defined elsewhere in applicable law.

(c) "Intermediary" means a person appointed by the court to pose questions to a child.

(d) "Record regarding a child" or "record" means any photograph, videotape, film, handwriting, typewriting, printing, electronic recording, computer data or print-out, or other memorialization, including any court document, indictment, complaint, or information, or any copy or reproduction of any of the foregoing, that contains the name, description, address, school, or any other personal identifying information about a child or the child's family and that is produced by or maintained by a public agency, private agency, or individual.

§ 8 Vertical Prosecution

Whenever practicable, the same prosecutor should handle all aspects of a case involving a child victim.

§ 9 Special Precautions for Child Witnesses

The court shall take steps to provide for the comfort and support of child witnesses and to protect children from coercion, intimidation, unnecessary psychological stress, and undue influence.

§ 10 Docket Priority

The court shall give docket priority to any criminal case involving a child victim. The court and the prosecutor shall take appropriate steps to insure a speedy trial in order to minimize the length of time the child must endure the stress of involvement in the proceedings.

§ 11 Continuances

Whenever a motion or other request for a delay or continuance is made in a case involving a child victim, the court shall grant the delay or continuance only for substantial reasons, and the court shall consider and give weight to the adverse impact the delay or continuance may have on the well-being of the child. The court shall make findings on the record when granting a continuance in cases involving a child victim.

§ 12 Court Preparation Programs

Programs designed to prepare children to testify serve the interests of justice and are encouraged. Judges are encouraged to participate in court preparation programs, and judicial participation in such programs is not a ground for recusal or disqualification. Judges should make their courtroom and staff available for court preparation programs. The fact that a child participated in a court participation program may not be used to impeach the child's credibility.

§ 13 Waiting Area for Child Witnesses

(a) The court shall provide a waiting area for children that is separate from waiting areas used by other persons. The child's waiting area should be furnished so as to make the child comfortable.

(b) Courts are encouraged to create special waiting areas for child witnesses.

§ 14 Guardian Ad Litem

(a) The court shall appoint a guardian ad litem for a child who was a victim of, or a witness to, a crime to protect the best interests of the child. In making the appointment, the court shall consider a prospective guardian's background in and familiarity with the judicial process, social service programs, and child development. The guardian ad litem shall not be a person who is a witness in a proceeding involving the child for whom the guardian is appointed. The guardian ad litem may, but need not, be an attorney. The guardian ad litem shall be notified of all proceedings.

(b) *Duties of guardian ad litem.* A guardian ad litem:

(1) May attend all interviews, depositions, hearings, and trial proceedings in which a child participates.

(2) Shall remain with the child in the courthouse or other location while the child waits to testify.

(3) May make recommendations to the court concerning the welfare of the child.

(4) May have access to all reports, evaluations, and records, except attorney's work product, necessary to effectively advocate for the child.

(5) May interview witnesses.

(6) Shall marshal and coordinate the delivery of resources and special services to the child.

(7) May request additional examinations by medical or mental health professionals if there is a compelling need for additional examination.

(8) Shall explain, in language understandable to the child, all legal proceedings, including police investigations, in which the child is involved.

(9) Shall, to the extent desired by the child and the child's family, assist the child and the child's family in coping with the emotional effects of crime and subsequent criminal or civil proceedings in which the child is involved.

(c) A guardian ad litem shall not be compelled to testify in any proceeding concerning any information, statement, or opinion received from the child in the course of serving as a guardian ad litem.

(d) A guardian ad litem shall be presumed to be acting in good faith and shall be immune from civil and criminal liability for complying with the guardian's duties described in section (b).

(e) A guardian ad litem shall not participate in the trial by way of juror voir dire, opening statement, closing argument, introducing or objecting to evidence, or examination of witnesses, including the child witness; provided that:

(1) A guardian ad litem, if the guardian ad litem is an attorney, may object during trial under section 33 that questions asked of a child are developmentally inappropriate.

(2) A guardian ad litem, whether or not an attorney, may communicate concerns regarding the child to the court at any time when court is not in session.

(3) A guardian ad litem, whether or not an attorney, may communicate concerns regarding the child to the court when court is in session through an officer of the court designated for that purpose by the court.

(4) A guardian ad litem, whether or not an attorney, may file motions pursuant to sections 20, 36, 37, 39 and 41(c).

§ 15 Support Persons

(a) A child testifying at or attending a judicial proceeding or deposition shall have the right to be accompanied by up to two persons of the child's own choosing, one of whom may be a witness, to provide emotional support to the child. Both support persons may remain in the courtroom or other room and in the child's sight during the child's testimony. One of the support persons may accompany the child to the witness stand, provided the support person does not completely obscure the child from the view of the defendant or the trier of fact. If needed for emotional support, the support person may hold the child's hand, hold the child on the support person's lap throughout the course of the proceeding, or take other steps appropriate to support the child.

(b) If a person chosen under section (a) is also a prosecuting witness, the court may disapprove the choice if the defense establishes by a preponderance of the evidence that the support person's attendance during the testimony of the child would pose a substantial risk of influencing or affecting the content of the child's testimony.

(c) If a person chosen under section (a) is also a prosecuting witness, the testimony of the support person shall be presented before the testimony of the child.

(d) A support person shall not provide the child with an answer to any question directed to the child during the course of the child's testimony or otherwise prompt the child. The court shall admonish the support person or persons not to prompt, sway, or influence the child during the child's testimony.

§ 16 Competency

Every child, irrespective of age, is qualified to be a witness unless the child lacks the ability to communicate, remember, distinguish truth from falsehood, or appreciate the duty to tell the truth in court. Every child is presumed to possess the requirements contained in this section.

§ 17 Competency Examination

(a) *When competency examination is allowed.* A court shall not hold a competency examination for a child unless the court, on its own motion or the motion of a party, determines that substantial doubt exists regarding the child's competence to testify. A party seeking a competency examination must present specific evidence that establishes that a competency examination is required. A child's age alone is not a sufficient reason for a competency examination.

(b) *Burden on party challenging competence.* If a court orders a competency examination, the burden of persuasion is on the party challenging the child's competence to rebut the presumption of competence established by section 16 and to prove by a preponderance of evidence that the child is not competent.

(c) *Persons present at examination.* The persons who may be present at a competency examination are limited to:

(1) the judge;

(2) the attorneys for the parties;

(3) the child's guardian ad litem;

(4) one or more support person for the child; and

(5) the defendant unless the defendant is excluded from the competency examination pursuant to section (d).

(d) *Excluding defendant from examination.* The defendant shall be excluded from the competency examination unless the court determines that competence cannot be fully evaluated in the absence of the defendant.

(e) *Examination outside jury's presence.* A competency examination shall be conducted out of the sight and hearing of the jury. A competency examination may be conducted in the judge's chambers or in some other location.

(f) *Questioning by the court.* Examination of a child related to competence shall normally be conducted by the court. Attorneys may submit questions to the court that the court may, in its discretion, ask the child. The court may permit an attorney to examine a child directly on competence if the court is satisfied that the child will not suffer emotional trauma as a result of the examination.

(g) *Developmentally appropriate questions.* The questions asked at the competency examination shall be appropriate to the age and developmental level of the child, shall not be related to the issues at trial, and shall focus on the child's ability to communicate, remember, understand the difference between truth and falsehood, and understand the duty to testify truthfully.

(h) *Psychological and psychiatric examinations regarding competence prohibited.* Psychological and psychiatric examinations to assess the competence of a child witness shall not be ordered.

(i) *Continuing duty to assess competence.* The court's responsibility to assess competence continues throughout the child's testimony.

§ 18 Oath or Affirmation

Before testifying, a child shall be required to declare that the child will testify truthfully, by oath or affirmation in a form calculated to awaken the child's conscience and impress the child's mind with the duty to do so. For a child under the age of 10, the court shall administer an affirmation in which the child promises to tell the truth.

§ 19 Interpreter for Child

(a) When a child is incapable of understanding the English language or is incapable, due to developmental level, fear, shyness, disability, or other reason, of communicating in the English language so as to be heard and understood directly by counsel, court, and jury, an interpreter whom the child can understand and who understands the child shall be sworn to interpret for the child.

(b) An interpreter should not be a witness in the case and should not have an interest in the case, provided that if a witness or member of the child's family is the only person who can serve as an interpreter for the child, then the witness or family member may serve as the child's interpreter. If the interpreter is also a witness, the interpreter shall testify before the child.

(c) An interpreter shall take an oath or affirmation to make a true and accurate interpretation.

§ 20 Intermediary to Pose Questions to Child

(a) A party or the child's guardian ad litem may apply for an order that an intermediary be appointed by the court. The court may appoint an intermediary on its own motion.

(b) The court may appoint an intermediary to pose questions to a child if the court finds that the child is unable to understand and/or respond to questions asked by counsel or the court.

(c) If the court appoints an intermediary to pose questions to the child, counsel for the parties shall not question the child. The intermediary shall pose questions desired by the prosecution and defense.

(d) Questions put to a child through an intermediary shall be either in the words selected by counsel or, if the child is not likely to understand the words selected by counsel, in words that are comprehensible to the child and which convey the meaning intended by counsel.

(e) An intermediary shall take an oath or affirmation to pose questions to the child accurately according to the meaning intended by counsel.

§ 21 Psychological and Psychiatric Examinations Regarding Credibility Prohibited

Psychological and psychiatric examinations to assess the credibility of a child witness shall not be ordered.

§ 22 Comfort Item

While testifying, a child shall be allowed to have a comfort item of the child's own choosing such as a blanket, toy, or doll.

§ 23 Testimonial Aids

The court shall permit a child to use dolls, anatomical dolls, puppets, drawings, mannequins, or any other demonstrative device the court deems appropriate for the purpose of assisting a child in testifying.

§ 24 Recesses During Child's Testimony

(a) The child may be allowed reasonable periods of relief from direct examination, cross-examination, and reexamination during which the child may retire from the courtroom. The court may allow other witnesses to testify while the child retires from the courtroom.

(b) In advance of the child's testimony, the court may order that relief from testimony will occur at regular intervals.

(c) Child witnesses age 8 and younger should normally be given relief from testimony every 30 minutes or more frequently.

§ 25 Persons Prohibited From Entering and Leaving Courtroom

The court may order that persons attending the trial shall not enter or leave the courtroom during the child's testimony.

§ 26 Testimony During Appropriate Hours

The court may order that the child's testimony be taken during a time of day when the child is well rested.

§ 27 Rearranging Courtroom

In the court's discretion, the judge, child, parties, witnesses, support persons, and court personnel may be relocated within the courtroom to facilitate a more comfortable environment for the child. The child may testify from a location in the courtroom other than the witness chair. The court shall supervise the spatial arrangements of the courtroom and the location, movement, and deportment of all persons in attendance. The witness chair or other place from which the child testifies may be turned to facilitate the child's testimony. The defendant and the trier of fact must have a frontal or profile view of the child during the child's testimony. Whenever the witness chair or other place from which the child testifies is turned pursuant to this section, the child must be able to see the defendant without having to turn the child's head more than 90 degrees if the child chooses to look at the defendant. Nothing in this section or any other provision of law, except official in-court identification provisions, shall be construed to require a child to look at the defendant. The judge may remove the judge's robe. Accommodations for the child under this section need not be supported by a finding of trauma to the child.

§ 28 Approaching the Witness

The court may prohibit an attorney from approaching a child if it appears that the child is fearful of the attorney or intimidated by the attorney.

§ 29 Mode and Order of Questioning

The court shall exercise control over the questioning of children so as to (1) make the questioning and presentation effective for the ascertainment of the truth, (2) avoid needless consumption of time, (3) protect children from harassment or undue embarrassment, and (4) ensure that questions are stated in a form appropriate to the age and understanding of the child.

§ 30 Questioning by Court

The court may question the child to clarify facts, ensure that the child understands questions asked by attorneys, and for other purposes.

§ 31 Leading Questions During Direct Examination

The court may allow leading questions during direct and redirect examination of a child if leading questions will further the interests of justice.

§ 32 Objections

The court may order that objections be made so as not to frighten, confuse, or intimidate the child.

§ 33 *Objection to Developmentally Inappropriate Question*

On its own motion, the objection of a party, or the objection of the child's guardian ad litem, the court shall forbid the asking of a question that is in a form that is not reasonably likely to be understood by a child of the age or developmental level of the child.

§ 34 *Sexual Abuse Shield Statute*

(a) *Evidence generally inadmissible.* The following evidence is not admissible in any criminal proceeding involving alleged child sexual abuse except as provided in subdivisions (b) and (c):

   (1) Evidence offered to prove that any alleged victim engaged in other sexual behavior.
   (2) Evidence offered to prove any alleged victim's sexual predisposition.

(b) *Exceptions.*

   (1) In a criminal case, the following evidence is admissible, if otherwise admissible under the law of this jurisdiction:

      (A) Evidence of specific instances of sexual behavior by the alleged victim to prove that a person other than the defendant was the source of semen, injury, or other physical evidence;
      (B) Evidence the exclusion of which would violate the constitutional rights of the defendant.

(c) *Procedure to determine admissibility.*

   (1) A party intending to offer evidence under subdivision (a) must:

      (A) File a written motion at least 14 days before trial specifically describing the evidence and stating the purpose for which it is offered unless the court, for good cause, requires a different time for filing or permits filing during trial; and
      (B) Serve the motion on all parties and the child's guardian ad litem.

   (2) Before admitting evidence under this section, the court must conduct a hearing in camera and afford the child, the child's guardian ad litem, and parties a right to attend and be heard. The motion, related papers, and the record of the hearing must be sealed and remain under seal and protected

by a protective order set forth in section 41(d). The child shall not be required to testify at the hearing in camera unless the child wishes to do so.

§ 35 Closing the Courtroom

When a child testifies, the court may order the exclusion from the courtroom of all persons, including members of the press, who do not have a direct interest in the case. Such an order may be made if the court determines on the record that requiring the child to testify in open court would cause psychological harm to the child or would result in the child's inability to effectively communicate due to embarrassment, fear, or timidity. In reaching its decision, the court shall consider the child's age, psychological maturity, the nature of the crime, the nature of the child's testimony regarding the crime, the relationship of the child to the defendant and to persons attending the trial, the desires of the child, and the interests of the child's parents or guardians. Such an order shall be narrowly tailored to serve the state's interests in protecting the child from psychological harm and ensuring complete testimony.

§ 36 Live-Link Television Testimony

(a) The prosecutor or the child's guardian ad litem may apply for an order that the child's testimony be taken in a room outside the courtroom and be televised to the courtroom by live-link television. Before the child's guardian ad litem applies for an order under this section, the guardian ad litem shall consult with the prosecutor and shall defer to the prosecutor's judgment regarding whether to apply for an order unless the guardian ad litem is convinced that the prosecutor's decision not to apply for an order will cause the child serious emotional trauma. The person seeking such an order shall apply at least 5 days before the trial date, unless the court finds on the record that the need for such an order was not reasonably foreseeable.

(b) The court may order that the testimony of the child be taken by live-link television as provided in section (a) if the court finds any of the following:

(1) The child is unable to testify fully in open court in the presence of the defendant due to fear of the defendant.

(2) There is a substantial likelihood that the child would suffer at least moderate nontransient emotional trauma from testifying in the presence of the defendant. The trauma need not be permanent, but must be more than the nervousness and anxiety experienced by most witnesses.

(3) Conduct by defendant or defense counsel causes the child to be unable to testify or continue testifying in the presence of defendant or defense counsel.

(c) The court shall support a ruling on use of live-link television on the record. The court shall consider the totality of the circumstances. Expert testimony may be considered, although expert testimony is not required to support a ruling allowing live-link television. The court may consider the following factors:

   (1) The child's age and level of development;

   (2) The child's physical and mental health, including any mental or physical disability;

   (3) Any physical, emotional, or psychological injury experienced by the child;

   (4) The nature of the alleged abuse;

   (5) Any threats against the child;

   (6) The child's relationship to the defendant;

   (7) The child's reaction to any prior encounters with the defendant in court or elsewhere;

   (8) The child's reaction prior to trial when the topic of testifying was discussed with the child by parents or professionals;

   (9) Specific symptoms of stress exhibited by the child in the days prior to testifying;

   (10) Testimony of lay witnesses;

   (11) The child's custodial situation and the attitude of members of the child's family regarding the events about which the child will testify;

   (12) Any other relevant factors.

(d) In ruling on a request for live-link television, the court may question the child in chambers, or at some other comfortable place other than the courtroom, on the record. The only other persons who may be present during the questioning include a support person for the child, the prosecutor, the child's guardian ad litem, and defense counsel. The defendant shall not attend the questioning. Questioning shall not be related to the issues at trial except that questions may relate to the child's feelings about testifying in the courtroom in the presence of the defendant.

(e) If the court orders the taking of testimony by live-link television, the prosecutor and the attorney for the defendant, not including a defendant representing himself or herself, shall be present in a room outside the courtroom with the child and the child shall be available for direct and cross-examination. The only other persons who may be permitted in the room with the child during the child's testimony are:

   (1) The child's guardian ad litem;

   (2) Persons necessary to operate the closed-circuit television equipment;

   (3) A court officer, appointed by the court;

(4) Other persons whose presence is determined by the court to be necessary to the welfare and well-being of the child; and

(5) One or both of the child's support persons.

(f) The child's testimony shall be transmitted by live-link television into the courtroom for viewing and hearing by the defendant, jury, judge, and public. The defendant shall be provided with a means of private, contemporaneous communication with the defendant's attorney during the testimony.

(g) While the child testifies it is not necessary that the child be able to view an image of the defendant.

(h) The court may set any other conditions and limitations on the taking of the testimony that it finds just and appropriate, taking into consideration the interests of the child, the rights of the defendant, and any other relevant facts.

(i) If it is necessary for the child to identify the defendant at trial, the court may allow the child to enter the courtroom for the limited purpose of identifying the defendant or the court may allow the child to identify the defendant by observing the defendant's image on a television monitor.

(j) The child's testimony shall be preserved on videotape. The videotape shall be made a part of the court record and shall be subject to a protective order as provided in section 41(d).

§ 37 Videotaped Deposition

(a) The prosecutor or child's guardian ad litem may apply for an order that a deposition be taken of the child's testimony and that the deposition be recorded and preserved on videotape. Before the child's guardian ad litem applies for an order under this section, the guardian ad litem shall consult with the prosecutor as required in section 36(a).

(b) On receipt of an application described in section 37(a), the court shall make a finding regarding whether at the time of trial the child is likely to be unable to testify in open court.

(c) If the court finds pursuant to section 36(b) that the child is likely to be unable to testify at trial, the court shall order that the child's deposition be taken and preserved by videotape.

(d) The court shall preside at the videotape deposition of a child. Objections to deposition testimony or evidence or parts thereof, and the grounds for the objection, shall be stated at the time of the taking of the deposition. The only other persons who may be permitted to be present at the proceeding are:

(1) The prosecutor;

(2) The attorney for the defendant;

(3) The child's guardian ad litem;

(4) Persons necessary to operate the videotape equipment;

(5) Subject to section 37(f), the defendant;

(6) Other persons whose presence is determined by the court to be necessary to the welfare and well-being of the child; and

(7) One or both of the child's support persons.

(e) The defendant shall be afforded the rights applicable to defendants during trial, including the right to an attorney, the right to be confronted with the child, and the right to cross-examine the child.

(f) If the finding of likely inability to testify under section 37(b) is based on evidence that the child is unable to testify in the physical presence of the defendant, the court may order that the defendant, including a defendant representing himself or herself, be excluded from the room in which the deposition is conducted. If the court orders that the defendant be excluded from the deposition room, the court shall order that live-link television equipment relay the child's image into the room where the defendant is located, and that the defendant be provided with a means of private, contemporaneous communication with the defendant's attorney during the deposition. If the defendant is excluded from the deposition, it is not necessary that the child be able to view an image of the defendant.

(g) The complete record of the examination of the child, including the image and voices of all persons who in any way participate in the examination, shall be made and preserved on videotape in addition to being stenographically recorded. The videotape shall be transmitted to the clerk of the court in which the action is pending and shall be made a part of the record.

(h) The court may set any other conditions and limitations on the taking of the deposition that it finds just and appropriate, taking into consideration the interests of the child, the rights of the defendant, and any other relevant factors.

(i) The videotape deposition shall be subject to a protective order as provided in section 41(d).

(j) If, at the time of trial, the court finds that the child is unable to testify for a reason described in section 36(b), or is unavailable for any reason described in [rule defining unavailability, e.g., Federal Rule of Evidence 804(a)], the court may admit into evidence the child's videotaped deposition in lieu of the child's testimony at the trial. The court shall support a ruling under this section with findings on the record.

(k) On timely receipt of notice that new evidence has been discovered after the original videotaping and before or during trial, the court, for good cause shown, may order an additional videotaped deposition. The testimony of the child shall be restricted to the matters specified by the court as the basis for granting the order.

§ 38 Videotaped Preliminary Hearing Testimony

(a) The prosecutor may apply at any time for an order that a child's testimony at a preliminary hearing, in addition to being stenographically recorded, be videotaped.

(b) On timely receipt of the application, the magistrate shall order that the testimony of the child given at the preliminary hearing be videotaped. The videotape shall be transmitted to the clerk of the court in which the action is pending and shall be made a part of the record.

(c) If, at the time of trial, the court finds that the child is unavailable to testify for a reason described in section 36(b), or is unavailable for any reason described in [rule defining unavailability, e.g., Federal Rule of Evidence 804(a)], the court may admit into evidence the child's videotaped preliminary hearing testimony as former testimony. The court shall support a ruling under this section with findings on the record.

(d) The child's videotaped preliminary hearing testimony shall be made a part of the court record and shall be subject to a protective order as provided in section 41(d).

§ 39 Screens and Other Devices to Shield Child From Defendant

(a) The prosecutor or the child's guardian ad litem may apply for an order that the child's chair be turned or that a screen or other device be placed in the courtroom so that the child cannot see the defendant while the child testifies in the courtroom. Before the child's guardian ad litem applies for an order under this section, the guardian ad litem shall consult with the prosecutor as required in section 36(a). The person seeking such an order shall apply for such an order at least 5 days before the trial date, unless the court finds on the record that the need for an order was not reasonably foreseeable.

(b) The court may order that the child be screened from viewing the defendant as provided in section (a) if the court finds any of the factors listed in section 36(b).

(c) The court shall support a ruling on screening the child from the defendant on the record. The court shall consider the factors in section 36(c).

(d) In ruling on an application to shield the child from the defendant during the child's testimony in the courtroom, the court may question the child as provided in section 36(d).

(e) If the court grants an application to shield the child from the defendant during the child's testimony in the courtroom, the court shall arrange the courtroom so that the defendant can view the child during the child's testimony.

(f) If the court grants an application made under section (a), the court shall describe for the record the courtroom arrangement approved by the court.

§ 40 Child Hearsay Exception

(a) A statement made by a child describing any act or attempted act of child abuse performed with or on the child by another, or describing any act or attempted act of child abuse witnessed by the declarant child, not otherwise admissible, is admissible in evidence in any civil, criminal, or administrative proceeding if:

   (1) The court finds, in a hearing conducted outside the presence of the jury, that the time content, and circumstances of the statement provide sufficient indicia of reliability; and

   (2) The child either:

      (A) Testifies at the proceedings; or

      (B) Is unavailable as a witness, provided that when the child is unavailable as a witness, such statement may be admitted only if there is corroborative evidence of the act.

(b) A statement may not be admitted under this section unless the proponent of the statement makes known to the adverse party the intention to offer the statement and the particulars of the statement sufficiently in advance of the proceedings to provide the adverse party with a fair opportunity to prepare to meet the statement.

§ 41 Protection of Child's Privacy and Safety

(a) *Records under seal.* Any record regarding a child that is part of the court record shall be confidential and under seal and shall not be released to anyone except the following:

   (1) Members of the court staff for administrative use;

   (2) The prosecuting attorney;

   (3) Defense counsel;

   (4) The child's guardian ad litem;

   (5) Agents of investigating law enforcement agencies;

   (6) Other persons on order of the court.

(b) *All government and private agencies to protect privacy.* Every agency of state or local government, and every private agency or person that provides services to children and/or their families, shall protect the confidentiality of records containing the identity of children who are or may be victims of crime. Children have the right not to have their name, address, telephone number, school, photograph, or other identifying information about them or their family disclosed by any law enforcement agency, prosecutor's office, state or local government agency, or private agency or person as defined herein, without the permission of the child if the child is of sufficient age and maturity to give informed consent to release, or the child's parent or guardian, to anyone except a law enforcement agency, prosecutor, defense counsel, guardian ad litem, or private or government agency or person that provides services to the child.

(c) *Identifying information deleted.* The name, address, telephone number, school, and other identifying information regarding a child and members of the child's family shall not appear on any indictment, complaint, information, pleading, motion, brief, or any other court document or legal record in the trial courts or appellate courts of this state. In place of the child's name shall appear initials or a fictitious name.

(d) *Protective order.* Any videotape or audiotape of a child that is part of the court record shall be under a protective order that provides as follows:

Protective Order

(1) For purposes of this order tape(s) means any videotape or audiotape of a child.

(2) Tapes may be viewed only by parties, their counsel and their counsel's employees, investigators and experts for the purpose of prosecuting or defending this action, and the child's guardian ad litem.

(3) No tape, or the substance of any portion thereof, shall be divulged by any person subject to this protective order to any other person, except as necessary for the trial or preparation for trial in this proceeding, and such information shall be used only for purposes of the trial and preparation for trial herein.

(4) No person shall be granted access to the tape, any transcription thereof, or the substance of any portion thereof unless that person has first signed an agreement in writing that the person has received and read a copy of this protective order, that the person submits to the court's jurisdiction with respect to the protective order, and that the person will be subject to the court's contempt powers for any violation of the protective order.

(5) Each of the tape cassettes and transcripts thereof available to the parties, their attorneys and respective agents shall bear the following legend:

This object or document and the contents thereof is subject to a protective order entered by the court in *State v.* _____. Case number _____.
This object or document and the contents thereof may not be examined, inspected, read, viewed, or copied by any person, or disclosed to any person, except as provided in the protective order. Any person violating

such protective order is be subject to the full contempt power of the court and may be guilty of a crime.

(6) Unless otherwise provided by order of this court, no additional copies of the tape or any portion of the tape shall be made without prior court order.

(7) The tape shall not be given, loaned, sold, or shown to any person except as provided by this order or by subsequent order of this court.

(8) On final disposition of this case, any and all copies of the tape and any transcripts thereof shall be returned to the court for safekeeping, except those tapes booked into and kept as evidence by the investigating law enforcement agencies. Those materials subject to this order so kept by any law enforcement agency shall remain subject to this order and those materials shall remain secured in evidence in accordance with the agency's policies and procedures.

(9) This protective order shall remain in full force and effect until further order of this court.

(e) *Additional protective orders.* The court may, on its own motion, or on the motion of any party, the child, the child's parents or guardian, or the child's guardian ad litem, enter any protective orders needed to protect the child's privacy in addition to the protective order required by section (d). A protective order may protect any record on a child.

(f) *Publication of identity unlawful.* Whoever publishes or causes to be published in any format the name, address, phone number, school, or other identifying information of a child who is or is alleged to be a victim of crime, or a member of the child's family, or who violates the protective order set forth in section (d) shall be guilty of a misdemeanor.

(g) *Physical safety of child; exclusion of evidence.* A child has a right at any court proceeding not to testify regarding personal identifying information including the child's name, address, telephone number, school, and other information that could lead to the whereabouts of the child or the child's family. The court may require the child to testify regarding personal identifying information that is required to be disclosed in the interest of justice.

(h) *Unauthorized release does not bar prosecution.* Any release of information in violation of this section does not bar prosecution or other legal action or provide grounds for dismissal of charges.

(i) *Destruction of videotapes and audiotapes.* Any videotape or audiotape of a child produced under the provisions of this code or otherwise made part of the court record shall be destroyed after 5 years have elapsed from the date of entry of judgment or other disposition, provided that if an appeal is filed, the tape shall not be destroyed until a final judgment on appeal has been rendered.

(j) The name of the defendant shall be available as part of the record to the extent permitted by law whether or not the defendant is a member of a child victim's family.

§ 42 Multidisciplinary Team Instigation; Interviewing

(a) Every county in the state shall create and maintain one or more multidisciplinary teams to investigate child abuse and interview children who witness abuse or who may be victims of abuse.

(b) Every county in the state, in conjunction with appropriate state, local, and private agencies, shall provide ongoing training to professionals who interview children. Training shall be provided to multidisciplinary teams and other professionals who interview children.

(c) Whenever it is necessary to interview a child regarding possible child abuse, efforts shall be made to have the child interviewed by a professional with training and experience interviewing children.

§ 43 Videotaping and Audiotaping Investigative Interviews

(a) Whenever child abuse is suspected and a child is interviewed by a member of a multidisciplinary team or a representative of law enforcement or child protective services, the interview shall be videotaped unless exigent circumstances render videotaping extremely difficult or impossible. If an interview is not videotaped, the interview shall be audiotaped unless audiotaping is impossible due to lack of proper equipment or an emergency.

(b) The requirements of this section regarding videotaping and audiotaping pertain to in-depth investigative interviews, commonly called disclosure interviews, where the goal of questioning is to determine whether child abuse occurred. Nothing in this section shall be construed to require videotaping or audiotaping of brief field contacts between children and representatives of law enforcement or child protective services that do not constitute in-depth investigative interviews.

(c) The fact that an investigative interview is or is not videotaped or audiotaped may be considered in determining the reliability of a child's statements describing abuse.

(d) The fact that an investigative interview is not videotaped or audiotaped as required by this section shall not by itself constitute a basis to exclude from evidence a child's out-of-court statements or testimony.

§ 44 Corroboration

Except as provided in § 40(a)(2)(B) of this code, corroboration shall not be required of a child's testimony, and a child's testimony, if believed, shall be sufficient to support a finding of fact, conclusion, or verdict.

§ 45 Jury Instruction Regarding Child's Testimony

On the request of a party, the court shall instruct the jury as follows:

In evaluating the testimony of a child you should consider all of the factors surrounding the child's testimony, including the age of the child and any evidence regarding the child's level of cognitive development. Although, because of age and level of cognitive development, a child may perform differently as a witness than an adult, that does not mean that a child is any more or less credible a witness than an adult. You should not discount or distrust the testimony of a child solely because he or she is a child.

§ 46 Severability

If any provision of this Child Witness Code or its application to any person or circumstance is held invalid, the remainder of the code or the application of the provision to other persons or circumstances is not affected.

14

Children as Witnesses
India Is Not Ready

UMA A. SEGAL

In a country such as India, 1,269,340 square miles in size, with a population of 852.4 million projected to reach 1 billion by the year 2000 (Population Reference Bureau, 1990), and where more than half the country lives below the poverty line, many of the problems children face are in the areas of health, nutrition, and education and are a result of impoverished economic conditions (Rane, Naidu, & Kapadia, 1986). India's child population under the age of 16 was 319.3 million in 1988 (UNICEF, 1990), 70.6 million more than the total population of the United States as reported by the 1990 census. Consequently, governmental agencies, nongovernmental organizations, and human service professionals have, almost by necessity, focused on the basic survival needs of children. However, a gradual increase in public and professional interest in the intrafamilial maltreatment of children suggests that child abuse may be an issue that warrants attention in India through the remainder of the 1990s and into the 21st century. As recently as 1988, nevertheless, there was a dearth of empirical data on the extent, nature, causes, and effects of different forms of child abuse in India. The First National Seminar on Child Abuse in India, held in New Delhi in 1988, revealed that there was practically no information about child abuse within the family.

This chapter presents an overview of the traditional Indian family and perceptions of children in India and explores the Indian Constitution, India's juvenile justice system, and the incidence of child abuse. Children's rights and available social services are discussed with a view to the use of child witnesses within the sociocultural context of the Indian subcontinent.

The Indian Family

Values have been shown to influence perception, affect problem solving, determine the selection of alternatives, and help coordinate and stabilize behaviors in social systems (Bamberger, 1986). At least five traditional values underpin the lifestyles of many Asians, including Indians, and serve to reinforce the joint family structure and specify relationships between parent and child:

1. Asians are allocentric or group oriented, and the individual is expected to make sacrifices for the good of the family (Hofstede, 1980; Segal; 1988; Triandis, Bontempo, Villareal, Asai, & Lucca, 1988).
2. Males are valued more than females. They act as the head of the household, primary wage earners, decision makers, and disciplinarians. Women are subordinate and serve as caretakers, and as children, they are groomed to move into and contribute to the well-being of the husband's family (Ho, 1988; Sue, 1981).
3. Children are docile and obedient. Their role is to bring honor to their families by exhibiting good behavior and high achievement and by contributing to the overall enhancement of the family (Dutt, 1989; Saran, 1985; Sinha, 1984).
4. High levels of dependency are fostered in the family. The female is expected to be dependent on the father, the husband, and the eldest son, in succession, throughout her life. Children are dependent emotionally, and often socially, on their parents for the duration of the parents' lives. Traditionally, all difficulties are handled within the family, whether these difficulties are familial, emotional, professional, financial, or health related (Ho, 1988; Sinha, 1984).
5. Two major concepts tend to permeate all significant relationships: obligation and shame. One is expected to be selfless and obligated to significant others, especially within the family. Furthermore, one's behavior should never bring shame on oneself or on one's family (Chathrathi, 1985; Ho, 1988; Sue, 1981).

It is within the constellation of these traditional values that one must view the Indian family structure, the role of children in that structure, and the rights of children in India.

Whereas the family is found to be an almost universal basic unit of society, it differs cross-culturally in form, and Indian values favor the joint family system. This structure is hierarchical in nature, and three or more generations may live together; age, gender, and generational status of individuals serve as the primary determinants of behavior and role relationships (Sue, 1981). Two or more family groupings of the same generation may be found in the joint family as sons bring their spouses to the parental home. A high premium is placed on conformity; interdependence is fostered, self-identity is inhibited (Sinha, 1984), and a conservative orientation, resistive to change, is rewarded.

In the joint family, each child has multiple role models, most of which model conformity (Sinha, 1984). Supervision of children is shared by all family members. Whereas infants are generally overindulged, young children are reared in an authoritarian atmosphere, in which autonomy is not tolerated (Whiting, 1961). As children enter their teen and young adult years, guilt, shame, and a sense of moral obligation are used as the primary mechanisms of control (Sue, 1981). This control model does have a positive aspect to it in that it provides a structure that maintains family integrity through a deep-seated belief in societal norms and obligation to duty. Western authors frequently overlook this aspect of Indian culture, which serves to bind the intergenerational family together (Segal, 1991a).

Belief in the integrity of the group provides the family with a group identity and strengthens family stability (Triandis et al., 1988). In addition, in most Third World and Asian countries, children are valued for their economic ability to contribute to the survival of the family and as a source of security for parents in their old age (Tanwar, 1988). Even among middle-class families, in which children are not expected to work until they complete their education, it is generally understood that they will eventually provide a home and support for their aging parents.

The transitional period of adolescence, during which children in the West renegotiate relationships with their parents, is relatively absent for the Indian teenager. Children continue to remain submissive to parents even after they get married, become employed, and leave the parental home (Sue, 1981). Because youth must always defer to age, the autocratic parent-child relationship tends to persist. Children are believed to be the property of their parents, and they continue to be perceived as extensions of their parents throughout the lifetime of the latter.

The Incidence of Child Abuse

In many nations, including India, traditional themes of the sanctity of the family, prerogatives of parents, and children viewed as parental property have protected abusive families from inspection and intervention by society. As a result of the increasing international recognition of the rights of the child, both developed and developing countries must take a closer look at the behavior of adults responsible for the care, nurture, and maintenance of children. However, child abuse in developing Third World countries is often camouflaged by the norms, values, and expectations of differing sociocultural traditions.

Although child abuse may be prevalent, it may not be perceived as such, because terms such as *harshness, discipline,* and *abuse* are culture specific. Professionals who come from similar cultural backgrounds may not recognize physical abuse as being problematic (Singh, 1988). Certainly, this was reinforced by a replication of Giovannoni and Becerra's (1979) study. The physical abuse of children was ranked by Indians as being sixth in severity, after sexual abuse, fostering delinquency, medical neglect, poor supervision, and the effects of parental sexual mores (Segal, 1992). Respondents in the United States ranked physical abuse second only to sexual abuse. Thus, it is not surprising that in 1992, the U.S. National Committee for the Prevention of Child Abuse (NCPCA) revealed that no prevalence/incidence studies had been conducted on child abuse in India. Although a central registry does exist for reports of child abuse and another for fatalities, and there is an official child abuse policy, the reporting system is voluntary and major focus is placed on societal abuses such as child prostitution, child labor, and street children (NCPCA, 1992).

Theoreticians, researchers, and practitioners at the National Seminar on Child Abuse in India in 1988 developed the following definition of child abuse:

Child Abuse and Neglect (CAN) is the intentional, non-accidental injury, or maltreatment of children by parents, caretakers, employers or others including those individuals representing governmental/non-governmental bodies which may lead to temporary or permanent impairment of their physical, mental and psycho-social development, disability or death. (National Institute of Public Cooperation and Child Development, 1988, p. 10)

Two points become readily apparent: (a) This definition of child abuse and neglect does not differentiate between familial and societal abuse, and (b) the definition, although broad enough to cover all forms of child abuse, will cause child welfare workers the same difficulties in operationalization as those experienced by their counterparts in the Western world (Segal, 1991b). The evolution of a definition is important in India and points to professionals' recognition of the need for society to pay heed to the injustices faced by several million children, yet it is merely a beginning in the long battle against child abuse and neglect in India.

Children can suffer a variety of forms of physical abuse at the hands of adults unrelated to them, but of special concern is the abuse and neglect children experience at the hands of their own parents and/or guardians. Within the structure of the family, abuse takes on a different dimension in that it violates the expected nurturant relationship between parent and child. Therefore, perhaps the abuse of children should be dichotomized as being either societal or parental/caregiver maltreatment, although these two categories may not be mutually exclusive.

Societal Abuse

Societal abuse constitutes those forms of abuse that are perpetuated by society, by its culture and values, or by its tendency to passively accept the existence of a problem. In India, child prostitution (Ashtekar, 1991; Simons, 1994), child beggary (Rane et al., 1986), child marriage (Jabbi, 1986), and child labor (Satyarthi, 1989), all concomitants of poverty, are increasingly becoming recognized as being abusive, because they involve both the exploitation of children by adults for personal gain and the deprivation of the basic ingredients necessary for childhood development. Although child prostitution, child beggary, and child marriage may be easy to identify and condemn, child labor becomes more nebulous. Is any job for which a child is paid (either monetarily or in kind) a form of exploitation? Are young domestic servants being exploited? Activists in India would claim that they are, because there is no dearth of adults who are unemployed and who could perform the same domestic functions; however, they would expect higher wages, shorter hours, and better benefits. Using this yardstick, then, is not the young boy or girl in the United States who baby-sits or mows lawns being exploited? An adult performing the same services would expect higher wages. Thus, it appears that societal abuse is often so intrinsic to the culture that it is not seen as being abusive unless a vocal advocate for change emerges.

Intrafamilial Physical Maltreatment

Literature suggests that physical abuse, sexual abuse, selective neglect, and failure-to-provide are some forms of physical maltreatment to which children in India may be subjected by their parents or caregivers.

Physical abuse. Although physical harm to a child should be both the least difficult to assess and the least controversial, except when physical abuse results in death or disfigurement, people are often in disagreement about what constitutes abuse. Recent articles in newspapers and popular magazines indicate that physical abuse may be prevalent in India, but few empirical studies have been conducted on this phenomenon. Most have been conducted on small samples of very young children by pediatricians (Bhattacharyya, 1982; Mehta, 1982); however, in Dave, Dave, and Mishra's (1982) study of 1,000 abused children admitted to a hospital, 81% had experienced physical injuries requiring medical attention. In a more recent study of the self-reports of a representative stratified random sample of 313 middle-class professionals in three Indian cities, 41.9% of the respondents indicated that they had used "abusive" violence, as defined by Straus (1979) on their children (Segal, 1995). Of the 515 children studied at intake into an observation home or a detention center, 79.4% reported having been subjected to "abusive" violence by their parents (Segal & Ashtekar, 1994). These findings clearly suggest that physical abuse does occur in India, although it has not yet received the attention of many researchers.

Sexual abuse. The sexual use of children by adults, especially by parents, has always been considered a very serious matter, not primarily because of the physical or psychological harm done to the child but because of the violation of a major societal taboo against incest (Giovannoni & Becerra, 1979). The extent of the problem in India is unknown; however, two studies (Castelino, 1985; Mehta, 1979) and the popular literature (Srinivasan, 1989) are beginning to indicate that it is a much more widespread phenomenon than has been heretofore acknowledged. Mehta (1979) found that of 100 female children who had been kidnapped, 29.1% had recently torn hymens; this did not include children who had been used for prostitution. Castelino's startling results of the self-reports of a group of middle-class graduate students in Bombay provided suggestion that 1 of every 3 girls and 1 of every 10 boys had been touched inappropriately or had sexual intercourse with an adult relative or close family friend in childhood.

Selective neglect and failure-to-provide. Because of the financial costs of raising daughters, who are often married at great expense to their parents and who often require a dowry to be considered marriageable, girls are less attractive to families than are boys, who are expected to be providers and social security for their aging parents. Disabled children are considered a drain on resources. Therefore, especially in the villages and among the very poor, where assets are nominal and female and/or disabled children are considered a liability, selective neglect is still perceived as a viable means for families to distribute meager resources and to practice population control. When resources are limited, parents tend to feed healthy male children first, and the nutritional and basic survival needs of female and disabled male children are considered less important. This is evident in the differences in the developmental and survival rates for boys and girls in different parts of the country (Rele & Kanitkar, 1979). Since the advent of free governmental immunization and preventive medical care programs in the past decade, medical care, which was often only sought for the more-valued male, is now readily accessible to all children. Because female and disabled children are a liability, despite the available governmental programs, parents in rural areas may still choose to neglect the physical and medical needs of these children. Medical neglect, lack of cleanliness, poor housing conditions, nutritional neglect, and lack of supervision may be categorized as failure-to-provide (Giovannoni & Becerra, 1979). Each of these is a concomitant of poverty and lack of education, and although there are no empirical data that address the scope of these problems, the Indian government and its social service agencies are actively involved in providing training to parents and other intervention services in these areas.

Juvenile Justice and Social Services for Children

Traditional beliefs that the family is the sole caretaker of children have been major impediments in the use of child welfare services in India (Phadke, 1987). Before industrialization and British rule, the child was left entirely to the care of the family; however, invasions and foreign rule (between the 11th and 20th centuries) resulted in movements from an agrarian economy to an industrial one, leaving social conditions of inequality and poverty in their wake (Somen, 1982). Early philanthropists were involved in the establishment of orphanages that were run on charity to provide custodial care to destitute children (Randive, Santos, & Shroff, 1985).

India has always been a country of paradoxes, with its extreme wealth and its abject poverty; with its rich culture of literature, art, and music and its widespread illiteracy; with its beauty constructed by human beings and its filth created by them. Likewise, on the one hand, children in India have no rights, in that they do not have a voice and cannot be independent in their thinking and their behavior; on the other hand, India realizes that children are an essential resource that must be protected from harm. Consequently, India has maintained the tradition of voluntary social service since the early years of philanthropists, and voluntary agencies have always been in the forefront of development programs for women, children, the elderly, and the disabled. Concern for the protection of children emerged as a major issue during India's freedom struggle against the British, as leaders such as Mohandas K. Gandhi and Jawaharlal Nehru recognized them as the resources of the future. Thus, although there is little general knowledge about child abuse as it is understood in the West, the Indian Constitution has made provisions to guard the interests and rights of children. Although no single legislation specifically addresses child abuse, several legislative acts proscribe the maltreatment of children. In 1960, the central government passed the Central Children's Act, which aims to protect children from assault, willful neglect, or harm that could cause unnecessary physical and mental suffering (Belavadi, 1989). The 1974 National Policy for Children expresses the obligation of the country to protect children from neglect, exploitation, and cruelty and stipulates the need for amending existing laws so that in all legal disputes, whether between children and their parents or children and institutions, the interests of children are most important (Nath & Kohli, 1988).

Additional laws were enacted to address more specifically particular forms of abuse prevalent in the country. The 1986 National Policy on Education calls for the exclusion of corporal punishment in the schools, and the 1986 Child Labour Act prohibits the employment of children in hazardous occupations and regulates the conditions of work in permissible occupations. This was especially important because India has the world's largest child labor market. There is enough evidence, nevertheless, that this act is not strictly enforced, and children continue to be employed for long hours and under dangerous conditions. Despite the Child Marriage Restraint Act of 1978, furthermore, child marriages are still very common in several parts of India, not only because of strong social custom but also for a number of psychological, religious, and economic reasons. The Juvenile Justice Act of 1986 aimed to bring uniformity to the acts and served to provide separate administrative mechanisms to deal with destitute and delinquent children. Prior to this act, destitute children received the same services as those who were found to be delinquent. An additional purpose of the act was to provide punishment to adult perpetrators who violated the rights of children, along with the Indian Penal Code, that clearly outlines punishable offenses against minors such as kidnapping, maiming, or raping (Belavadi, 1989). Existing laws such as the Indian Penal Code and the Children Acts provide for the punishment for all offenses against children, but unfortunately, they are rarely enforced because of weak implementing machines and the absence of a child welfare orientation of officials, including those in the police force and the judiciary system (Rane, 1991).

There are no accurate figures of the extent of child abuse because incidents are neither reported nor punished. Although the phenomenon may be widespread, it is still not taken seriously by government authorities and physicians, especially because the abusers are often parents and close family members ("Child Abuse," 1987) and belief in the sanctity of the family is firmly entrenched in Indian society. At a workshop led by the author in 1991 on child abuse for residents in psychiatry in Bombay, participants questioned the value both of focusing on intrafamilial child abuse in the absence of intervention services and of investing limited social service resources in preventive and parental education programs.

With the size of the child population in India and the number of children who live below the poverty line, the need for child welfare services is monumental, and the financial resources of the country are not sufficient to meet this need. India has been highly cognizant of the general plight of a large percentage of the children, therefore, the country has passed the many acts discussed. However, with a lack of funds, these cannot be operationalized or applied, and although throughout this century there has existed a highly sophisticated network of social services for children in India (see Figure 14.1), most resources address the health, education, and survival needs of children and families. These services and programs can be classified as statutory or nonstatutory, as institutional or noninstitutional, and may also be classified into the categories of developmental, preventive, or rehabilitative services. Developmental services are the main focus of governmental intervention and target all children with an aim to promote health, nutrition, education, and recreation. Preventive services, on the other hand, focus on preventing delinquency, vagrancy, and emotional distress, and rehabilitative services include services to physically disabled children as well as to those who have been subjected to societal abuse, neglect, or destitution. Although focus has primarily been toward eradicating illiteracy, malnutrition, and disease and to providing safe housing for destitute, delinquent, and unwanted children, there now are a few preventive efforts directed toward educating parents to avoid traditionally sanctioned abusive practices, but these are still in an embryonic stage.

The Use of Child Witnesses

Nothing in the literature or discussions of directions for policy suggests use of the voice of children in the prosecution of perpetrators. One isolated statement of an academic voicing his opinion regarding his perception of the use of a child witness in Britain was, "Expecting children to give evidence before strangers in a court room is . . . quite unrealistic." (Singh, 1988, p. 106). It is unclear whether Singh believes that the evidence of children may not be accurate or whether their involvement in the adult legal system in this capacity is too traumatizing.

Ashtekar (1991) indicates that sexually abused girls are brought before the juvenile court under Section 78 of the Bombay Children Act of 1948, which is an earlier, regional version of the Central Children's Act that protects children from willful harm. Adults are charged under Section 57 of the act, which pertains to the punishment of the adult accused for the seduction of a minor. Ashtekar further states, however, that in a majority

CLASSIFICATION OF CHILD WELFARE SERVICES*

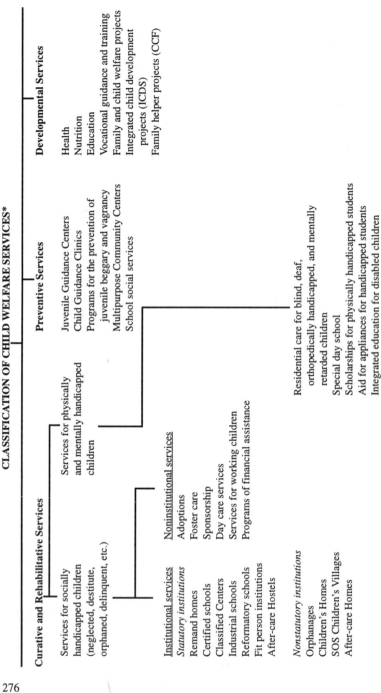

Curative and Rehabilitative Services

Services for socially
handicapped children
(neglected, destitute,
orphaned, delinquent, etc.)

Services for physically
and mentally handicapped
children

Institutional services
Statutory institutions
Remand homes
Certified schools
Classified Centers
Industrial schools
Reformatory schools
Fit person institutions
After-care Hostels

Nonstatutory institutions
Orphanages
Children's Homes
SOS Children's Villages
After-care Homes

Noninstitutional services
Adoptions
Foster care
Sponsorship
Day care services
Services for working children
Programs of financial assistance

Residential care for blind, deaf,
orthopedically handicapped, and mentally
retarded children
Special day school
Scholarships for physically handicapped students
Aid for appliances for handicapped students
Integrated education for disabled children

Preventive Services

Juvenile Guidance Centers
Child Guidance Clinics
Programs for the prevention of
juvenile beggary and vagrancy
Multipurpose Community Centers
School social services

Developmental Services

Health
Nutrition
Education
Vocational guidance and training
Family and child welfare projects
Integrated child development
projects (ICDS)
Family helper projects (CCF)

Figure 14.1. Classification of Child Welfare Services
SOURCE: Rane (1989).

of the cases, the accused adult is acquitted by the adult court for want of definite evidence and adult witnesses, because children cannot serve in the capacity of witness. Juvenile officers can report what children have discussed previously. In her study, Ashtekar found that charges were only pressed by the parents of victims and the girls were exempt from being present in the court in many cases. Because of the long and drawn-out process, after a few hearings, even the girls' parents lost interest and stopped attending court proceedings. This clearly suggests that child witnesses are not considered in the case of sexual abuse.

As is made clear by the Juvenile Justice Act of 1986, children in the legal system are viewed either as victims or as perpetrators. As perpetrators, they are provided rehabilitative services or are placed in remand homes, which are similar to detention centers in the United States. As victims, they are often also placed in remand homes, but their cases are presented to juvenile judges through the juvenile officer, who serves as an advocate for the child. The Juvenile Justice Act merely identifies the right of the children to be treated humanely and to have their basic physical needs met. At no point is there discussion of the child's appearance as a witness against adults. It is not evident whether children are perceived as being incapable of testifying or whether expecting them to testify is believed to expose them to more unnecessary harm.

Currently, there are no recommendations being discussed in India regarding the need to accommodate child witnesses in the legal system, and there are no relevant case precedents. Children may not testify against adults either on their own behalf or on the behalf of others. For example, it is not infrequent that children are witness to dowry deaths; this is a relatively new method of spousal abuse, in which women are burned to death by their spouses and/or their in-laws so that the husband may remarry for another dowry. Even when children may have witnessed dowry deaths, their testimony is not admissible in court. The only condition under which they may appear in court in cases related to adults is when their parents are seeking a divorce. If they are over 10 years of age, they may be included in court proceedings and allowed to state whether they wish to live with the mother or the father. Here, too, the level of involvement is limited to stating their preference, but reasons for the preference are not explored.

As is evident from a recent study of a remand home in Bombay, most children who come to the attention of the juvenile justice system are those who have run away or become lost, those who have exhibited aggressive behavior, those who have been found begging, or those prostituting themselves (Segal & Ashtekar, 1994). Although the study revealed that many of the children had run away because of abuse, intervention and tertiary prevention are not the focal points of the program. The primary aim is to reunite parent and child, regardless of the reason for the separation, and no follow-up or supportive services are provided. In essence, cases involving the intrafamilial abuse of children are not handled in Indian courts. Abuses against children that do come to the attention of the courts are cases of societal abuse, such as child labor, child prostitution, child beggary, and child marriage. Even so, children are not involved in the adult justice system, and their testimony is not used in court. Medical and other experts may provide evidence against adults, but more often than not, it is the juvenile officers who present the information to which they have had access.

The West has used child witnesses for a number of years now, and often their contributions have been instrumental in affecting decisions. Why, then, is this resource not used in India? The answer may well lie in differing societies' perceptions of their children. In India, children are socialized to be docile and submissive and to accept adult values and directions. Children are expected to be seen and not heard. They are mere extensions of the family, and their achievements bring recognition to the family just as their indiscretions bring shame. Furthermore, children are not considered capable of making sound decisions, and although it is believed that they are an important resource for the country, the potential of this resource does not get realized until they reach adulthood. Until that time, they are believed to be highly vulnerable and in need of protection; this may include being protected from the trauma of having to raise their voices against adults who may have harmed them. In addition, recognition of the rights of children in India does not truly include recognizing their ability to make choices or their fortitude to serve as witnesses on their own behalf.

Certainly, one must be aware that the independence of children is an Occidental concept. In India, youth must always defer to age, which may well preclude the use of child witnesses against adults. Unless there is a strong push from children's advocates to hear the voices of children, children will not serve as witnesses. Before Indian child advocates take a step in this direction, they must recognize the importance of having children speak on their own behalf on a regular basis. Unfortunately, such advocacy may not be forthcoming in the near future. These advocates are themselves products of the culture that expects children to be obedient, docile, vulnerable, and voiceless. Although the champions of the cause of children may urge policy changes, the implementation of child protection laws, and responsiveness to the needs of children, they may not truly believe that children can have a hand in significantly affecting their own futures.

Summary and Conclusions

Despite the several services available to children in India, the primary aim of these services is in the area of development with a focus on health, education, and welfare. This has also included addressing the needs of delinquent and destitute children. More recently, child advocates have become cognizant of the many abuses adults perpetrate on children, but stress has been placed on alleviating societal abuses that allow children to be involved in child prostitution, child labor, child beggary, and child marriage. The abuse of children by caregivers has only begun receiving some attention in the past 5 years. However, given the scope of the problems faced by this developing country, where the size of the population is continuing to grow dramatically each year, where poverty, illiteracy, malnutrition, and disease are overwhelming, and where children have few rights, it is commendable that the governmental framework for protecting children is in place. The phenomenal network of social services that operates for children on shoestring budgets helps meet some of the many needs of a large number of children, and free preventive medical care is now available in every area of the country. Furthermore, in a land of scarce resources, where the survival needs of children are so great, both public and private social service organizations have not had the capability to provide the intensive types of intervention programs or alternative care methods to serve the needs of children subjected to abuse by their caregivers. Often, the fact that the abused child has a home and a caregiver is, itself, considered a blessing in a country where there are so many destitute and street children.

However, through all this, it remains true that children do not have a voice in India, and certainly not a voice against adults. Given the country's norms, values, and perceptions of role relationships and the rigidly hierarchical structure of the family, it is highly unlikely that child witnesses will be used in the near future. In addition, because the whole realm of child abuse and inspection of the family by outsiders is such virgin territory, perhaps the use of child witnesses at all is a novel idea, and therefore, to address the status of child witness research in India is premature. As practitioners, educators, and researchers become increasingly sensitized to the rights of children, and with the globalization of society as a whole, perhaps some less functional family relationships will begin to be questioned in Indian society on a much wider scale than is done currently. When, and if, that occurs, India may be ready to use child witnesses to press charges against adult perpetrators.

References

Ashtekar, A. (1991). Abused girls under statutory institutional care. In Tata Institute of Social Sciences (TISS) Unit for Family Studies (Ed.), *Research on families with problems in India: Issues and implications* (Vol. 2, pp. 472-482). Bombay, India: TISS.

Bamberger, I. (1986). Values and strategic behavior. *Management International Review, 26,* 57-69.

Belavadi, R. N. (1989). The Juvenile Justice Act, 1986. *Indian Journal of Social Work, 50,* 239-243.

Bhattacharyya, A. K. (1982). Child abuse in India and nutritionally battered child. *Child Abuse & Neglect, 3,* 607-614.

Castelino, C. T. (1985). *Child sexual abuse: A retrospective study.* Unpublished manuscript, Tata Institute of Social Sciences, Bombay, India.

Chathrathi, S. (1985, September 13). Growing up in the U.S.—An identity crisis. *India Abroad, 15,* 2.

Child abuse: Tragically widespread. (1987, January 31). *India Today,* pp. 116, 118.

Dave, A. B., Dave, P. B., & Mishra, K. D. (1982). Child abuse and neglect (CAN) practices in Durg District of Madhya Pradesh. *Indian Paediatrics, 19,* 905-912.

Dutt, E. (1989, October 13). Becoming a 2d generation. *India Abroad, 20*(2), 16.

Giovannoni, J. M., & Becerra, R. M. (1979). *Defining child abuse.* New York: Free Press.

Ho, M. K. (1988). *Family therapy with ethnic minorities.* Beverly Hills, CA: Sage.

Hofstede, G. (1980). *Culture's consequences.* Newbury Park, CA: Sage.

Jabbi, M. K. (1986). Child marriages in Rajasthan. *Social Change, 16*(1), 3-9.

Mehta, M. N. (1979). Kidnapping: A social evil in India. *Child Abuse & Neglect, 3,* 678-682.

Mehta, M. N. (1982). Physical abuse of abandoned children in India. *Child Abuse & Neglect, 6,* 171-175.

Nath, N., & Kohli, M. (1988). Child abuse in India: Some issues. In National Institute of Public Cooperation and Child Development (NIPCCD), *National Seminar on Child Abuse in India: 22-24 June, 1988* (pp. 137-151). New Delhi, India: NIPCCD.

National Committee for the Prevention of Child Abuse. (NCPCA) (1992). *World perspectives on child abuse: An international resource book.* Chicago: Author.

Phadke, S. V. (1987). Child welfare policy. In *Encyclopaedia of social work in India* (Vol. 1, pp. 89-100). New Delhi: Government of India, Publications Division, Ministry of Information and Broadcasting.

Population Reference Bureau. (1990). *1990 world population data sheet.* Washington, DC: Author.

Randive, S., Santos, N., & Shroff, K. (1985). New trends in programmes for children. In *Developing a national perspective for social work education in the field of family and child welfare* (pp. 121-137). Bombay, India: Tata Institute of Social Sciences.

Rane, A. J. (1989). *Child welfare policy and programmes in India.* Unpublished manuscript, Tata Institute of Social Sciences, Bombay, India.

Rane, A. J. (1991). Research on child abuse in families: Review and implications. In Tata Institute of Social Sciences (TISS) Unit for Family Studies (Ed.), *Research on families with problems in India: Issues and implications* (Vol. 2, pp. 451-461). Bombay, India: TISS.

Rane, A. J., Naidu, U. S., & Kapadia, K. R. (1986). *Children in difficult situations in India: A review.* Bombay, India: Tata Institute of Social Sciences.

Rele, J. R., & Kanitkar, T. (1979). Demographic profile of an Indian child. In S. D. Gokhale & N. K. Sohoni (Eds.), *Child in India* (pp. 33-48). Bombay, India: Somnaiya.

Saran, P. (1985). *The Asian Indian experience in the United States.* New Delhi, India: Vikas.

Satyarthi, K. (1989, June/July). *Child bonded labour in South Asia: An overview.* Paper presented at the South Asian Seminar on Child Servitude, New Delhi, India.

Segal, U. A. (1988). Career choice correlates: An Indian perspective. *Indian Journal of Social Work, 69,* 338-348.

Segal, U. A. (1991a). Cultural variables in Asian Indian families. *Families in Society, 72,* 233-242.

Segal, U. A. (1991b). Child abuse in India: A theoretical overview. *Indian Journal of Social Work, 52,* 293-302.

Segal, U. A. (1992). Child abuse in India: An empirical report on perceptions. *Child Abuse & Neglect, 16,* 887-908.

Segal, U. A. (1995). Child abuse by the middle class? A study of professionals in India. *Child Abuse & Neglect, 19,* 213-227.

Segal, U. A., & Ashtekar, A. (1994). Detection of intrafamilial child abuse: Children at intake at a Children's Observation Home in India. *Child Abuse & Neglect, 18,* 957-967.

Simons, M. (1994, January 16). The littlest prostitutes. *New York Times Magazine,* pp. 30-35.

Singh, R. R. (1988). Role of social workers and community in the prevention and management of child abuse. In National Institute of Public Cooperation and Child Development (NIPCCD), *National Seminar on Child Abuse in India: 22-24 June, 1988* (pp. 93-120). New Delhi, India: NIPCCD.

Sinha, D. (1984). Some recent changes in the Indian family and their implications for socialization. *Indian Journal of Social Work, 45,* 271-286.

Somen, S. (1982). *National planning and policy for children in India: An appraisal.* Unpublished manuscript, Tata Institute of Social Sciences, Bombay, India.

Srinivasan, S. (1989, July 8-14). No one talks about it. *Eve's Weekly,* pp. 50-53.

Straus, M. D. (1979). Measuring intrafamily violence: The Conflicts Tactics (CT) Scales. *Journal of Marriage and the Family, 41*(1), 75-88.

Sue, D. W. (1981). *Counseling the culturally different.* New York: Wiley.

Tanwar, T. (1988). Media and child abuse. In National Institute of Public Cooperation and Child Development (NIPCCD), *National Seminar on Child Abuse in India: 22-24 June, 1988* (pp. 120-136). New Delhi, India: NIPCCD.

Triandis, H. C., Bontempo, R., Villareal, M. J., Asai, M., & Lucca, N. (1988). Individualism and collectivism: Cross-cultural perspectives on self-ingroup relationships. *Journal of Personality and Social Psychology, 19,* 323-338.

UNICEF. (1990). *The state of the world's children.* Delhi, India: Author.

Whiting, J. W. M. (1961). Socialization process and personality. In F. L. K. Hsu (Ed.), *Psychological anthropology: Approaches to culture and personality* (pp. 355-399). Homewood, IL: Dorsey.

Index

About the Editors

Bette L. Bottoms is Assistant Professor of Psychology at the University of Illinois at Chicago. She received her BA from Randolph-Macon Woman's College, her MA from the University of Denver, and her PhD in social psychology from the State University of New York at Buffalo. Her research has focused on issues of psychological and legal interest, including the reliability of children's eyewitness testimony, jurors' perceptions of child sexual assault victims, religion-related child abuse allegations, and adults' claims of repressed memories of child abuse. Her work has culminated in published journal articles and book chapters. She is coeditor (with Gail Goodman) of the book *Child Victims, Child Witnesses: Understanding and Improving Testimony* (1993, Guilford).

Gail S. Goodman is Professor of Psychology at the University of California, Davis. She obtained her doctoral degree in developmental psychology from the University of California, Los Angeles in 1977 and conducted postdoctoral research at the University of Denver and the Universite Rene Descartes in Paris, France. She has published numerous scientific articles, books, and chapters on child abuse, child witnesses, and children's testimony. In addition, she has served as president of the Division of Child, Youth, and Family Services of the American Psychological Association (APA) and is a founding member of the American Professional Society on the Abuse of Children (APSAC). She is President-Elect of the American Psychology-Law Society. She has also received a number of awards for her writings, including the 1994 Robert Chin Award from the Society for the Psychological Study of Social Issues of APA and APSAC's 1992 Research Career Achievement Award. The recipient of a number of federal grants for her research, her studies have been cited in several U.S. Supreme Court and lower court decisions. For instance, a study of children's reactions to criminal court involvement, funded by the National Institute of Justice, was cited pivotally by the majority in the *Maryland v. Craig* (1990) decision, which concerned children's testimony.

About the Contributors

Eugene Borgida is Professor of Psychology and Adjunct Professor of Law and Political Science at the University of Minnesota. He currently serves as Director of the social psychology PhD program. He received his undergraduate degree from Wesleyan University and his PhD in social psychology from the University of Michigan. His research interests include psychology and law, social cognition, and political psychology. He is currently working on a psychology and law monograph for the Westview Press series New Directions in Social Psychology, which will include a chapter on children as witnesses.

Frank Buffing is a senior associate at the A.B.J., a forensic institute for the assessment and treatment of victims of child maltreatment and the assessment and treatment of perpetrators of sexual abuse. After receiving his master's degree in orthopedagogics from the Vrije Universiteit (Amsterdam), he was a coresearcher in a foster-parenting project and a research assistant in the Lamers-Winkelman research project on sexual abuse of young children. He is now directing the research project on the sexual knowledge of nonabused young children at the Vrije Universiteit. He is also working as a consultant for social workers of the Child Protection Board in The Hague, the Netherlands. He is coauthor of several articles on foster parenting and indicators of child abuse.

Ray Bull, PhD, is Head of the Department of Psychology at the University of Portsmouth in England. He has conducted research on witnessing since the late 1970s and on child witnesses since 1987, and he regularly acts as an expert in legal cases involving witness evidence. He has authored/ coauthored over 75 articles and chapters; coauthored three books (one of which was chosen by the American Library Association as "one of the outstanding textbooks of the year"); and coedited two books (*Handbook of Psychology in Legal Contexts,* 1995, and *Children's Evidence in Legal Proceedings,* 1990). He was cofounding editor of the journal *Expert Evidence: The International Digest of Human Behaviour, Science and Law.* In 1991, he was asked (together with a professor of law) by the Home Office to write the first working draft of the *Memorandum of Good Practice on Video Recorded Interviews with Child Witnesses for Criminal Proceedings* (published by Her Majesty's Stationery Office in 1992). From 1992 to 1995, he was Chair of the U.K. Association of University Heads of Psychology Departments, and in 1995 he became Chair of the Committee of Professors at the University of Portsmouth. In 1995, he was awarded a Higher Doctorate (Doctor of Science).

Graham Davies, PhD, is Professor of Psychology at the University of Leicester, United Kingdom. His main research interests lie in the area of eyewitness testimony and identification in adults and children. His co-authored publications include *Perceiving and Remembering Faces, Identification Evidence: A Psychological Evaluation, Memory in Context: Context in Memory, Memory in Everyday Life,* and some 100 articles in learned journals. He is editor of the journal *Applied Cognitive Psychology.* At the request of the Home Office, he has undertaken evaluations of two procedural innovations for child witnesses: the "live link" and the use of videotaped interviews as a substitute for the child's live examination at court. The report on videotaped evidence appeared recently (G. Davies, C. Wilson, R. Mitchell, and J. Milsom, 1995, *Videotaped Evidence: An Evaluation.* London: Home Office). He is a fellow of the British Psychological Society and a Chartered Forensic Psychologist.

Rhona Flin, PhD, is Professor of Applied Psychology at the Robert Gordon University, Aberdeen, Scotland. In conjunction with Graham Davies and Ray Bull, she completed two studies of child witnesses funded by the Scottish Home and Health Department. She is coauthor, with John Spencer, of *The Evidence of Children* (1993).

Kevin Gowdey received his bachelor of laws in 1981 from the University of Western Ontario. He was called to the Ontario Bar in 1983. Since 1991, he has been Crown Attorney in St. Thomas, Ontario, a small community in southwestern Ontario. Before that he worked for 6 years as Assistant Crown Attorney in Chatham and London, Ontario. He has a special interest in child sexual abuse cases. He is on the advisory board for the Child Witness Project at the London Family Court Clinic and has been working to take advantage of and develop the procedures for the use of closed-circuit television in the courtroom.

Susan Hayes has a doctorate in psychology and is a clinical forensic psychologist, practicing primarily in the area of accused persons with mental retardation. She is Associate Professor and Head of the Department of Behavioral Sciences in Medicine at the University of Sydney. She has published extensively in the field of rights of minority groups, focusing on people with mental retardation and children. Her other interests include research into medical education and communication between doctor and patient. She is a member of the New South Wales Guardianship Board, and Honorary Consultant to the New South Wales Law Reform Commission. Between 1986 and 1988, she was a commissioner in the New South Wales Department of Corrective Services, and she maintains an interest in conditions for prisoners with mental retardation. She has achieved international recognition in the area of people with mental retardation in the criminal justice system.

Mark Henaghan graduated from the University of Otago in Dunedin, New Zealand, in 1978, with an Honours degree in law and a degree in political science. He is currently Associate Professor in Law at the University of Otago. In 1987-1988, he was a visiting scholar at Stanford University in California. He is a member of the New Zealand Committee for the Prevention of Child Abuse and the New Zealand Committee for Children. These committees were responsible for lobbying for change of the position of child witnesses in New Zealand. He is coauthor of *Family Law Policy in New Zealand* (Oxford University Press) and *Family Law in New Zealand* (Butterworths). He is editor of Butterworth's *Family Law*

Service and the *New Zealand Family Law Journal.* He has a particular interest in children's rights, has written a number of articles about children as witnesses in the New Zealand court system, and was co-organizer of a national conference on children as witnesses, held in Dunedin, in 1993.

Irit Hershkowitz is Assistant Professor of Social Work at Haifa University, Israel. She has taught undergraduate and graduate courses on child development and related topics as well as family violence issues, specifically, stress and the coping resources of violent spouses. Her current research is focused on child witnesses. In this area, much of her efforts have been devoted to the development and field testing of interviewing strategies for child witnesses. In cooperation with youth investigators in Israel and collaborators at the National Institute of Child Health and Human Development, she has focused on the relative effectiveness of different types of questioning in eliciting richer information from alleged victims of sexual abuse. She is also involved in attempts to assess the credibility of children's statements. She obtained her BA from Bar-Ilan University, Israel, and received her MA and PhD from Haifa University. From 1991 to 1994, she was a postdoctoral fellow at the National Institute of Child Health and Human Development.

Ting-Pong Ho, MD, MRCPsych, is a consultant child psychiatrist in the Department of Psychiatry, Queen Mary Hospital. He graduated from the University of Hong Kong. In 1991, he obtained a Croucher Foundation Fellowship and received further training in child and adolescent psychiatry in the Maudsley Hospital in London. He is a member of the Royal College of Psychiatrists in the United Kingdom and a founding fellow of the Hong Kong Academy of Medicine. He has been an adviser to the Education Department, Rehabilitation Division of the Hong Kong Government, Save the Children's Fund (Hong Kong Branch), and St. James' Settlement, a voluntary agency in Hong Kong. His research interests include childhood hyperactivity, child sexual abuse, and youth suicide.

Brian Kearney has been a sheriff in Scotland for 21 years. He is author of *Ordinary Civil Procedure in the Sheriff Court* (1981) and *Children's Hearing and the Sheriff Court* (19897), and he has contributed to Butterworth's *Family Law Service* (1995). He has lectured extensively in

Britain and abroad, including an address (with Kathleen Murray) to the American Bar Association in 1987.

Margaret Bull Kovera is Assistant Professor of Psychology at Florida International University. She received her BA from Northwestern University and her 1994 PhD from the University of Minnesota. Her research interests include media effects on jury decision making, expert testimony, child witnesses, hearsay evidence, political accountability, and attitudes and persuasion. Her research has been published in journals such as *Personality and Social Psychology Bulletin, Law and Human Behavior,* and the *Minnesota Law Review.*

Michael E. Lamb has been Head of the Section on Social and Emotional Development at the National Institute of Child Health and Human Development in Bethesda, Maryland, since 1987. Prior to that, he was Professor of Psychology, Pediatrics, and Psychiatry at the University of Utah in Salt Lake City, and he also served on the faculty of the Universities of Wisconsin (USA), Michigan (USA), Hokkaido (Japan), and Haifa (Israel) since receiving his PhD from Yale University. His current research is concerned with the evaluation, validation, and facilitation of children's accounts of sexual abuse; the effects of domestic violence on children's development; the effects of contrasting patterns of early child care on children and their families; and the description of early patterns of infant care in diverse sociocultural ecologies. He is coauthor of *Development in Infancy, Socialization and Personality Development, Infant-Mother Attachment,* and *Child Psychology Today.* He has edited several book on the role of the father in child development, founded and coedited the Advances in Developmental Psychology series, and has edited about two dozen other books on various aspects of child development, most recently, *Images of Childhood* (in press). He has received two national awards from the American Psychological Association—The Young Psychologist Award (1976) and the Boyd-McCandless Young Scientist Award (1978)—and is a fellow of the American Psychological Society. He was awarded an honorary doctorate by the University of Göteborg (Sweden) in 1995.

Francien Lamers-Winkelman, PhD, is a research scientist at the Vrije Universiteit (Amsterdam) and a registered psychomotor therapist at the Medical Day Treatment Center (Aerdenhout, the Netherlands). Her clinical practice includes the assessment of alleged sexual abuse victims and the treatment of sexual and physical abuse in very young children. She has served as a court-appointed expert witness in many cases of alleged sexual abuse and has written numerous articles (in Dutch and German) in the area of child sexual abuse. She is a senior trainer in the Mental Health Project of Medicins sans Frontieres (Doctors Without Frontiers) in Sarajevo (former Yugoslavia) and has lectured several times in this besieged town on war-related trauma in children.

Dap Louw received his PhD in criminology from the University of Pretoria and his PhD in psychology from the Potchefstroom University. He is registered as a clinical psychologist at the South African Medical and Dental Council. He studied at Rutgers University and Temple University and was a visiting professor at the University of Idaho and the University of Colorado. At present, he is Head of the Center of Behavioral Sciences and Professor in the Department of Psychology at the University of the Orange Free State. He has published widely and is the author or coauthor of 12 books, some of which are widely read in South Africa, and has presented several papers at international conventions. He belongs to several professional organizations and, among others, served on the board of directors of the International Council of Psychologists and as President of the South African Society for Forensic Psychology.

Lucy S. McGough is the Vinson and Elkins Professor of Law at Louisiana State University Law School. She received her BA from Agnes Scott College, JD from Emory University Law School, and LLM from Harvard University Law School. As a Kellogg National Fellow (1981–1984), she began her interdisciplinary research focusing on child development. Her book *Child Witnesses in the American Legal System: Fragile Voices* (Yale Press, 1994) was honored by the 1995 Honorable Mention Book Award by the American Society of Writers on Legal Subjects.

Kathleen Murray, MA, MEd, C. Psychol. A.F.B.Ps.S., is Research Consultant and Honorary Research Fellow at the Centre for the Study of the Child & Society at Glasgow University, Scotland. She has authored and coedited five books and numerous papers on the Scottish juvenile justice system and related topics.

John E. B. Myers, JD, is Professor of Law at the University of the Pacific, McGeorge School of Law in Sacramento, California. He is editor of *The Backlash: Child Protection Under Fire* (1994, Sage) and author of *A Mother's Nightmare, Incest: A Practical Legal Guide for Parents and Professionals* (in press), *Evidence in Child Abuse and Neglect Cases* (1992), *Legal Issues in Child Abuse and Neglect* (1992, Sage), and *Legal and Educational Issues Affecting Autistic Children* (with W. Jenson and W. McMahon; 1986). He is author of numerous articles on child maltreatment and is on the faculty of the National Judicial College, the National Council of Juvenile and Family Court Judges, and the National Center for Prosecution of Child Abuse.

Kim Oates is Professor of Pediatrics and Child Health at the University of Sydney and Chairman of the Division of Medicine at the Royal Alexandra Hospital for Children. He is also Chairman of the board of directors of NAPCAN, Australia's National Association for the Prevention of Child Abuse and Neglect. Kim is a past president of the International Society for the Prevention of Child Abuse and Neglect, Associate Editor of the journal *Child Abuse & Neglect,* and in 1993 was Director of the Kempe Center in Denver. One of his interests is the long-term outcomes of child abuse.

Pierre Olivier received his LLB from the University of Pretoria and his LLD from the University of Leiden in the Netherlands. He was Professor in the College of Law at the University of Port Elizabeth and the University of the Orange Free State. After 1973, he practiced as an advocate in Bloemfontein. In 1985, he was appointed as a judge of the Supreme Court, and early in 1986 he was seconded to the S.A. Law Commission in Pretoria as a full-time member. In 1995, he was appointed as judge at the Appeal Court in Bloemfontein. The author and coauthor of two standard textbooks in South Africa, he has published widely in legal journals. He is also widely known for his work in the field of human rights and constitutional matters.

Margaret-Ellen Pipe has a PhD from the University of Auckland, New Zealand. She is a developmental psychologist, with research interests in memory development and children's eyewitness testimony. She has taught developmental psychology at the University of Otago since 1985, where she is currently a senior lecturer in the Psychology Department. She is

Associate Editor of the *New Zealand Journal of Psychology* and is on the editorial board of *Applied Cognitive Psychology.*

Louise Dezwirek Sas, PhD 1980, University of Western Ontario, is Director of the Child Witness Program and heads research concerning child witnesses and child sexual abuse at the London Family Court Clinic, in London, Ontario, Canada. She is an adjunct professor of psychology at the University of Western Ontario. As a clinical child psychologist, she conducts court-ordered assessments and frequently provides expert testimony in court on matters related to child sexual abuse and the competency of child witnesses. She has been invited to present briefs to Canadian parliamentary committees regarding legislative amendments pertaining to child witnesses, and she has served on numerous provincial and national committees. Over the past 7 years, she has been funded by Health Canada to evaluate the efficacy of court preparation and monitor implementation of new legislation, and most recently, she has completed a 2-year study on disclosure patterns in child sexual abuse: *Tipping the Balance to Tell the Secret: The Public Discovery of Child Sexual Abuse* (with Alison Hatch Cunningham). She has published numerous journal articles and several book chapters, and is currently involved in providing training for the Canadian judiciary on the effect of emotional and sexual abuse on children.

Uma A. Segal, PhD, LCSW, is Associate Professor of Social Work at the University of Missouri–St. Louis, where she is also Research Associate in the Center of International Studies and a fellow with the Public Policy Research Centers. She has focused on the study of child abuse in cross-cultural context and its implications for social service delivery and is particularly interested in the parental maltreatment of children of Eastern countries and cultures. She is currently studying child abuse among Southeast Asian refugees in the United States and is working on a pilot comparison between Japan, India, and the United States. She has received several grants to study child abuse and neglect and has published in journals such as *Child Abuse & Neglect, International Social Work, Children and Youth Services Review, Journal of International and Comparative Social Welfare,* and *Families in Society.* In addition to her teaching, research, and service responsibilities at the University of Missouri, she serves as program evaluator for the International Institute in St. Louis;

is a grant reviewer for the Department of Health and Human Services' Administration for Children, Youth, and Families; and is a member of boards of several local and national organizations. She received her BA from Barnard College of Columbia University, her MSSW from the Graduate School of Social Work at the University of Texas at Arlington, and her PhD from Washington University in St. Louis.

Sandra Shrimpton is a doctoral student at the University of Sydney, Australia. She received her BA from Macquarie University (1981) and her postgraduate qualification from the University of Melbourne in adolescent and child psychology (1987). Her research interests include child witness testimony and early intervention with high-risk children. Areas of work interests include families in crisis and children at risk.

Kathleen J. Sternberg is currently Chair of the Research Committee of the Federal Interagency Task Force on Child Abuse and Neglect. She has worked as a research psychologist at the National Institute of Child Health and Human Development (NICHD) since 1988. During the past 7 years, most of her research has focused on applied issues in developmental psychology, including the longitudinal effects of domestic violence on children's development, the evaluation and development of interview techniques with children who have made allegations of sexual abuse, and effects of day care on children's development. She has a long-standing interest in how culture affects human development and how the study of both normative and pathological phenomena benefit from a cross-cultural approach. She has coordinated a number of research projects that involve community and mental health professionals. In addition to her work as a researcher, she has taught a number of courses and seminars focusing on the definition and effects of maltreatment, cross-cultural aspects of developmental psychology, and interviewing techniques.

Amye R. Warren is a University of Chattanooga Foundation Professor of Psychology at the University of Tennessee in Chattanooga. She received her PhD in experimental psychology in 1984 from the Georgia Institute of Technology. She has published articles and chapters on suggestibility in child witnesses, language development and linguistic factors in questioning children, and memory for emotional events. She is a member of the American Psychological Association, the American Psychology-Law

Society, and the Society for Research in Child Development. She also serves on the review board of the journal *Law and Human Behavior* and as a consultant to her local Children's Advocacy Center and attorneys involved in child abuse cases.

David A. Wolfe, PhD 1980, University of South Florida, is Professor of Psychology and Psychiatry at the University of Western Ontario in London, Canada, and a member of the board of the university's Centre for Research on Violence Against Women and Children. He holds a diploma in clinical psychology from the American Board of Professional Psychology and maintains a practice in child clinical psychology with the Children's Aid Society of London/Middlesex. He received the "Contribution to Knowledge Award" from the Ontario Psychological Foundation in 1988 for his work with children of battered women. He was made a fellow of the American Psychological Association in 1991 and has served on a number of provincial, national, and international panels concerned with violence against women and children. His books include *Children of Battered Women* (1990; with P. Jaffe and S. Wilson); *Child Abuse: Implications for Child Development and Psychopathology* (1987), *Preventing Physical and Emotional Abuse of Children* (1991), and *Empowering Youth to Promote Nonviolence: Issues and Solutions* (in press).